DISTRIBUTIONS OF THE SENSIBLE

DISTRIBUTIONS OF THE SENSIBLE

Rancière, between Aesthetics and Politics

Edited by Scott Durham and Dilip Gaonkar

With an afterword by Jacques Rancière

Northwestern University Press
Evanston, Illinois

Northwestern University Press
www.nupress.northwestern.edu

Printed in the United States of America

10 9 8 7 6 5 4 3 2 1

Library of Congress Cataloging-in-Publication Data

Names: Durham, Scott, 1960– editor. | Gaonkar, Dilip Parameshwar, 1945– editor. | Rancière, Jacques, writer of afterword.
Title: Distributions of the sensible : Rancière between aesthetics and politics / edited by Scott Durham and Dilip Gaonkar ; with an afterword by Jacques Rancière.
Description: Evanston, Illinois : Northwestern University Press, 2019. | Includes index.
Identifiers: LCCN 2019007711 | ISBN 9780810140271 (paper text : alk. paper) | ISBN 9780810140288 (cloth text : alk. paper) | ISBN 9780810140295 (e-book)
Subjects: LCSH: Rancière, Jacques—Political and social views. | Rancière, Jacques—Aesthetics. | Political science—Philosophy. | Equality—Philosophy.
Classification: LCC B2430.R274 D57 2019 | DDC 194—dc23
LC record available at https://lccn.loc.gov/2019007711

Contents

A Preface to Rancière

Dilip Gaonkar

The singularity of Jacques Rancière's oeuvre and its relevance today in 2018, exactly half a century after the May 1968 uprisings and civil unrest in France, which profoundly shaped young Rancière's political thinking and aesthetic sensibilities, turns on three key thematically charged concepts: equality, dissensus, and the distribution of the sensible. To foreground and privilege three concepts and themes out of a massive oeuvre, nearly six decades in the making, is a bit of an oversimplification. However, these conceptual/thematic threads run through Rancière's thinking and writing consistently and ubiquitously across his multiple intellectual engagements both in the academy and in the public sphere. These concepts and themes are also at the very heart of Rancière's relevance today and his growing interdisciplinary appeal and influence in France and beyond, especially in the English-speaking world in the last two decades. Moreover, these three concepts and themes are fully engaged and interrogated in this volume of critical essays on Rancière's seminal writings, which dwell on and radically reimagine the nexus between politics and aesthetics.

We are indeed living through times of extraordinary dissensus everywhere, virtually in every national/cultural space across the globe, and that dissensus has much to do with the question of equality and its erosions. Those erosions promulgated and naturalized by the ideologies of postpolitics, such as neoliberalism and good governance, seek to curb and ostracize dissensus, that which, for Rancière is constitutive of politics as such. The link between equality and dissensus is made visible, however fleetingly and fugitively, by a derangement of perceptual fields of hierarchically structured bodies, things, and words, a "police" order where allegedly everything has its proper station. These disruptions, both quotidian and eventful, flow both from dissensual enunciations and assertions of equality by speaking subjects in political struggles and from the quiet appearance and presence of things, a veritable plenitude of all and sundry bereft of hierarchy, made perceptible in aesthetic practices and artifacts. The contingent crossing of these disruptive flows keeps shifting and destabilizing given hegemonic distributions of the sensible: known and unknown, said and unsaid, visible and invisible. Thus, a molecular democracy, a fugitive democracy, is born and reborn, time and again.

By focusing on these concepts/themes, Rancière is also able to defer, if not completely avoid, the twin temptations of ontology and teleology: the former characteristic of philosophical and economic discourses and the latter characteristic of historical accounts and narratives. This is most evident in Rancière's treatment of equality. Equality, as Rancière insists, is not telic. Unlike liberty, equality has no "ends," no arrivals, no progressive emancipatory grand narratives in which it can play the protagonist. Equality is a point of departure, a volatile spread one traverses laterally from one encounter to the next, gathering nuances and differences in variable circumstances and across heterogeneous situations. Unlike Karl Popper's negative model of "conjectures and refutations" to account for the growth of scientific knowledge,[1] Rancière offers an affirmative, but noncumulative model of "supposition and verification" to describe a phenomenology of egalitarian struggles. Every scene of equality, ungrounded, begins anew. No truth of philosophical anthropology or of moral psychology or of divine providence can guarantee the claim of equality. It stands alone, whenever and wherever one takes a stand, a shivering reed sustained by dissensus, uncounted and anomalous, in the police order of the day.

Rancière's notion of dissensus is also counterintuitive. It is not simply the opposite of consensus. Nor is it simply polemical, although it partakes in polemics. It marks the essential "litigiousness constitutive of politics," especially of democratic politics, something effaced and occluded both by consensual institutional models, where the social trumps the political, and by rule-governed constitutional models, where the normative trumps the political. From Aristotle to Habermas, it is routinely assumed that politics is grounded in the distinctive human capacity for speech and communication and in its corollary, the human disposition to live with and among others in communities. This anthropological universal is augmented with the sociohistorical generalization that living together in communities necessarily embeds humans in a dialectic of conflict and cooperation, in a clash of interests and values among individuals, factions, and groups that needs to be addressed and reconciled for communities to endure. These two propositions are braided with the third normative proviso that, given the unique affordances of speech, conflicts immanent to living in communities ought to be addressed and reconciled by open-ended discussion, deliberation, and due process. This is what distinguishes humans from other species. Rancière does not summarily dismiss this grounding package for the advent of democratic politics; he modifies and subverts it.

He shifts from what distinguishes humans from other species to what divides them from within the folds of the common, that which triggers and releases the political. "Political dissensus," he observes, "is not a discussion between speaking people who would confront their interests and values. It is a conflict about who speaks and who does not speak, about what has to be heard as the voice of pain and what has to be heard as an argument of justice."[2] Rancière dwells on Aristotle's claim that "slaves *understand* language, but don't *possess* it." A slave may register a wrong, *blaberon*, in a cry of pain, but that cry is bereft of reason. Someone else must speak, think, and reason on her behalf. In a police order, or in a politics of police, only those with allotted stations and functions based on their alleged competencies and accreditations can speak and advance their interests and values in the name of the common. Those with no such allocation in the structured social body, the uncounted, "the part with no part," cannot speak; if they speak, it is not heard; if heard, it is deemed unintelligible in the prevailing perceptual order. Such is the police distribution of the sensible.

Rancière challenges this notion of politics within the folds of police, as elaborated and justified not only by an avowed antidemocrat like Plato in *The Republic,* but also by many renowned champions of the demos, the poor. In his groundbreaking early work *The Philosopher and His Poor* (1983), Rancière shows how Marx, Sartre, and Bourdieu, each in his own way, like Althusser in his refusal to support students and workers in 1968 in the name of a correct "scientific" line of analysis, engage in Platonic exclusion and silencing of "the part that has no part" in the police order. For Marx, the workers, while embodying a transformative revolutionary future, are unable to grasp it; for Sartre, the workers are unable to think for themselves because they are too tired and have no time; and for Bourdieu, the common people cannot reflexively grasp the social forces and mechanisms that operate behind their backs to injure and wrong them. They need help; they need someone to think and speak for them, for instance, the party as anointed by Sartre or a school of social scientists as proposed by Bourdieu. Rancière's masterful historical reading of the careers of Gabriel Gauny, the plebeian philosopher in *Proletarian Nights,*[3] and Joseph Jacotot, the radical egalitarian pedagogue in *The Ignorant Schoolmaster,*[4] decisively undercuts and debunks this allegedly noble Platonic lie and its afterlife.

By contrast, for Rancière, dissensual politics commences precisely when the uncounted insists on speaking and insists on being heard. "Being part of no part," the uncounted cannot speak for any part, but for the whole. This is neither a totalizing move nor a strategic move. It is performative, a mode of appearing. There is no politics until one begins to disagree about what politics is, and this disagreement cannot be settled by invoking an ethical idea of the common. Here Rancière is not offering an ideology-critique or engaging in a hermeneutic of suspicion that would unmask a collection of private interests masquerading as the common good or as the general will. Like Foucault, with whom he shares deep affinities in theory and in practice, Rancière is content to dwell on and map the surface.

For Rancière, unlike Hannah Arendt, there is no distinct sphere of politics, the sphere of speech and action untouched or unencumbered by the social. There is no political life as such, that of *vita activa*. There is no "pure politics," stemming from a place outside of the police. Politics has no proper or privileged objects. As Rancière puts it: "Politics 'takes place' in the space of police, by rephrasing and restaging social issues, police problems, and so on."[5] What we have is a political stage, already compromised by the police, where heterogeneous scenes of dissensus unfold. Every staging of the demos, the people, enacts a wrong, a breach of equality, and a demand to address it by the uncounted, hitherto invisible and inaudible. "Politics," Rancière writes, "has its own universal, its own measure that is equality. The measure never applies directly. It applies only through the enactment of a wrong."[6] But that wrong is not grounded in the "excess of being" or in the ontological gap or in any version of the "ethical absoluticization of wrong" (as with Lyotard and Agamben). Instead, wrong turns on the contingency of being born "here or there," on the "specificity of difference," and, more than anything else, on "the excess inherent in any process of nomination" that arbitrarily binds names and bodies together, giving few the qualification to rule and to speak about the common while relegating others to the silence of obedience.[7] Thus, Rancière's egalitarian politics of dissensus vigilantly resists the varied temptations to dissolve "politics on behalf of some historico-ontological destinary process."[8]

Rancière is also deeply committed to deciphering and exploring this play of equality and dissensus in the aesthetic realm, which parallels and interrupts the political realm, but the two are not commensurable. When Rancière speaks of the aesthetic realm, he does not equate it with what is subsumed under art and literature generally. He distinguishes between three distinct sensorial and perceptual regimes governing art and literature: the ethical regime of images, the representative regime of art, and the aesthetic regime of art.[9] Each regime is governed by a set of protocols as to what is visible and intelligible and what is not, whether artifacts, actions, or agents. According to Rancière, the ethical regime associated with Platonism is not properly about art. What becomes visible under this regime, say a statue of a deity, is made intelligible in terms of how the origins, ends, uses, and effects of that image are incorporated within the totalizing ethos of the community. The representative regime, governed by Aristotle's principle of mimesis, is primarily about speech and action, about speakers of words and doers of deeds. But only a few, of noble visage, speak and initiate actions; and, how, when, and where those few speak and act is governed by the precepts of classical rhetoric, of propriety and decorum. What is visible and intelligible within this regime, especially the play of human wills and how they are formed and deformed, is hierarchically structured, characteristic of an order of the police. In the aesthetic regime, disclosed in the works of Flaubert, Mallarmé, and many others, and also in Hollywood films, the hierarchically privileged speaking subject is dislodged not only by the rising din of hitherto inaudible popular voices but also by the mute clutter of things, bodies, and signs, placed and displaced on an equal footing. Thus, the sensory fabric of everyday social space, the constitutive background of aesthetic imaginings and experiences, made visible and intelligible within this regime, imparts a quiet lesson of the equality of mute entities and an intimation of a molecular democracy of senses and perceptions always already at play.[10]

Starting with Scott Durham's framing introduction, this volume offers a rich array of essays which, among other things, energetically interrogate and interpret Rancière's three pivotal concepts and themes mentioned above. These essays are also composed with a presentist bent. They reiterate insistently the importance of Rancière's oeuvre in making sense of our troubled times. They tell us in different ways that the "lesson of Rancière"—unlike that of his early mentor, Althusser, from whom he broke in 1968[11]—is that there are *no lessons* once we give up the lures of ontological guarantees and teleological consolations. The supposition of equality must be asserted, fought for, and verified in pedagogy, no less than in politics and in art. We are equally on our own and equally with and among others as we engage this challenging dissensual present. For readers already familiar with Rancière's oeuvre, it is hoped that this volume will provide new provocations and openings to explore his work further and more deeply. And for those who are beginning to notice the growing interdisciplinary influence of and references to Rancière's writings, it is hoped that this volume will provide a set of critical starting points and nodes to engage his work, especially in the region where politics and aesthetics are made to cross and uncross so deftly as to "redistribute the sensible" and to alter our perceptual fields that would disclose a million mutinies afoot now, here and there and everywhere.

Notes

1. Karl Popper, *Conjectures and Refutations: The Growth of Scientific Knowledge* (Oxford: Routledge & Kegan Paul, 1963).

2. Jacques Rancière, "The Thinking of Dissensus: Politics and Aesthetics," in *Reading Rancière*, ed. Paul Bowman and Richard Stamp (New York: Continuum, 2011), 2.

3. Jacques Rancière, *Proletarian Nights: The Workers' Dream in Nineteenth-Century France*, trans. John Drury (London: Verso, 2012; French original, 1981).

4. Jacques Rancière, *The Ignorant Schoolmaster: Five Lessons in Intellectual Emancipation*, trans. Kristin Ross (Stanford, Calif.: Stanford University Press, 1991; French original, 1987).

5. Rancière, "The Thinking of Dissensus," 8.

6. Rancière, "The Thinking of Dissensus," 4.

7. Rancière, "The Thinking of Dissensus," 12.

8. Rancière, "The Thinking of Dissensus," 12.

9. Jacques Rancière, *The Politics of Aesthetics*, trans. and ed. Gabriel Rockhill (New York: Continuum, 2004; French original, 2000).

10. See Jacques Rancière, "The Politics of Literature," in *The Politics of Literature*, trans. Julie Rose (Cambridge: Polity, 2011; French original, 2006), 3–30.

11. See Jacques Rancière, *Althusser's Lesson*, trans. Emiliano Battista (New York: Continuum, 2011; French original, 1974).

Acknowledgments

The editors would like to thank the Center for Global Culture and Communication, an initiative of Northwestern University's School of Communication, and the Department of French and Italian at Northwestern University for their support of this project at its various stages. We wish to thank the anonymous readers of our manuscript for their thoughtful and insightful readings of the collection. We would like to thank Liam Mayes for contributing his astuteness as a reader to the preparation of this manuscript. We would especially like to thank Caitlyn Doyle, whose acute critical intelligence and unerring editorial judgment have been indispensable at every phase of this project. Above all, we would like to express our profound gratitude to Jacques Rancière himself for his intellectual and personal generosity in sharing with us the multiple dimensions of a body of work that has fundamentally rethought the relations of politics to aesthetics—as well as for his generous contribution of a significant original essay as the afterword to this volume, and his graciousness in working with us to bring the project to fruition.

Editors' Note

Just as *le partage du sensible* is translated in a number of ways (including, in this volume, "distribution of the sensible," "partition of the sensible," and "partition of the perceptible"), the editors wish to alert the reader that our contributors variously render Rancière's key term *subjectivation* into English as "subjectification," "subjectivization," and "subjectivation."

DISTRIBUTIONS OF THE SENSIBLE

Introduction

Between Two Equalities

Scott Durham

> There was nothing else to do but to persist in indicating the extravagant path that consists in seizing in every sentence, in every act, *the side of equality*. Equality was not an end to attain, but a point of departure, a *supposition* to maintain in every circumstance. Never would truth speak up for it. Never would equality exist except in its verification and at the price of being verified always and everywhere.
>
> —Jacques Rancière, *The Ignorant Schoolmaster*

From Politics to Aesthetics: The Verification of Equalities

Rancière begins with equality neither as a foundational claim nor as a teleological horizon, but as a working supposition that must be verified. The immediate appeal of this approach across the disciplines (in political theory on the one hand and in literature, film, and media studies on the other) lies in part in the fact that it bypasses many of the interminable debates that have internally divided these disciplines—debates that have largely turned on claims of ontological foundation or historical necessity. The affirmation of democracy—which, whether it be aesthetic or political, can appear everywhere and anywhere in the absence of an *arkhē*—has no need to appeal to a foundation preceding, underlying, or beyond it. Democracy seeks its legitimacy neither by grounding the moments and forms of its appearance in ontology nor by having recourse to a teleological narrative or founding myth that reveals its original or historical truth.[1]

But it is precisely for this reason that the verification of the supposition of equality, far from referring us to some noumenal realm, is itself of the order of appearance. For in Rancière, the appearance of equality is affirmed in two incommensurate forms: it is sometimes proclaimed in the "empty word" of a political actor that does not yet exist, and sometimes lived in the sensible excess of a "molecular democracy" in which all lives, bodies, affects, and sensations are experienced (in contravention of their hierarchical distribution within the aesthetic fabric of social space) as being on an equal footing.[2] The paradox which all of the essays in this volume address in one form or another lies in this: that, as a principle with neither origin nor telos beyond the destabilizing effects of its appearance within the reigning order, equality cannot be verified by an appeal to a truth beyond appearance. It can be verified only by linking two moments or two forms of appearance itself—that is, by linking the appearance of new subjects laying claim to equality within the field of political speech to a new configuration of bodies as they might appear in a new distribution of the sensible.

In political theory, this can take the form—as in Jason Frank's discussion of a scene in James Baldwin in light of Rancière's *Disagreement* —of finding a correlative of the enunciative acts of emerging political subjects (who have no place as yet within the existing body politic) in the implicit political acts performed by a body when it shifts "from the place assigned to it" and "makes visible what has no business being seen."[3] The scene unfolds at an airport in the Jim Crow South where Baldwin, as his plane's only Negro passenger, observes a black chauffeur, who is there to meet the "beaming" and "delighted" white woman who is his employer. "If she were smiling at me that way," Baldwin remarks, "I would expect to shake her hand." This imagined handshake would in itself, no doubt, be a small gesture. But Baldwin goes on to tell us that it would nonetheless be enough to " 'blow up' " a town, and, with it, the unspoken web of " 'signs and nuances' " that structures the perceptible and symbolic relations woven into Jim Crow's distribution of the sensible.[4] Such symbolic acts render perceptible in the field of embodied everyday experience a heretofore unimaginable subject of emancipation. But they do not do so by identifying that subject with a collective body incarnating a new people. On the contrary, as Frank goes on to argue in the present volume, subjectivation "is first and foremost a mode of disidentification" with the distribution of places and roles in the existing body politic. The emergence of a democratic subject is enacted in the unexpected gap (like that produced by Baldwin's imagined handshake) between "the practical choreography of gesture and movement" that embodies hierarchy in the reigning distribution of the sensible and the new world of equality to which an as-yet-unimaginable subject of emancipation lays claim.[5]

Indeed, as Frank suggests in his discussion of the art of Glenn Ligon, it is arguably in this key dimension of political subjectivation as disidentification—as a dissensual " 'removal from the naturalness of a place' " —that Rancièrian politics encounters art.[6] Frank explores how Ligon's works, such as *Hands* and *The Day of Absence* (both of which take up media images of the Million Man March), can be read as reexamining in light of political disidentification what is at stake in images memorializing the enactment of " 'the people's liberation.' "[7] In so doing, he argues, Ligon at times advances a critique of the "imperative of visibility" discernible in forms of protest seeking recognition for preconstituted roles and identities (" 'Why do we need to raise our hands in that symbolic space again and again and again to be present in this country?' ").[8] At other times, Ligon leads us to reflect, not so much on "the object or identity made visible, [as on] the process of appearance or staging itself." In both cases, Frank finds in Ligon's works an aesthetic practice which, far from representing the identity of a liberated people in an image that would fulfill the collective promise of an act of speech, instead makes visible the forms and processes through which the dissensual effects of political subjectivation are verified in an embodied experience of disidentification—in the gaps, displacements, and absences that such "removal[s] from the naturalness of a place" produce in the sensuous fabric within which we habitually weave our consensual identities.

But as Benjamin Arditi shows, one can also begin with the excesses and deviations of bodies from their assigned place in the police order prior to political subjectivation—deviations whose proto-political content as resistance to that order only becomes visible in light of a democratic speech which, as yet unanchored in any recognized collective body, itself remains, in Rancière's phrase, an "empty word without a referent."[9] As Arditi observes, it is precisely because it is empty speech—a supplement, without any recognized social content of its own—that the language of democracy makes visible what should not be seen, and makes heard a discourse where once there was only place for noise. And yet if it is possible for such local flashes of equality to be rendered visible or audible once they are resituated within a social whole reconfigured by the emergence of new political actors, it must be because they were in some sense there to be seen or heard all along, even if they have never had a place in the police order's mapping of the places and functions it distributes within social space. It is in light of this insight that Arditi takes up Rancière's revision of Althusser's archetypal encounter with the police on the street, which is less a matter of interpellating demonstrators (as in the hailing, "Hey, you there!," that is the prototype of ideology in Althusser) than of declaring the supposed obviousness of what is and what is not to be seen ("Move along! There is nothing to see here!," as the police actually say when they break up crowds). As Arditi points out, if the police say that there is nothing to see, it is "precisely because there *is*" something to see which, from the police perspective, "should not be seen by those passing by or should be of no concern to them." There is, in other words, an as yet unacknowledged and unnamed excess in the social body—a part of the social body which obstinately refuses to know its place—that must be foreclosed for the supposed plenitude of the police order to be maintained. Nor are such encounters with an unremarked or invisible remainder the least bit unusual, since, every day and everywhere, "people can deviate from the given *without* putting into question" the police order as such. Arditi acknowledges the relative rarity of politics as Rancière defines it, since it involves a fundamental calling-into-question of who and what counts as political. But it is precisely because the emergence of new collective actors is so rare that we must be attentive to those perceptible deviations from the given which appear within the police order as the immanent possibility of politics—a possibility which will only rarely give rise to an emergent subject capable of retrospectively grasping such a deviation as political. In this light, dissensual aesthetic experience, as an instance of resistance to the police order that is not yet fully political, can serve as a privileged moment for grasping how resistance within the framework of the police order becomes politics in Rancière's sense. But it also invites us to consider the limits and possibilities of those everyday deviations from, or resistance to, the given that remain protopolitical: that is, of those local experiences of, or struggles for, equality that do not in themselves call into question the global structure of the police order, which Arditi (developing a concept from Samuel Chambers) calls the politics of the police.

Both Frank and Arditi can thus be said, despite their differences in other respects, to accord such deviations and excesses in the aesthetic fabric of sensuous experience the privilege of serving as the horizon or potential point of emergence of politics in their readings of Rancière. Both appeal in different ways to aesthetic experience (in the expansive sense in which Rancière often uses the term)[10] as the supplementary medium or correlative field through which the possibilities or effects of political dissensus might be imagined, although in neither case does it serve politics either as the utopian site in which its fundamental antagonisms would be reconciled, or as the expression of a prepolitical ontology (such as the being of a people) that might precede it as its ground. If "empty" democratic speech seeks its verification (Frank) or its possibility (Arditi) in aesthetic experience, it is not because that experience provides it with the fullness or harmony of a collective body of which democratic speech would be the lack. On the contrary, for both Frank and Arditi, the body invoked by democratic speech itself appears as a rupture in the fabric of the police order in which the occasion or effects of a potential political redivision of the whole are felt or seen in a dissensual displacement or deviation of its parts.

Meanwhile, art and aesthetics have their own way of thinking their relationship with politics, which, for Rancière, begins with the working assumption that Joseph Tanke (in his account of Rancière's reinterpretation of classical German aesthetics) identifies as the "egalitarian kernel" of his discussions of art, literature, and aesthetic philosophy: namely, that what defines aesthetic experience as such is the sensible appearance of the "suspension of . . . hierarchies" characteristic of the police order. The notion that aesthetic experience gives rise to an "experience of equality" appears in various forms in Rancière's readings of works of art and literature, ranging from the representation of social content;[11] to the egalitarian recomposition and redistribution of literary and theatrical publics that give rise to a "literariness" of circulating speech "without any specific addressee," where "situations, characters and expressions [are] freely available to anyone who feels like grabbing hold of them";[12] to the *livre en style*'s suspension of the hierarchical binaries embedded within the logic of narrative action characteristic of the "representative régime."[13] The Schillerian reading of the free play of faculties in Kantian aesthetics cited by Tanke—where Rancière sees the suspension of the hierarchical relationship between reason and sense as rehearsing a challenge to a " 'distribution of the sensible that identifies the order of domination with the differences between two humanities' "—is thus one of many examples.

From the perspective of intellectual and cultural history, the grouping of these otherwise heterogeneous instances (drawn as they are from different aspects and levels of aesthetic practice and experience) under the sign of democracy might appear debatable. For Rancière's "aesthetic régime" is not ultimately a structural or periodizing concept like the discursive formation in Foucault or the cultural dominant in Jameson, which might provide an archaeological or hermeneutic frame permitting us to grasp these instances of equality as symptomatic expressions on different levels of the same underlying institutional dynamic, structural logic, or historical tendency. What links these moments in Rancière is neither a hermeneutic nor an archaeology, but (as Tanke puts it) the "political promise" they offer us: that of an embodied community of equals. The supposition that they can be grasped as instances of equality is thus not affirmed in Rancière as a historical or ontological truth, but is most productively understood as a polemical thrust that reads them against the grain of a literary and aesthetic tradition that, even as it claims the power to assimilate the percepts and affects of any and every life for a common world of aesthetic experience, nonetheless distinguishes between that part of humanity endowed with the capacity to grasp their true meaning from those lives which merely unconsciously reproduce those sensations as aesthetic effects without being able to articulate their truth.

It is within this gap between sensation and meaning in aesthetic experience that the dissensual space of the politics of literature characteristic of the aesthetic régime emerges: the gap between an egalitarian experience of sensation, on the one hand (which frees up elements of the sensible from their hierarchical distribution), and, on the other, the authorial style or hermeneutic language that claims for itself the capacity to make visible the being or name the truth in which these disconnected parts participate. In Flaubert's *Madame Bovary*, for example, the literary division of labor between the epistemic authority of the writer and the sensuous experience of the character—which affirms the democracy of the lived sensations that they have in common, even as it marks the difference between the respective capacities of "two humanities" to think their truth—is, as Rancière argues, the prototype of all those methods of symptomatic reading and ideological critique that, serving, like literature, as a "machine for making life speak," lay claim to giving conscious expression to the truth of a people which is as yet incapable of saying what it is.[14]

Rancière himself, however, as Tanke observes, risks enacting a version of this contradiction when he follows Schiller in reading the free play of faculties in aesthetic experience as an allegory of a community to come. For through the interpretive act by which he "assigns a meaning, namely that of equality" to aesthetic experience, Rancière would seem to impose a determinate meaning on an experience whose democratic possibilities depend precisely on its indeterminacy—that is, on the fact that its interpretation is up for grabs for the very community of equals of which it is supposed to offer the prefiguration. Against this allegorizing temptation, Tanke turns to the Rancière of *The Emancipated Spectator*, where the authority of a narrator or commentator no longer imposes a determinate meaning on the indeterminate relations between sensible elements dislodged by the aesthetic work from their place in the reigning distribution of the sensible. For here, as Tanke puts it, it is not a commentator or allegorist but viewers themselves who "constantly interpret, select, and navigate their way through a given arrangement, in a sense recompleting it each time." For the meaning of any aesthetic reconfiguration of the sensible cannot be assigned in advance. The egalitarian community cannot be assumed to be the allegorical significance or utopian telos of the work without collapsing the gap between concept and sensation on which the very possibility of a democratic aesthetic politics depends.

Indeed, as Codruţa Morari argues in her analysis of the politics of film reception in postwar Paris, the tension between aesthetic democracy and interpretive authority is precisely what concretely constitutes a group of spectators as an aesthetic community. On the one hand, the community of postwar cinephiles (out of which emerged both the critics of *Cahiers du cinéma* and the filmmakers of the *Nouvelle Vague*) affirmed the seventh art as the democratic medium par excellence. For not only did this community's experience of cinémathèques along with neighborhood cinemas bring art films into relation with "disparaged" Hollywood films, linking " 'the cult of art to the democracy of entertainment and emotions.' "[15] It also discovered in the space of cinema a "common territory" in which any and every lover of the cinematic image, without regard to any claims to interpretive authority or cultural legitimacy, could learn to see anew.

On the other hand, as Morari further shows, the elaboration by these cinephiles of a politics of vision to which any and all in principle have access went hand-in-hand with the valorization of cinematic mise-en-scène in accordance with a *politique des auteurs* which tended to reproduce within this most democratic of media the same dissensual relations between disparate abilities of different viewers to grasp the truth of what they see (and, with it, the hierarchical distinction between two kinds of humanity) that Rancière identifies in Flaubert's politics of literature. If cinema emerges as a "common territory" for postwar cinephilia, it is thus not as a utopian destination, but as a space of contestation and dissensus. And if these aesthetic works continually rediscover the same antinomies—active and passive, sensation and signification, lived experience and theoretical truth—it is because it is only through the tension between these forms that we can attempt, however provisionally, to bridge the gap between a hierarchical distribution of the sensible and the life of a community of equals.

Nowhere is the cultivation of such antinomies so striking as when Rancière's commentators foreground the effects on critical discourse itself of the unresolved tension between politics and aesthetics in the relationship of commentary to its object. Critical accounts of modern political art, as Rancière suggests in *The Politics of Literature*, have historically depended on two contradictory ways of relating art to politics. On the one hand, art appears as a mode of mediated action, which intervenes in a social sphere from which it is autonomous only in and through the work it performs on the materiality of its own language and the forms of its medium considered as such. On the other hand, the critic's identification of what counts as political in art—namely, the specific injustice against which it intervenes—turns on a consideration of the work from the outside as an object whose formal characteristics can be understood only as the instrumental means for advancing a project whose truths fundamentally lie beyond it: in the commitments of an authorial intention, and in the effect it produces on its public. In other words, the measure of the political engagement of a literary work is approached by treating it as an instrument of communication like any other—and thus negating everything that is specific to it as literature.[16]

Sudeep Dasgupta's account of Rancière's strategy for evading these contradictions of political art as traditionally conceived begins by evoking an insight from Adorno, whose aesthetic thought, Dasgupta argues, has a deep affinity with that of Rancière. If the work appears as a contradictory object in criticism's attempts to determine the meaning of political art (as Rancière shows in his account of the "vicious circle" into which Sartre is led in elaborating his concept of *la littérature engagée* in *What Is Literature?*),[17] it is in part because art is irreducible to the status of an object, since "its very meaning . . . is the *suspension* of objectification."[18] As a privileged site for the critique of bourgeois culture's universal reification and instrumentalization of the world, the work of art resists the relegation of sensuous experience to the one-dimensionality of an instrument or mere illustration of a concept, by weaving the elements of that experience into a web of polyvocal and multivalent relations.

Where Rancière differs from the Frankfurt School, Dasgupta continues, is in his framing of aesthetic autonomy. For the Frankfurt School, art resists reification by retreating into the autonomy of an aesthetic sphere that might serve as a site of refuge or utopian compensation. For Rancière, by contrast, the work of art intervenes directly in the reigning distribution of the sensible, as it introduces indeterminacy into the sensuous fabric of our experience by unknotting and reweaving the relations between its elements. For Rancière, art's politics lies not in a movement toward autonomy, but in the immanent practice of the "aesthetics of displacement," which, as Dasgupta suggests, he nonetheless shares with Adorno. For both, art redraws the map separating and relating concepts and sensations, instrumental and poetic language, forms of expression and forms of life. But Rancière reveals the immanent political possibilities implicit in Adorno's critique of the reification of the work of art, which must resist treating the work of art as an aesthetic object endowed with a political meaning if it is not to exclude from the outset the dissensual movement of displacement—between politics and aesthetics, art and life—which is the real "meaning" of the work of art.

Meanwhile, if the politics of aesthetics can only be affirmed by destabilizing art's status as an object, an analogous movement, as Nico Baumbach shows, may be found at the opposing pole of the dialectic of commentary and its object: namely, in Rancière's performance of the discourse of critical theory itself. As Baumbach notes, much of the critical debate around Rancière concerns the way in which he has reframed the objects of the disciplinary discourses—political theory, literary and film studies, and so forth—of which he has been critical. But the literature on Rancière's work has, he argues, largely focused on the effects of such reframings within those disciplinary fields themselves, and on the challenges they pose to the concepts dominant within those fields. Thus, the scholar of film studies or literature foregrounds the way in which Rancière's concepts redefine "what makes art art," just as the political theorist explores how he rethinks "what makes politics politics." Baumbach, by contrast, turns his attention to what is less often explicitly discussed in critical responses to Rancière: namely, the questions posed in his work with regard to "the place or function of the very discourse within which these debates about art and politics take place." Just as Dasgupta reflects on Rancière's rethinking of Adorno's conception of aesthetics as a form of theoretical knowledge without an object, Baumbach emphasizes the implications for our notions of disciplinary authority of Rancière's critical style, which seeks to keep faith with the mobility and extraterritoriality of aesthetic experience, rather than maintaining a theoretical metalanguage that must rigorously separate itself from its object in order to speak that object's truth from a position of transcendence.

In film theory, a prominent example of a theoretical metalanguage which presupposes just the sort of clean break between the language of commentary and its object that Rancière's critical practice is calculated to subvert is the school of ideology critique, derived from the work of Rancière's teacher and adversary Louis Althusser, set forth by such critics as Jean-Louis Comolli and Jean Narboni in the pages of *Cahiers du cinéma*. Baumbach argues that ideology critique of this sort, with its enabling distinction of ideology from science, needs to distinguish the immanence of aesthetic experience from critical thought's transcendence of its object in order to speak from a position of mastery, since its fundamental problem is to explain the underlying logic that produces ideology's (imaginary) surface effects. And yet, Baumbach continues, the privileged aesthetic objects of this critical tendency are cinematic and literary works (those of Brecht and Godard may serve as examples) that endeavor, precisely, to lay bare and undo the effects of ideology within their own aesthetic fabric by exploring the effects of truth produced by aesthetic forms themselves. What is most significant for Baumbach about such " 'returns to sender' " (to use Rancière's own formula)—in which the work has already carried out on itself the critique of the ideological mechanisms it would in principle be the task of the critic to unmask—is not so much that the work of ideology critique is thereby rendered superfluous.[19] It is, rather, that the critic's task ceases to lie in a symptomatic reading aimed at making visible the underlying cause or "other scene," which would be the absent truth of the work's discontinuities and displacements.

On the contrary, the role of the critic now becomes that of espousing and inhabiting the gaps and leaps woven into the work's mise-en-scène (between the hierarchical world of the police order and that of the community of equals, but also between the equality of affects and sensations and that of political or social actants) in order to make of its dissensual fabric the very site for thinking the problem of democracy. For Baumbach, in short, critical thought must model itself on the movement of interruption and displacement that, for Dasgupta, characterizes the experience of the aesthetic object. "Theory," as it reflects on the relationship between politics and aesthetics, would thus have its own aesthetic politics—one that both inhabits the "gaps" (to use Rancière's term from *Les écarts du cinéma*) between domains of knowledge and experience, and maps unexpected connections between them: not only between art and politics, but also between the discourse of knowledge and the aesthetic fabric of the sensible. In this, Baumbach argues, Rancière's critical practice leads us to call into question the place and function of critical discourse in a way that goes beyond interdisciplinarity in any conventional sense, inviting us to work "against the idea of disciplines"—and, with it, disciplinary authority—as such.

Equality, History, Narrative

Equality, as we have seen, is not the attribute or claim of a preexisting actor, nor is it an ontological ground in the name of which such claims might be made. Equality presupposes nothing, since it is itself "always and everywhere" an absolute, if always provisional, point of departure. This gives Rancière's approach an immediate political appeal beyond that of the potential for renewal that it offers debates internal to the academy. For by beginning with the supposition that democracy requires no presupposition other than itself—that the principle of equality need not pass through the thickets of an ontological or historical preamble—it authorizes us to act on the provisional assumption that, here and now, whatever the "objective conditions" might seem to be, another world is possible.

In this light, Rancière's political thought is perhaps, as Giuseppina Mecchia suggests, uniquely suited to the needs of radical thought in a period of reaction. For it renders possible a radical discourse even in the face of a global situation that seems to preclude it. Indeed, as Mecchia argues, this accounts for the initial rise of Rancière's thought to prominence in the 1990s, a moment in which "the wholesale liquidation of communist models of sociopolitical organization" was coupled with "the triumph of the Western capitalist model of social organization." Rancière's affirmation that the many retained "both the linguistic ability and the historical pretext to rise up and demonstrate their fundamental equality with their rulers" could only appear as a welcome corrective to the technocracy's claims to have put an end to "the age of political struggle." It is above all the strategic value of his invocation of democracy in that historical conjuncture that Mecchia underscores in her reading of Rancière. And yet, Mecchia suggests, the enabling condition of Rancière's untimely insistence on the possibility of a democratic politics in any situation—which she identifies as the possibility available to any subject of language to affirm in the adjudication of a wrong its equality with any other—also potentially limits its political and analytical force. For, she argues, in the very act of freeing itself from the need to ground its claim to speak in the name of an emergent collective subject in a history, substance, or process that would constitute the being of a collective body, Rancière's concept of politics runs the risk of abstracting the process of subjectivation manifested in actual social movements from the material forms of embodiment that define them in their historical specificity and ultimate political effects. The same rejection of any Spinozian ontology or Marxist historical necessity that allows Rancière to find the possibility of democratic contestation in any historical conjuncture, Mecchia suggests, also makes it difficult to determine on what conceptual grounds one can differentiate one such contestation from another—whether this be a matter of a historical reflection on what might distinguish the democratic politics of the Aventine secession from that of the Arab Spring, or of distinguishing the "real politics" giving rise to a new people from rioting without any ultimate political significance (as Rancière attempted in commenting on the uprising of youth of Arab and African descent across France in 2005).

Like Mecchia, Pheng Cheah takes the measure of the strategic value of Rancière's political thought in relation to a contemporary historical situation—a situation Cheah frames in terms of postcolonial theory's attempts to imagine the emergence of new subjects within (and against) the framework of the contemporary global system and its international division of labor. In so doing, Cheah contrasts Rancière's account of the emergence of a new and "contentless" subject from the interruption of the continuity of the existing world's "order and routine" and the attendant suspension of recognized social identities—a dissensual suspension of the police order's mapping of bodies and roles which permits that subject both to lay claim to the experience of a "new envisioned world" and to argue for its "*capacity for* and *right to* visibility"—with Fanon's dialectical narrative of the emergence of revolutionary subjectivity through the development of a nascent national culture.

In Fanon, as Cheah reminds us, the conditions for political action are prepared by the emergence of new forms of cultural expression contesting the subjugation, divisions, and passivity woven into the fabric of colonial experience—cultural forms that ultimately make it possible for a nascent collective actor to come to recognize itself as such. But whatever philosophical or strategic value this dialectical narrative in which the sovereign nation emerges as "a self-causing being" might have had at the moment of decolonization, it is "no longer viable" in the very different situation of "contemporary globalization." For this new moment is defined, he argues, both by forms of "biopolitical technologies" and "calculative reason" resistant to their dialectical reappropriation by a free and autonomous subject, and by an organization of the division of labor on a scale too vast to find its dialectical reversal in a narrative of national resistance.

Rancière's conception of a "contentless" subject of democratic politics offers, Cheah continues, a promising alternative to Fanon's for thinking the emergence in the global South of counterhegemonic collective protagonists that would contest the forms of hierarchy characteristic of the international division of labor which defines our contemporary political situation, where potential subjects of political struggle can no longer presuppose the content of a preexisting national culture as the ground out of which they might emerge. And yet, he suggests, if Rancière's account of emergence is to provide the theoretical language in which the appearance of new political subjects in the global South might be thought, Rancière's conception of politics must address its own "socio-anthropologistic" presuppositions. As Cheah observes, the contestation of hierarchy cannot be formulated (as in the critique of the Platonic distinction between "two humanities") as a demand for the inclusion of the heretofore invisible and unrecognized workers on the periphery of the global system in the juridical and political structures of global governance (even if that inclusion is staged in the paradoxical form of a subject arguing for the right to exist of a world in which it could speak and be heard). This is first because labor, far from being stigmatized in the contemporary world system, is a condition for participation in discourses of governance and its structure of rights, whose hierarchical effects are produced by an obligatory inclusion which accords each nation a place in the global community commensurate with its function in the international division of labor. But it is even more fundamentally the case because resistance on the part of those subaltern and indigenous groups actually excluded from that international division of labor does not take the form of an argument contesting (in however paradoxical a form) its account of who by rights should count within it. As Cheah argues in a reading of Amitav Ghosh's novel *The Hungry Tide*, the heretofore unimaginable world in the name of which such subaltern collective protagonists contest the subsumption of forms of life for which the "calculative reason" of the global system has no place—but which Ghosh's narrative of emergence nonetheless renders visible and audible—privileges cultural experiences of "inhuman forces" (notably, in Ghosh's invocations of animism) incommensurate with a conception of the political defined by "making or receiving a dissenting human argument."

Meanwhile, it is also possible, as Eleanor Kaufman argues, to read the relationship of Rancière's political thought to his historical moment against the grain. Kaufman situates Rancière's writing on politics of the early 1980s, alongside the work of such contemporaries as Alain Badiou and Jacques Derrida, as part of a broader turn away from "the terrain of the economic to that of the political in late twentieth-century French thought." As Kaufman points out, the most crucial insights of twentieth-century French thought had up to that point been "grouped under a rubric or logic of the economic . . . in distinction from the political"—and, indeed, presupposed (in Fredric Jameson's formulation with regard to Marxism) the "*structural* priority of economics over politics."[20] The forms of thought Kaufman groups under her far-reaching concept of the economic (which encompasses, not only various Marxisms and libidinal economies, but also economies of excess in the tradition of Mauss and Bataille) may all, in one sense or another, be characterized as manifestations of the ontological thinking from which Rancière seeks to free the thought of politics as such. They are all versions of what Rancière refers to as "metapolitical interpretation,"[21] which reads political speech and action as fundamentally symptomatic expressions of a deep structure that can be rendered visible only through the interpretive powers of the theorist capable of seeing beyond appearances to the other scene in which their truth resides.

Taken on its own terms, the strategic value of Rancière's rejection of such metapolitical ontologies as clearing a space for political action, as Mecchia suggests, must be weighed against the claims of economic thought to account for the play of forces within the social body that give rise to (but also delimit the possibilities of) such action. But Kaufman, in a provocative reading of Rancière's reflections in *The Nights of Labor* on the imbalanced "'cenobitic economy'" of rebellious worker intellectuals on the margins of the factory system, poses a different question: to what degree does Rancière's turn to politics succeed in differentiating itself from the economic thought from which it seeks to free the possibility of politics? The powerful resonances of the interplay of forces of labor and desire in Rancière's portrait of Gabriel Gauny with the imbalanced economies of sacrifice and expenditure Kaufman evokes in discussing such thinkers as Bataille and Lyotard invite us to interrogate the extent to which it is possible (or, indeed, desirable) for politics to finally dispense with thinking the unconscious dynamics of social structures, or the entanglement of individual and collective bodies in the interplay of power, desire, and resistance. Indeed, it might be argued that, as with Derridean deconstruction (to which it has sometimes been compared), what Samuel Chambers calls Rancière's "impure politics"[22] cannot simply declare itself to have done away with ontology along with metapolitics, any more than Sartre's Roquentin can ultimately cleanse himself of the sin of existing. On this point, Kaufman's commentary overlaps with Mecchia's critique of Rancière. For both argue, from very different perspectives, that the historical and material economies of power and resistance that Rancière's political *epoché* rejects along with every form of ontology and metapolitics continue to haunt his thought, whether from the outside, as Mecchia argues (in the form of a collective body whose materiality is unthinkable as such in what she sees as Rancière's language-centered problematic), or, as Kaufman suggests, from within, as a return of the repressed force of economic thought within Rancière's account of democratic politics itself.

Tom Conley situates Rancière's thought in relation to another experience: not to the "consensual times" of the supposed end of history and politics against which Rancière's profile as a philosopher of dissensus has largely been defined for contemporary readers, but to the Paris of the 1960s. It was there—out of his encounters both with Marxism and the prerevolutionary atmosphere that would culminate in May '68, and with the world of cinephilic democracy evoked by Morari, where European art film was viewed alongside the (then-devalued) films of the Hollywood studio system—that Rancière's emerging thought took shape. Moving between the attempt to come to grips with inequality in philosophy and politics, and screenings of such films as Rossellini's *Europa '51* (1952) or Walsh's *Colorado Territory* (1949), the young Rancière confronted the task of working out for himself how struggles for political equality might relate to the pleasures of an equality of quite another sort: the democratic sublime revealed on a screen where even the most apparently insignificant figure or object normally consigned to the background—the dust kicked up in the course of a gunfight, or the shadow unconsciously cast on a cliff face by a rifleman—emerges with its own splendor into the projector's light.

By evoking this experience, however, Conley is not offering a biographical or historical explanation of Rancière's democratic turn. He is, rather, recounting with regard to Rancière's democratic problematic what one might call the "fable" of its emergence. As Rancière reminds us in *Film Fables*, the story of young John Mohune in Lang's *Moonfleet* (1955) stages before our eyes the very self-education in the art of democratic vision to which the film invites us as viewers. Similarly, if the story of the young Rancière's movement back and forth between two incommensurate fields is exemplary, it is not because it provides us with a narrative foundation to the problem of equality, but because it allows us to imagine, through the story of an individual life, the problem we confront as both viewers and political actors as we move between two equally compelling but distinct forms of equality: the problem of negotiating the gap between the pleasures of aesthetic equality and the "common and collective battle against social inequality." This problem is that which Conley, following Rancière, identifies (in contradistinction to the *politique de l'auteur*) as that of a *politique de l'amateur*: an aesthetic politics defined, neither by expertise nor by reference to first principles, but by the "deviations" through which we trace multiple paths between these two incommensurate experiences of equality. As in cinematic montage, this movement allows each pole to be affected by the other, while at the same time measuring the distance between them.

But to approach the thought of equality in this way, as a kind of intercutting that opens up an indeterminate relation between incommensurate forms—one articulated in the political struggle against hierarchy, and the other lived in the cinephilic experience of equality of affects and sensations—is to underscore the fact that, from the moment of its emergence, democratic thought in Rancière does not seek to resolve the tension between aesthetic and political equality. On the contrary, Conley finds the originality of Rancière's thought in the way that it identifies equality as the common problem that at once links and separates these two forms (much as the sayable and the visible in Foucault are, as Deleuze has argued, brought into relation on the basis of their difference),[23] obliging us to reflect on what is produced (and what is lost) each time we traverse the gap between them.

The fable of equality's discovery thus will neither recount a return to origins, nor take the form of an evolving and uninterrupted narrative that reveals over the course of its history the concrete possibilities latent within its concept. Because it is not fundamentally ontological but polemical, the formulation of the problem of equality in any historically determinate police order cannot presuppose an underlying being of a democratic people which would provide the common horizon for both its collective actors and the subjects of egalitarian vision. In a given historical situation, equality is verified only by the intercutting that allows us to see the undoing of hierarchical relations within disparate forms of appearance (the reconfiguration of relations between recognized social actors, and aesthetic intervention in the reigning distribution of the sensible) as distinct but indissociable dimensions of the same political problem. Similarly, it is precisely because it is not conceived as an endpoint or solution that this problem can neither be limited to a specific localizable historical horizon, nor recounted as a continuous and uninterrupted narrative which would unfold from the "miracle" of democracy in Athens to the Aventine secession, or from Wordsworth's impressions of the French Revolution to the Boulevard Saint Michel in May '68. Because, in each historical instance, it is articulated in its polemical relation to the hierarchical forms that it problematizes, equality (in contrast to liberty) necessarily takes the form of interruption: it is verified in scenes of political equality and tableaux of democratic experience that (to recall our discussion of Pheng Cheah) interrupt the historically specific continuities on which the coherence of a given police order depends. The history of equality, accordingly, does not unfold along a straight and single path, but moves along the diagonal, tracing a broken line from interruption to interruption and from one problematization to the next, in each case weaving a new montage of the relations across the gaps between disparate spaces of social practice and incommensurate forms of experience.[24]

Rancière contra Foucault: From a History of Power to the Narration of Equality

It is on the related question of the theoretical emplotment of emergent democratic subjects' contestation of relations of domination—and the rewriting of the "cartography of the perceptible and the thinkable" from which such contestation is inseparable—that Rancière, in his own contribution to this volume, frames his relationship to (and divergences from) the thought of Michel Foucault. Rancière remarks on the affinity of his work, beginning with *The Nights of Labor*, with Deleuze and Foucault's rethinking of the relationship of theory to practice in their 1972 interview, "Intellectuals and Power," as expressed in his citation of a key formulation of Deleuze: "A theory is always local and related to a limited field, and it is applied in another sphere, more or less distant from it."[25] Rancière sees this as marking a break with the form in which the relationship of theory to practice has been narrated from Plato to Althusser: namely, one that distinguishes in principle between the privileged point of view of the theorist, who alone is in a position to grasp the structure of the totality as "the nexus of social causes," and the "restricted field of vision" of subjects of social praxis, who (like the prisoners in Plato's cave) are incapable of grasping the extent to which their lived experience is the effect of a structure invisible to them. "The difference," as Rancière puts it, "is that the former sees the connection of the laws that govern this world while the latter only see the effects estranged from their cause." Theory would thus provide the subjects of social practice with a "viewpoint . . . inaccessible to them due to their very position."

But, as Rancière notes, Deleuze and Foucault remap this "cartography of the perceptible and the thinkable" by calling into question the notion that there is any privileged point "from which the global nexus of causes could be given." Nor can theory, armed with its supposed knowledge of the whole, prescribe from the summit of that totalizing point of view the course of action that must be pursued locally by subjects of social action (who would otherwise labor in blind isolation) if they are to transform the structure of the whole itself. For Deleuze and Foucault, theory begins by confronting the relations of power and resistance at play in a specific situation, such as the prison, as at once a political problem to be made visible and named, and as a philosophical problem to be thought.

This means, first of all, that theory enters into a direct (rather than a mediated) relationship with the local field in which it intervenes. Such was, writes Rancière, the relationship of Foucault's Prison Information Group to the prisoners who resisted the prison's relations of domination along with its forms of knowledge. The task of theory was no longer to reveal to the prisoners a truth of the whole that they were not capable of seeing for themselves. It was, rather, to create with them the conditions under which they could lay claim to a discourse and make visible the realities of power that they already knew quite well, but for which the dominant forms of knowledge had no place. In short, the task of theory was to ally itself with what Foucault has elsewhere called "the insurrection of subjugated knowledges."[26]

But it also means that when theory moves between two distinct situations, it no longer does so by passing through a concept of the system in whose logic social actors ignorant of the whole might come to see their truth. On the contrary, in constructing "relay[s] from one practice to another,"[27] theory continually reinvents its concepts in relation to the different relations of power and resistance that it discovers in "another sphere, more or less distant from it."[28] Theory thus does not move vertically, from the partial or occluded view of the local situation to a panoramic map of the whole. Rather, it discovers, as Rancière puts it, "new and unexpected effects" in its lateral movement from site to site, contributing, in the process, "to a new mapping and a new territory."

Rancière underscores his own affinity with Deleuze and Foucault's rearticulation of the relationship of theory to practice in "Intellectuals and Power," which in many respects parallels the movement of his own thought beginning with *The Nights of Labor*. But it is also in the name of this Foucauldian rethinking of the politics of theory with specific reference to prisoners and the prison that Rancière critiques the implicit politics of *Discipline and Punish*. For in that work, he alleges, Foucault recounts the history of the prison beginning with the whole, as it is imagined from a privileged point of view. For Rancière, the scenes Foucault describes of local exercises of power—as in his celebrated tableaux of the mid-eighteenth-century execution of the regicide Damiens, and the exhaustive rules governing the conduct of boys interned in a nineteenth-century reformatory—serve less as maps of local relations of power/knowledge than as exemplary figures of a historical shift in the logic of the system as a whole, as an ancien régime governed according to a logic of power based on sovereignty, law, and deduction (*prélèvement*) is succeeded by increasingly pervasive disciplinary technologies more adept at policing "rebellious popular bodies."

It is in this context that Rancière brings us back to the question of the emplotment of narratives of resistance and emancipation. For Rancière's critique of Foucault's history of the prison does not turn on a "question of political inclination"—that is, on the accusation that Foucault himself sees the world from the totalizing perspective of power and its archives instead of listening to "the voices from below." It turns, rather, on his observation that Foucault chooses a form of narrative that privileges structural causes in its way of linking local effects. It is to this choice of narrative form privileging the "viewpoint from the hill of science on the machinery of the cave" that Rancière attributes the depoliticizing effects of Foucault's history. For such a narrative, in which resistance appears as what disciplinary power turns in various ways to its own ends in its conquest of the body politic, hardly lends itself, Rancière observes, to "fostering the spirit of rebellion."

Meanwhile it is, Rancière goes on to suggest, precisely because there is no place for rebellion in his emplotment of the history of the prison that Foucault must find a place for it elsewhere, in another, more literary form. Such, he argues, are the poetic figures of resistance invoked by Foucault in "The Life of Infamous Men," where Foucault registers the momentary emergence from the margins of the police order of those ill-fated or monstrous existences which, seemingly having no relationship with the world organized by the dominant forms of power, appear to incarnate in their fugitive encounters and clashes with that power an outside which power is incapable of naming or imagining.[29] Resistance, Rancière suggests, is here given an absolute and literary form—one in which it appears as the thought of the outside—precisely because there is no place for it in Foucault's historical narrative. The politics of theory implicit in the form of that narrative—in what Rancière calls its "poetics of knowledge"—thus gives rise to a division between two forms: a historical narrative that recounts how power structures the logic of the whole, and a literary narrative, which supplements the narration of that history with a lyrical expression of the life of the outside as the being of resistance.

What is perhaps most striking about Rancière's account of Foucault—which brings to the fore both the affinities and the points of divergence between their styles of thought—is the extent to which his critique is ultimately articulated in formal terms. The politics of Foucault's account of the history of the prison turns on the narrative form in which it narrates (or is incapable of narrating) the appearance of resistance. Nor does Rancière address the notion of forces of resistance themselves, considered as the "other side" or "absent cause" of power—that is, as a potential for resistance which might find its absolute expression in the "unseen abysses" of the life of infamous men—as a Nietzschean or Spinozian ontological claim. Refusing to follow Foucault into the depths, it is enough for Rancière to show that Foucault must give resistance an absolute expression in one place because he has been unable to narrate it historically in another. According to Rancière, in other words, a literary ontology of resistance serves to supplement the lack of political resistance in Foucault's history—an absence that follows from the latter's choice of narrative form.

A Foucauldian might well object that Rancière's critique brackets precisely what marks the originality of the conception of power Foucault advances in *Discipline and Punish.* For the strategies of power for Foucault are not oriented by a view from the hill, nor are they "totalizing," whether in the sense that power could subordinate all possible resistance to its ends, or in the sense that its local effects would be the consequences of a transformation of the structure of the whole. On the contrary, Foucault quite explicitly elaborates a conception of power for which any map of the whole only appears as the effect of innumerable local struggles involving distinct relations of forces.

Moreover, in the relation between power and resistance played out in such struggles, resistance comes first for Foucault, as the risk of an emergent counterpower that must be confronted by the dominant powers whenever they assemble a multiplicity of individuals (whether the latter are brought together to be witnesses of their sovereign's execution of a regicide, or as delinquents to be disciplined in a reformatory). From this perspective, the first question we must pose in analyzing power relations in a given social field is: in terms of what strategic logic does power pose the problem of its relation to resistance?

In this light, the historical question raised by Foucault's juxtaposition of the two scenes opening *Discipline and Punish* is not that of the structure of the whole (as with the Marxist concept of mode of production), but of two "styles" in which power is exercised, and in terms of which the relationship of power to resistance is problematized.[30] Is the problem posed, for example, as one of prohibition and deduction, according to the logic of sovereignty? Or is it, rather, posed, according to the logic of the disciplines, as one of investing the forces of the social body (including the forces of resistance) in detail in order to render them more productive? In this light, what links the various islands of the carceral archipelago—what makes "prisons resemble factories, schools, barracks, [and] hospitals, which all resemble prisons"[31]—would be not some structure in dominance that one might grasp from a height but, precisely, the "style" of correction and formation in terms of which power poses the problem of resistance in each instance: a problem that each institution imperfectly resolves according to the power relations immanent to it.

Rancière's critique thus arguably brackets everything specifically Foucauldian in the concept of power articulated in *Discipline and Punish*—and, above all, Foucault's conception of power as a relation that presupposes resistance as primary. But this is not to say that Rancière simply misrepresents Foucault. For Rancière's reframing allows us to see the extent to which resistance—as the omnipresent other term through which, according to his concept of power, the exercise of power must pass—is effaced from Foucault's narrative. Indeed, that narrative, as Rancière argues, for the most part focuses not on the "revolts, spontaneous organizations, coalitions—anything that may establish conjunctions" that can arise anywhere in the social body where an "organized multiplicity"[32] is assembled (which Foucault enumerates in articulating his concept of power)—but rather on the story of the progressive spread and consolidation of disciplinary power in every domain of society. In short, disciplinary power, rather than plebeian resistance to it, ends up being the protagonist of Foucault's narrative. Indeed, where resistance briefly takes center stage in *Discipline and Punish* is, precisely, in the lyrical coda, recalling the aesthetic of "The Life of Infamous Men," with which Foucault concludes his chapter titled "Illegalities and Delinquency." There we read of the ephemeral appearance in court (memorialized for posterity by a Fourierist newspaper, *La Phalange*) of a vagabond—a young man with neither parents, nor trade, nor employer, nor fixed domicile—who declares before an incredulous judge his right to live outside every form of discipline.[33]

It is thus by bracketing what is specific to Foucault's problematization of power in order to focus on the form of his narrative that Rancière is able to foreground a dissensual tension between the form in which

Foucault narrates power and his articulation of its concept. Meanwhile, a fundamental question for Rancière in developing his own poetics of knowledge is that of elaborating a mode of theoretical narration which will give such moments of contestation their due without either romanticizing or lending false continuity to the local and discontinuous forms of their appearance. Everything will turn on the effects Rancière draws from the scenes of dissensus out of which he builds his theoretical narrative. This is first of all a matter of emplotment. He must develop a narrative form which moves neither forward in a continuous horizontal line, nor vertically, from the local description of the part to the global structure of the whole, but (as we have already suggested in our discussion of Rancière's relationship to history) along the diagonal from scene to scene—not to reconstruct a sequence of causes but, rather, to take stock of the resonances and differences between distinct stagings of the problem of equality from one site to the next.

But it also involves, more fundamentally, a different way of staging in each scene the relationship of life to the forms of theoretical or literary language that articulate its truth. "As a 'theoretical' form," writes Rancière in the afterword, "the scene is the staging of the process through which a life affirms its capacity to be an object of thought for itself." The task of the writer of such scenes is thus no longer either to name the form of power it makes visible, nor even to recount in literary form the force of resistance inherent in a deviant life incapable of recounting its own legend. It is, rather, to capture those moments when plebeian men and women, "[borrowing] the 'language from above,'" cross the border separating the practice of life from its theoretical or literary truth "into the universe of writing." Such moments give rise to dissensual scenes, where the infamous can call into question the power that marginalizes them, and resistance can recount its own history.

The task of theory, from this perspective, is no longer one of discerning relations of power and resistance, but one of memorializing such scenes of dissensus in "an archive of 'the writing of the people,'" which bears witness to those fugitive moments when "those who are not supposed to write get into the world of writing." As Rancière insists, the verification of the claim to equality staged in these scenes demands not only that these voices be heard, but that they be woven into a theoretical narrative whose form does not replicate the narratives of power. It is thus that *The Nights of Labor* stages Rancière's response to the problem of resistance posed by Foucault in *Discipline and Punish*: not only by staging plebeian contestations of disciplinary power, but by undoing the latter's forms of knowledge, through the creation of a counterarchive where the effects of aesthetic and political equality will be intricately interwoven.

Notes

1. I thus cannot follow Oliver Marchart in assimilating Rancière to a "left-Heideggerian" postfoundational political thought which would play out within political philosophy the aporias of the ontological difference. See Oliver Marchart, *Post-Foundational Political Thought: Political Difference in Nancy, Lefort, Badiou, and Laclau* (Edinburgh: Edinburgh University Press, 2007). For, as Benjamin Arditi cogently argues below, while Rancière's method of equality shares with such thinkers what Rancière himself describes as an "enactment of the aporia of foundation," Rancière refuses "to ontologize the aporia."

2. Jacques Rancière, *The Politics of Literature*, trans. Julie Rose (Cambridge: Polity, 2011), 41, 26.

3. Jacques Rancière, *Disagreement: Politics and Philosophy*, trans. Julie Rose (Minneapolis: University of Minnesota Press, 1998), 30. For Frank's discussion of this scene in Baldwin, see Jason Frank, *Constituent Moments: Enacting the People in Postrevolutionary America* (Durham, N.C.: Duke University Press, 2009), 231–32.

4. Baldwin, quoted in Frank, *Constituent Moments*, 231.

5. Frank, *Constituent Moments*, 232.

6. Rancière, *Disagreement*, 36.

7. Million Man March National Organizing Committee, quoted in Frank.

8. Ligon, quoted in Frank.

9. Rancière, *The Politics of Literature*, 41.

10. On this point, see Jacques Rancière, *The Politics of Aesthetics*, trans. Gabriel Rockhill (New York: Continuum, 2004), 13: "If the reader is fond of analogy, aesthetics can be defined in a Kantian sense—re-examined perhaps by Foucault—as the system of *a priori* forms determining what presents itself to sense experience. It is a delimitation of spaces and times, of the visible and the invisible, of speech and noise, that simultaneously determines the place and the stakes of politics as a form of experience." It is only when one begins with the expansive frame of this "primary aesthetics," Rancière argues, that it is possible to consider what is at stake in the aesthetic practices of works of art. For "artistic practices are 'ways of doing and making' that intervene in the general distribution of ways of doing and making as well as in the relationships they maintain to modes of being and forms of visibility" (13). In other words, the aesthetics of artistic practices relate to politics as interventions in aesthetics in this expansive Kantian or Foucauldian sense—as interventions in the distribution of the sensible.

11. See Rancière's discussion of the dissolution of the system of genres that linked the style of expression to the social rank of the character, which gives way to "the antigeneric principle of the equality of all represented subjects," in *Mute Speech: Literature, Critical Theory and Politics*, trans. Gabriel Rockhill (New York: Columbia University Press, 2011), 50.

12. Rancière, *The Politics of Literature*, 12–13.

13. See Rancière's discussion of Flaubert in "The Book in Style," in *Mute Speech*, 113–27.

14. Rancière, *The Politics of Literature*, 14, translation modified. For Rancière, Madame Bovary is exemplary of the "politics of literature" and the "aesthetic régime" in that its aesthetic politics is defined by the tension between "two ways of identifying art and life." For that politics is played out in the gap between a provincial nobody's appetite to savor and possess all of the circulating percepts and affects that the democratization of culture makes available to her, and the style of the writer who, in contemplating this dance of sensations from an appropriate distance, allows readers more sophisticated than his heroine both to hear the music of the whole that animates them and to diagnose the democratic fever that gives rise in Emma to the fatal illusion that the truth of aesthetic experience lies in their possession as an object of desire. See Rancière, "The Putting to Death of Madame Bovary," in *The Politics of Literature*, 49–71.

15. Rancière, quoted in Morari.

16. "Literary modernity has been styled as the implementation of an intransitive use of language as opposed to its communicative use. In determining the relationship between politics and literature, this was a most problematic criterion, one that quickly led to a dilemma: either the autonomy of literary language was contrasted with some political use, considered as an instrumentalization of literature; or a solidarity between literary intransitivity, seen as the affirmation of the materiality of the signifier, was authoritatively asserted, along with the materialist rationality of revolutionary practice." Rancière, *The Politics of Literature*, 5. For Rancière, the impasses into which Sartre is led by his attempt to contrast "poetic intransitivity" with a "literary transitivity" (5) characteristic of *la littérature engagée* are exemplary of this dilemma.

17. See Rancière, *The Politics of Literature*, 5–8.

18. T. W. Adorno, "Cultural Criticism and Society," in *Prisms*, trans. Shierry Weber Nicholson and Samuel Weber (Cambridge, MA: MIT Press), 22.

19. Rancière, *The Politics of Literature*, 23.

20. Fredric Jameson, "Lenin and Revisionism," in *Lenin Reloaded: Toward a Politics of Truth*, ed. Sebastian Budgen, Stathis Kouvelakis, and Slavoj Žižek (Durham, N.C.: Duke University Press, 2007), 66.

21. Rancière, *Disagreement*, 82.

22. See Samuel Chambers, *The Lessons of Rancière* (Oxford: Oxford University Press, 2012).

23. See Gilles Deleuze, *Foucault*, trans. and ed. Seán Hand (Minneapolis: University of Minnesota Press, 1988), 64–69.

24. That is why, as both Morari and Conley insist from their distinct angles on the question, the relationship of equality to hierarchy in cinephilic reception can never be settled once and for all, but remains a problem that we, as viewers, confront today, albeit in the forms specific to our political conjuncture and media landscape.

25. Michel Foucault and Gilles Deleuze, "Intellectuals and Power: A Conversation between Michel Foucault and Gilles Deleuze," in *Language, Counter-memory, Practice: Selected Essays and Interviews*, ed. Donald Bouchard, trans. Donald Bouchard and Sherry Simon (Ithaca, N.Y.: Cornell University Press, 1977), 206.

26. Michel Foucault, *"Society Must Be Defended": Lectures at the Collège de France, 1975–1976*, ed. Mauro Bertani and Alessandro Fontana, trans. David Macey (New York: Picador, 2003), 7.

27. Foucault and Deleuze, "Intellectuals and Power," 206.

28. Deleuze, from Foucault and Deleuze, "Intellectuals and Power," 206.

29. Michel Foucault, "The Life of Infamous Men," in *Michel Foucault: Power, Truth, Strategy*, ed. Meaghan Morris and Paul Patton (Sydney: Feral Publications, 1979), 76–91.

30. "We have, then, a public execution and a time-table. They do not punish the same crimes or the same type of delinquent. But they each define a certain penal style." Michel Foucault, *Discipline and Punish: The Birth of the Prison*, trans. Alan Sheridan (New York: Vintage, 1977), 7.

31. Foucault, *Discipline and Punish*, 228.

32. Foucault, *Discipline and Punish*, 219.

33. See Foucault, *Discipline and Punish*, 290–92.

Jacques Rancière's Politics of the Ordinary

Jason Frank

> Exclusive consensus comes unstuck not only at exceptional moments . . . It comes unstuck as often as specific worlds of community open up, worlds of disagreement and dissension. Politics occurs wherever a community with the capacity to argue and to make metaphors is likely, at any time and through anyone's intervention, to crop up.
>
> —Jacques Rancière, *Disagreement: Politics and Philosophy*

For Jacques Rancière, democracy is defined by an astounding but usually disavowed principle: that "those who rule—the people—do it on the ground that there is no reason why some persons should rule over others, except the fact that there is no reason." Democracy—organized by ancient Athenians in the random drawing of lots and "complete absence of the entitlement to govern"—reveals that "the very ground for the power of ruling is that there is no ground at all," that all of the natural qualifications for rule—whether they be the qualifications of wealth or birth, prophecy or knowledge, charisma or skill—are equally fictive.[1] Rancière's an-archic principle of democracy breaks with all theories of democracy that focus on different justifications or legitimations of popular rule, which is to say, with most democratic theory as traditionally understood.

My interest in Rancière is primarily as a democratic theorist, even though his complex and provocative work in democratic theory moves and blends with his equally complex and provocative work in aesthetics, philosophy, historiography, education, literature, and film and media studies; it is an appropriately wide-ranging itinerary for a thinker who works under the sign of "indisciplinarity."[2] However, this essay does not attempt to provide a systematic explanation, much less defense, of Rancière's democratic theory, or even attempt to trace its networked connections to other regions of his thought. This is being ably done by the growing number of political theorists currently engaging Rancière's work.[3] Instead, I want to make a case for Rancière's importance to contemporary democratic theory that is empirically focused on the forms of political speech and action that his work allows us to perceive—and to theoretically engage—that would otherwise be unavailable or obscured, and would certainly be so if we were compelled to engage political life primarily through the myopic conceptual lenses provided by dominant approaches to democratic theorizing in the Anglophone world, whether aggregationist or deliberative, communitarian or liberal, and even many of the radical or agonistic democrats with whom Rancière is usually associated. Rancière's democratic theory affirms not only an an-archic antifoundationalism, as suggested above, but also an everyday theory of political subjectivization, through which "the power of the people" is "re-enacted ceaselessly by political subjects that challenge the police distribution of parts, places or competences, and that re-stage the anarchic foundation of the political."[4] This essay focuses on Rancière's conceptualization of the relationship between democracy as a politics without arche, rule without qualification, and the singular acts of political subjectivization that bring this contingency to light and enact it on the public stage.

I will not claim that the forms of political speech and action I will be examining are the only ones that are democratically important, much less that they are the only ones that can be properly designated "political." I agree with critics who charge that in trying to avoid what he dismisses as the purity of politics, on the one hand (for example, in the work of Hannah Arendt), and the "everything is political" analysis of power, on the other (sometimes, rightly or wrongly, associated with the middle-period work of Foucault), Rancière may too narrowly delimit his account of political subjectivization.[5] I only want to argue that attentiveness to such forms should provoke a more rigorous and thoroughgoing account of their significance for democratic politics, enliven awareness of their dynamics and appearance, and suggest new avenues for democratic theorizing not built around norms of justification or formal procedures of deliberation, but engaged with the textured weave of ordinary political utterances and enactments. Rancière's work should provoke historically and aesthetically situated democratic theorizing along the lines of his own investigations into radical educational reformers, proletarian poets, nineteenth-century socialism, and contemporary cinema, rather than a stream of rigidifying commentary on his "theory." His scholarship is better approached as an inspiring exemplar rather than an object of exegesis. Rancière's work orients a different kind of attention to the political world than that provided by prevailing forms of democratic theorizing primarily through its theoretical engagement with singular examples. I take this approach to be very much in the spirit of verification and extension that Rancière envisions for his own work when he claims it offers "tools with which we can draw a new topography in order to account for what happens to us and with which we can try to weave modes of investigation and action equally distant from the consent to things as they are as from the hyperboles of an imaginary radicalism."[6]

In taking this more modest route into Rancière's democratic theory I hope to contest, if somewhat indirectly, the prevailing reception of his work in contemporary political theory. This reception has typically placed Rancière alongside other influential theorists of the event, the revolutionary, the ruptural; Rancière is presented alongside such influential theorists as Carl Schmitt, Giorgio Agamben, and Alain Badiou, as another theorist captivated by the indelible drama of the exception in political life. Thus, Todd May argues that for Rancière "democratic politics is an extraordinary and rare event"; Joseph Tanke draws a contrast between the disruptive political world and what he calls the "everyday world of the police"; Peter Hallward examines the limitations of Rancière's "rare and ephemeral" conception of politics; and Slavoj Žižek celebrates this same conception and its insistence on "magic, violently poetic moments."[7] Elsewhere I have described this as the evental reading of Rancière.[8] I do not think this familiar emphasis is entirely wrong, but I do think it distracts readers from other resources in Rancière's writing that resist its central preoccupations and terms. There are many passages that confirm it too, of course, as when Rancière describes democracy as "a state of exception where no oppositions can function," or when he writes that democracy must be grasped as a "rupture in the logic of the arche" and that "the normal state of things equals the non-existence of politics."[9] He also notes at several points that politics is "rare" and "provisional."[10] But what this familiar reception of Rancière's works most insistently obscures is his distinctive approach to the politics of the ordinary. In contemporary political theory the politics of the ordinary is usually associated with theorists influenced by ordinary language philosophy and Stanley Cavell, on the one hand, or those taking up Foucauldian or Deleuzian investigations into "micropolitics," on the other (or some combination of the two).[11] Rancière belongs at least as much to this contemporary theoretical constellation as he does with the one preoccupied with "the axioms of rupture," emergency, or what he dismisses as the "supposedly radical experience of the heterogeneous."[12] Rancière suggests as much in some of his recent writing. When confronted with the evental reading of his work in a recent interview, for example, he responded as follows: "I didn't mean to suggest that equality exists only on the barricades, and that once the barricades come down it is over, and we go back to listlessness. I am not a thinker of the event, of the upsurge, but rather of emancipation as something with its own tradition, with a history that isn't just made up of great striking deeds, but also of the ongoing effort to create forms of the common different from the ones on offer from the state and the democratic consensus."[13]

That Rancière would be engaged with the politics of the ordinary is not surprising in itself, considering the broad preoccupation with these issues among French political thinkers on the Left after May '68, especially among former students and colleagues of Althusser. This is a common set of theoretical preoccupations that has been firmly established by intellectual historians, both those who criticize post–May '68 thinking in France, like Richard Wolin in his book on French Maoism, and those who admire it, like Kristin Ross in her seminal study of May '68 and its afterlives.[14] However, Rancière's engagement with these issues is highly distinctive on a number of registers, and very clearly opposed to the politics of the ordinary associated with such influential contemporaries as Michel de Certeau (through his concept of resistant popular cultures, transgressive walking, and tactics), Pierre Bourdieu (through his influential concept of the habitus), but also Foucault (and his affirmation of microresistance at the capillary level of disciplinary power). As Ross notes, Rancière's return to the ordinary is not an affirmation of situated practices that resist the imposition of rationalist grids of administration and knowledge, and he does not celebrate forms of politics that emerge defensively from challenges to "unchanging . . . customs, hobbies, and dispositions."[15] Rancière does not begin with "culture" or some other stand-in for the term, because doing so would efface the very dynamic process of subjectivization that has preoccupied him for decades. Rancière's intellectual trajectory since the time of his break from the epistemic inequality affirmed in Althusser's scientism and theoreticism can be understood as an extended affirmation of the capacities of ordinary people to think, a prolonged examination of the myriad consequences that follow from the presumption of a fundamental equality of intelligence and capacity. "This equality is not given," as he writes in the *Ignorant Schoolmaster*, the text that brings this preoccupation most clearly into view with its blurring of the voices of Rancière and Joseph Jacotot, "nor is it claimed; it is practiced, it is verified."[16] This equality is without determinate content, but instead enacted in everyday capacities to be other than the nominations and classifications that bestow identity. It is, in his words, the capacity to convert subjects into a "double being" that removes them from their assigned place, a mimetic act of splitting in two that disaggregates the governing designations of particular functions and roles. Equality is the practical refusal of the injunction first articulated by Plato and reiterated by philosophy and antiphilosophy ever since: "Let all do their own business and develop the virtue specific to their condition."[17] Rancière's work since the mid-1970s is populated with artisans who write poetry, blacksmiths who love philosophy, rational plebs, and active spectators. Aesthetics provides an essential conceptual apparatus for thinking through this presumption of ordinary equality because, as Rancière takes it through his appropriation of Kant, its "as if" implies this suspension of functions (or interests). It means that "the eyes of the worker can be disconnected from his hands, that his belief can be disconnected from his condition."[18] Aesthetic experience also suspends the unitary logic of sensation, or, as Davide Panagia has put it, "the sensual intensities of everyday life are crucial to the agentic potential of human beings regardless of class or stature."[19]

This essay is divided into two parts. In the first, I will elaborate on what I take to be the most significant aspects of Rancière's politics of the ordinary, and how it illuminates forms of speech and action—in short, forms of political subjectivization—that are obscured by the prevailing frameworks of democratic theory. I am particularly interested in the vexed relationship between speech and action in Rancière's work, the extent to which politics requires a space of interlocution, or whether its "staging of dissensus" may be extended beyond the linguistic paradigm emphasized in *Disagreement.* The examples in the essay's second part—a remarkable series of images created by the contemporary artist Glenn Ligon that critically engage with the Nation of Islam's 1995 Million Man March—extend this discussion further and provide an occasion for thinking in more historically and aesthetically detailed ways about the forms of everyday political speech and action that Rancière's work might help bring into view.

I

Read from the perspective of Rancière's work, most democratic theory in the United States is blind to the dissensus that defines democratic politics and its declassifying affirmation of equality and instead embraces, however unwittingly, consensus and the inequalities of order and rank that are built upon it. This is true even when—or perhaps especially when—democratic theory proclaims its recognition of pluralism and political conflict, whether this conflict is construed in the compromises and shifting coalitions of interest group politics, the deliberative exchange of different opinions filtered through the clarifying medium of public reason, the fusion of horizons over the meaning and inheritance of a shared political tradition, the entrenchments of class conflicts and social struggles, and even the deep pluralism of an agonistic multiculturalism or a radical democratic theory of intersectional difference. The political dispute that Rancière conceptualizes in the terms of dissensus is not a "discussion between partners" and is distinct "from all conflicts of interest between constituted parties of the population."[20] Political philosophy more broadly, and contemporary democratic theory in particular, is, according to Rancière, built on the fundamental disavowal of this dissensus. This disavowal takes different forms, which Rancière divides into three basic categories: Archipolitics, Metapolitics, and Parapolitics. Contemporary political theory in the United States has its versions of Archipolitics (in lingering forms of communitarianism, some versions of republicanism, but perhaps especially in the classical visions of politeia endorsed by some Straussians). It also has its proponents of Metapolitics (in the relatively few Marxist theorists), but most of its dominant articulations past and present must be grouped under the heading of Parapolitics (including the contending approaches of aggregative versus deliberative democrats). While most of these approaches to democratic theorizing embrace their normativity, which partly secures or justifies their continued existence in American political science departments, and while most of them also criticize the value-free pretensions of their positivist social science colleagues, each of them also has a clear empirical component because they establish an orientation to the political world that allows certain enunciations and enactments to appear as politically significant or legible while filtering others out. The expression of community values and ideals is key to communitarian approaches; Marxists and early twentieth-century progressives identified economic class interests behind every political utterance and enactment; aggregative democrats identify group contention around competing interests; rational choice theorists turn to the formal modeling of individual preferences; and deliberationists envision one or another version of ratio-critical public reason giving when deciding issues of basic constitutional significance. More recently, democratic theorists influenced by affect theory have turned to dispositions, weak ontology, and the ethos of critical responsiveness or presumptive generosity to envision a more robustly pluralist and democratic public.[21] But from the perspective of Rancière's work these theories are oriented not around the torsion of politics, its fundamental dissensus, but around the preconstituted identities, however provisional, of the police. He proposes the term "policing" for "what normally goes by the name of politics."[22]

In his clearest formulation of his concept of police, Rancière writes that it is "first an order of bodies that defines the allocation of ways of doing, ways of being, and ways of saying, and sees that those bodies are assigned by name to a particular place and task; it is an order of the visible and the sayable that sees that a particular activity is visible and another is not, that this speech is understood as discourse and another as noise."[23] While many commentators have focused on the operations of exclusion in Rancière's conception of the police, of equal importance is his insistence on a kind of mandatory field of visibility, an insistence that resonates clearly with Foucault's work on panopticism and disciplinary power. Rancière's police order establishes and sustains a field of ontic positivity or presence. It distributes bodies without remainder and leaves nothing unaccounted for. Rancière conceptualizes this imperative in terms of "realism," which he describes as "the absorption of all reality and all truth in the category of the only thing possible."[24] To be of the order of the police is to be "caught in the structure of the visible where everything is on show and where there is thus no longer any place for appearance." That distinction between visibility and appearance is important, and I will return to it in my discussion of Ligon's work below. It is a distinction also implied by the contrast Rancière draws between his account of the police and Althusser's concept of interpellation. Rather than the policeman's "Hey, you there!" which hails the responsive/responsible subject in Althusser's "Ideological State Apparatuses" essay, Rancière's police recalls "the obviousness of what there is, or rather what there is not. Its slogan is 'Move along! There's nothing to see here.' Or, perhaps it might be said that there is nothing to see here, except that which everyone sees, that which is given and is subject to count."[25] The police, as Rancière writes, "only counts empirical parts—actual groups defined by differences in birth, by different functions, locations, and interests that constitute the social body, without any supplement."[26] Rancière therefore frequently criticizes the poverty of empiricism in understanding politics, the constitutive blindness of sociology and history for example. His work attempts to bring into view that which is not only denied by the founding pretensions of political philosophy, but that which cannot be seen by counterveiling pretensions of empirical antiphilosophy. From the perspective of this essay, he aims to show the poverty of both normative political philosophy and positivist political science. One of Rancière's most important contributions to democratic theory is his attempt to bring into view what he calls democracy's "impossible object," the vital supplement of the people.

Rancière understands the people as neither an empirical entity nor a normative ideal. It is not the aggregation of interested individuals conceptualized in terms of the population, or an entirely juridical entity, a sovereign power at once constituted and constrained by formal law. It is neither Rousseau's will of all nor his general will. Instead, Rancière conceptualizes the people "as the supplement that disjoins the population from itself, by suspending all logics of legitimation."[27] Rancière's people is the appearance of that subject which makes visible the supplementary void denied by the positivity or mandatory visibility of the police order. This is what leads Rancière to write that "the people only exists as a rupture within the logic of the arche, a rupture with the logic of commencement/commandment."[28] The details of Rancière's rich engagement with the Platonic and Aristotelian conceptions of the demos are not important here, but it is important for the argument I want to make concerning the politics of the ordinary, and the forms of speech and action that Rancière's work makes visible, that this invocation of rupture not be misunderstood. Rancière does not limit this rupture to revolutionary challenges to the juridical order of the police—as in some contemporary radical democratic arguments about constituent power. The police order is, of course, not limited to formal legal or political institutions—it is, as already cited, an "allocation of ways of doing, ways of being, and ways of saying"—and its rupture need not occur on the barricades, as it were, but in the tear in those allocations enacted on the presupposition of equality. It is, as Rancière writes, "from the demos that those who have no business speaking speak, and those who have no business taking part take part thereby enacting a reconfiguration of the sensible." "To be of the demos," he writes, "is to be outside of the count" as this is revealed through the "singular mechanism of subjectification."[29]

This term "subjectivization" is a broader category under which the democratic subjectivization of the people is a smaller subset; it is a difference often overlooked in the scholarship on Rancière. If subjectivization is "the production through a series of actions of a body and a capacity for enunciation not previously identifiable within a given field of experience, [and] whose identification is thus part of the reconfiguration of the field of experience," that is, if subjectivization is first and foremost a mode of disidentification, "a removal from the naturalness of a place," then the democratic subjectivization that Rancière associates with the people is captured in the famous formula "the part that has no part in the name of the whole."[30] The political subjectification of the people (the people is not a subject or entity) is the mode of disidentification where the part that has no part proclaims against the constitutive wrong of the community, and does so in the name of the very community founded and established by that wrong. The people "through which democracy occurs"—democracy presented as an event, a dynamic enactment—"is a unity that does not consist of any social group but that superimposes the effectiveness of a part of those who have no part on the reckoning of society's parties. Democracy is the designation of subjects that do not coincide with the parties of the state or of society, floating subjects that deregulate all representation of places and portions."[31] This is a unity that is enacted through division, or through the very dissensus that defines politics for Rancière. Dissensus is conceived not as a conflict between existing parties, but as a dispute over the very staging of the criteria for a party to count as disputant.

Rancière offers a recurrent set of examples to demonstrate this dynamic form of political subjectivization. During the French Revolution, Olympe de Gouges demands the political rights of women and rejects the republican discourse around their inherent domestic particularity. She does so by arguing that "since women were qualified to mount the scaffold, they were qualified to mount the platform of the assembly." By proclaiming that the universality of the death sentence undermines the self-evident distinction between political life and domestic life, she shows that "women did not have the rights they had and had the rights that they did not have." Through their very protest, women "demonstrated a political capacity they were said not to have, and showed that since they could enact those rights they actually possessed them."[32] Similarly, in 1849 Jean Deroin presents herself in a French legislative election in which she cannot run. "This demonstration," Rancière writes, "is not a simple denunciation of an inconsistency or a lie regarding the universal. It is also the staging of the very contradiction between police logic and political logic which is at the heart of the republican definition of community." It is "the contradiction of two worlds in a single world."[33] The example that Rancière recurs to most frequently is the plebeian revolt and secession at Aventine recorded by Livy in his *History of Rome* and rearticulated by Pierre-Simon Ballanche in 1829. As the patrician Menenius Agrippa comes to restore order to the city, he appeals to the natural hierarchies of the body politic and urges the restoration of the plebeian's subordinate role. "There is no place for discussion with the plebs for the simple reason that the plebs do not speak . . . They do not speak because they are deprived of logos." However, in making his commands Agrippa must speak to the plebs and persuade them. He must rely on their intelligence and understanding, and must therefore presume the very equality that his appeal to natural command and inequality denies. "In speaking to them as men," even through commandment, as Rancière writes, "he makes them men." The plebeians, conversely, have to establish their own conflictual or paradoxical stage, because the patricians cannot understand what they say; they hear only noises, a "fugitive sound," "lowing" (they have phone and no logos). In order to be audibly understood and visibly recognized as political beings, the plebeians don't simply provide arguments and justifications for their position—there is no equal space of communicative exchange or dialogue—but instead must "construct the scene of argumentation in such a manner that the patricians recognize it as a world in common." "The plebs gathered on the Aventine," as Rancière writes, to:

> establish another order, another partition of the perceptible, by constituting themselves . . . as speaking beings sharing the same properties as those who deny them these. They thereby execute a series of speech acts that mimic those of the patricians: they pronounce imprecations and apotheoses; they delegate one of their number to go and consult *their* oracles; they give themselves representatives by rebaptizing them. In a word, they conduct themselves like beings with names. Through transgression, they find that they too . . . are endowed with speech that does not simply express want, suffering, or rage, but intelligence.[34]

All of these recurrent examples of political subjectivization, as well as others not discussed here—like the revolutionary Auguste Blanqui's proclamation that his profession was "a proletarian" at his criminal trial in 1832, or May '68 demonstrators in Paris claiming, "We are all German Jews"—seem to turn on dilemmas of speech, on the troubled boundary between phone and logos, on strange scenes of interlocution, and the at once political and poetic dimensions of language's world-disclosive power. In *Disagreement*, Rancière distinguishes his account of political subjectivization from both the purportedly universal but "closed-world forms of arguing and validating" endorsed by Habermas, and the incommensurable language games of Lyotard's "differend."[35] He refuses the "trap" that insists the only alternative to our normative commitment to procedures of ratio-critical communication is the violence of irreducible difference. At times his account of political subjectivization seems to be just as speech-centric as these other influential versions of postlinguistic turn democratic theory. He defines "disagreement" itself, after all, as "a determined kind of speech situation" where "contention over what speaking means constitutes the very rationality of the speech situation."[36] "Dis-agreement bears on what it means to be a being that uses words to argue," he writes, and "comes down to a dispute over the object of discussion and over the capacity of those who are making an object of it."[37] "At the heart of all arguing and all litigious argument of a political nature lies a basic quarrel as to what understanding language implies."[38] In the afterword to the English edition of *The Philosopher and His Poor*, Rancière goes so far as to write that "the status of speech that gives rise to the form of subjectivization associated with politics is the vital thread tying together all of [his] research."[39] Jane Bennett has criticized Rancière on just these grounds in *Vibrant Matter*—for reducing "eruptive events" to "argumentative utterances"—while also recognizing that there are resources in his work for moving beyond its focus on speech.[40] Rancière too is aware of these resources, of course, and insists that disagreement is not about "words alone," but generally "bears on the very situation in which speaking parties find themselves."[41]

Rancière's account of interlocution points beyond the dilemmas of locution primarily through his account of "staging" and "demonstration." Politics is always about creating a stage, Rancière writes: "It always takes the form more or less of the establishment of a theater,"[42] and "every political subject is first and foremost a sort of local and provisional theatrical configuration."[43] A number of scholars, most notably Peter Hallward and Richard Halperin, have examined Rancière's conception of "theatocracy," and I will not go into the details of the account here. What seems to be of crucial importance in his idea of staging is "the putting of two worlds in one world," and doing it publicly, in a space of appearances. This enactive or world-disclosive phenomenon of staging brings about another world of political commonality through its antagonism. It is not enough that Jeanne Deroin "makes the argument for women's political equality," for example; "she has to enact it."[44] Politics as Rancière understands it is "primarily conflict over the existence of a common stage and over the existence and status of those present on it."[45] As with the plebeians at Aventine Hill, this stage is not simply one of difference, opposition, or conflict—it is not the contending warring parties of the Scythians—but rather the insistence on an equal commonality not acknowledged by the patricians. The assertion of a common world thus happens through what Rancière calls a "paradoxical *mise-en-scène*." It presumes that such a common stage exists when it does not, and acting on this assumption—what he will elsewhere call the verification of equality that "brings the community and the noncommunity together." This staging of dissensus not only overturns "legitimate situations of communication," like those either presumed or idealized by advocates of deliberative democracy, but also "the legitimate parceling out of worlds and languages." It "redistributes the way speaking bodies are distributed," Rancière writes, "in an articulation between the order of saying, the order of doing, and the order of being." "The *demonstration* proper to politics is always both argument and opening up the world where argument can be received and have an impact—argument about the very existence of such a world."[46]

One of the most important theoretical questions raised by Rancière's account of political subjectivization as a distinctive example of the politics of the ordinary is whether the redistribution and repartition that he emphasizes must be as firmly anchored in the dilemmas of speech and argument as he sometimes suggests. If the essential work of politics is "the configuration of its own space, to get the world of its subjects and its operations to be seen," why need it be so centrally preoccupied with the status of the speaking subject, with the division between phone and logos? Why is language so central to the account? "If there is someone you do not wish to recognize as a political being," he writes, "you begin by not seeing him as the bearer of signs of politicality, by not understanding what he says, by not hearing what issues from his mouth as discourse."[47] This dynamic does indeed have a long history, but at times Rancière seems to essentialize its centrality to the dispute that defines politics.

All of these invocations of the redistribution of speaking bodies in the passages quoted above are obviously meant to invoke Rancière's influential concept of the partition of the sensible (*le partage du sensible*), that is, "the system of self-evident facts of sense perception that simultaneously discloses the existence of something common and the delimitations that define the respective parts and positions within it," "the cluster of perceptions and practices that shape and sustain a common world and our orientation to it."[48] This concept establishes a theoretical terrain for promising engagements with a broader discourse around the politics of the ordinary because it knits forms of macrodomination and authority to the micro level, to the level of sensation and sense-making. It also opens up a discourse as to how reconfigurations on the micro level can come to resonate within larger structures of power. Rancière's concept of the partition of the sensible offers a conceptual vocabulary for thinking the relationship between the macro- and the micropolitical. Because "it is a dividing up of the world and of people," Rancière writes, it provides the *nemein* (Greek for "appropriation" and "distributions") on which the *nomoi* (or laws) of the community are founded.[49] Power is inscribed in the very partition of perception, in other words, before it ossifies and is made available in legal rules and institutions, or their formal and explicit justifications.

This partition of the sensible is, of course, also what unites politics and aesthetics in Rancière's work, not by collapsing these spheres into each other but by illuminating their shared conceptual terrain. "The cutting up of the perceptual world" that Rancière associates with aisthesis "anticipates through its sensible evidence, the distribution of shares and social parties. And this distribution itself presupposes a cutting up of what is visible and what is not, of what can be heard and what cannot."[50] Davide Panagia, who has engaged these issues through an examination of what he calls the politics of the sensorium, writes that "within any regime of perception there exists a micropolitics of appraisal that formulates the shared condition of sense making. . . . A distribution of the sensible therefore addresses the modes of attending to the world that align our organoleptic practices with our bodily postures, our cognitive attunements, and our practices of sense making."[51] Panagia's primary interest is to examine how the capacity for perceptual reconfiguration is given by sensation itself, that is, how the distribution of the sensible creates "the perceptual conditions for a political community and for its dissensus." My own interest in Rancière's account of political subjectivization as a politics of the ordinary departs from Panagia's emphasis on the transformative capacities inherent in perception, in the tension he identifies between "an act of perception and what is taken to be a preconstituted object worthy of perception," or the gap it opens up between sense and sense. Panagia affirms sensation itself as a kind of radical democratic moment of aesthetic judgment in that sensory experience interrupts our perceptual givens, creating occasions to suspend authority and inviting "occasions and actions for reconfiguring our associational lives."[52] The capacity of politics and aesthetics to enact such redistributions provides their shared conceptual terrain in his work. But Rancière insists also, and importantly, on their nonidentity:

> A political declaration or manifestation, like an artistic form, is an arrangement of words, a montage of gestures, an occupation of spaces. In both cases what is produced is a modification of the fabric of the sensible, a transformation of the visible given, intensities, names that one can give to things, the landscape of the possible. What truly distinguishes political actions is that these operations are the acts of a collective subject offering itself as a representative of everyone, and of the capacity of everyone. This type of creativity is specific, but it is based on modifications to the fabric of the sensible, produced in particular by artistic reconfigurations of space and time, forms and meanings.[53]

While Rancière is interested in the landscape that unites "artistic practice and political practice," denying a pure sphere of politics as well as a pure sphere of art, he is also insistent on the "blurring but not the collapse of the boundaries" between them. My worry is that Panagia's approach to "the aesthetic-political dimensions of democratic life," while importantly correcting the evental reading of Rancière, takes it too quickly to the opposite extreme, obscuring what is specific about political subjectivization in Rancière's work.[54] I want to maintain Rancière's focus on political specificity, while also attending to the importance of sensational reconfiguration. There is no criteria that can determine the line between these spheres in advance; this can only be achieved through the examination of singular examples that demonstrate the necessity and indistinction of that line.

II

"The afterlife of slavery," Saidiya Hartman writes, "is not only a political and a social problem but an aesthetic one as well," which means we must learn to "listen for the politics of the lower frequencies."[55] While Hartman echoes here the final lines of Ellison's Invisible Man—"Who knows but that, on the lower frequencies, I speak for you?"—her comments are directed to, and elicited by, the work of Glenn Ligon, a contemporary American artist working in the Afro-modern tradition of black radical critique.[56] On Hartman's reading, Ligon's work offers powerful occasions for thinking the entanglements of the political and aesthetic "afterlife of slavery," and for listening more attentively to the "politics of the lower frequencies." I will not present Ligon's works here as mere illustrations of Rancière's theory of everyday political subjectivization, but rather as examples that at once are illuminated by that theory and challenge it in different ways. Ligon's work is engaged with several of the problems I have explored above: the fraught relationship between identification and subjectivization, visibility and appearance, and the aesthetic and political distributions and redistributions of the sensible. Ligon's work is crucially focused, I think, on the necessary indistinctions of the line between aesthetics and politics.

Ligon is probably best known for his text-based paintings, works that incorporate the words of such writers as Langston Hughes, Jean Genet, Zora Neale Hurston, Richard Pryor, and especially James Baldwin. He is often associated with a group of contemporary artists preoccupied with intersectional constructions of racial, sexual, and gender identity, and with the politics of representation more broadly construed. He was a prominent participant in the famous Whitney Biennial of 1993, which scandalized some critics because of its focus on the politics of abjection and social marginalization, leading Robert Hughes to notoriously describe it as a "big fiesta of whining agitprop."[57]

Some of Ligon's work is focused on the semiotic mechanisms of inclusion and exclusion, and can be placed alongside the work of such contemporaries as Kara Walker and Ellen Gallagher, but Ligon's work is also always more than an exercise in decoding and demystification, or the mobilization of counterhegemonic images and representations, and I never think his work transmits a clear ideological message, or aims to politicize the audience in any obvious way. The work seems to actively resist the transmission of a message, sometimes quite literally, as when his gobs of black paint or charcoal disfigure letters to render texts illegible. Ligon, as one critic has pointed out, was influenced by "conceptualism's linguistic turn, minimalism's phenomenological address, and feminist critiques of media imagery," but his work does not easily fit the rubric of "political art" that Rancière has criticized so relentlessly in "The Emancipated Spectator" and other essays, that is, stultifying art that aims to establish a pedagogical hierarchy with its viewer and to make its audience or spectator feel exactly as the artist or director would intend.[58] Ligon has said about his own work that it is animated by "a pessimism about making things explicit or understanding things and transmitting that understanding."[59] Ligon's work exemplifies the kind of artwork that "opens up new passages toward new forms of political subjectification" and "introduces dissensus into the world of shared appearances and meanings."[60]

It is not my purpose to engage here with Rancière's account of the ethical, the representative, and the aesthetic regimes of art, or to situate Ligon's work in relation to his aesthetics, but instead to suggest proximities in their concerns and ask how one of Ligon's most prominent works might productively engage with Rancière's account of political subjectivization, and in doing so enliven an appreciation or attentiveness to the distinctive account of the politics of the ordinary that it offers. The work I am thinking about is a series that Ligon completed for an exhibition at the San Francisco Museum of Modern Art in 1996 entitled *The Day of Absence.* The exhibition consisted of four large silkscreened and unstretched canvases depicting reframed and resized news photographs of the Million Man March / Day of Absence, which had been organized the previous year by Louis Farrakhan and the Nation of Islam. The dual title of that event referred to the fact that black women wishing to support the march were asked not to attend the march itself but to instead absent themselves from work on that day. By borrowing the second half of that title for his installation, Ligon emphasized the ways in which male presence was tied to female absence, both at the march itself and in the newspaper photographs documenting it, but I do not take the work to be primarily preoccupied with constitutive exclusions, nor to be a simple call for greater inclusivity—of women or of gay men, for example—although this is primarily how the work was received and reviewed in the press. I take Ligon's work to be primarily not a critique of exclusions but, rather, a visual dramatization of the power of disidentification and an attempt to envision dissensual forms of demonstration and appearance based on a declassifying and markedly impersonal equality. These are works engaged with the evanescence of appearance as much as they are engaged with struggles to attain visibility. They seem to capture the precariousness of such demonstrations, demonstrations that as Rancière insists throughout his work are always on the verge of their own disappearance.

The shared premise of Ligon's installation and the Million Man March might be said to be that "the distribution of the visible itself is part of the configuration of domination and subjection."[61] Both Ligon and the march organizers are focused on how power is created and sustained through the circulation of images, and on how power may also be effectively countered or reconfigured through redeployments of these images. The march organizers made this purpose explicit in their initial press release, writing that "the Million Man March is the Holy Day of Atonement and Reconciliation for, and by, Black men in the United States of America who will March on Washington DC to convey to the world a vastly different picture of the Black male."[62] The march, its organizers insisted, would counter dominant media depictions of black male pathology and affirm instead the "dignified representation" of black men as responsible fathers and heads of household, paternalist images it stated were necessary not just for the health of the family but for "the people's liberation."[63] The march, as Ligon notes in an interview given at the time of the installation, "emphasized the interrelated goals of male responsibility, black solidarity, and self-reliance."[64]

Ligon demonstrates his shared concern with this effort to "heighten the visibility of black men as a social force in this country" by taking widely circulated newspaper images of the march as his primary source material, but then manipulating them to discreetly disrupt their anticipated circulation and conveyance. Doing so, he offers a very different take on the mechanisms of power and visibility than the march's organizers. Instead of making visible an identity that had been historically denigrated and abused, and treating this greater visibility as a means of achieving greater economic, cultural, and political power, Ligon's *Day of Absence* suggests the traps that await a politics oriented wholly around identity and visibility, and the unexplored possibilities of political appearance that breaks from the anticipated markers even of demonstration, protest, and resistance. It is not simply a question of his countering the heteronormative or patriarchal vision of the black identity affirmed by Farrakhan and the march's organizers, in other words—to contest the terms of their normative vision of blackness would be to adopt the same strategy but put it to different ends—but to question the imperative of visibility itself.

Ligon challenges the identity politics of the march by both showing how it participates in the dominant distribution of the sensible even as—or especially as—it challenges that order. *Day of Absence* alerts its viewers to how dominant forms of protest visibility—on the National Mall, say, addressed by leaders and to political representatives—can work to sustain the dominant distribution of the sensible even as they contest it. It aims not to make present an excluded part, or to reverse the "hierarchy of already positively constituted groups," but to "introduce new subjects and heterogeneous objects into the field of perception."[65] I don't think it is too much to say that the refigured collectivities presented in Ligon's dynamic reappropriations point to "lines of fracture and their disincorporation into imaginary collective bodies" that Rancière associates with the demonstration of politics, the staging of dissensus. These works envision the "uncertain communities that call into question the reigning distribution

Figure 1. Glenn Ligon, *Hands*, 1996. Silkscreen ink and gesso on unstretched canvas, 82 × 144 in. (208.3 × 365.8 cm.). © Glenn Ligon; reproduced courtesy of the artist; Luhring Augustine, New York; Regen Projects, Los Angeles; and Thomas Dane Gallery, London.

of roles, territories, and languages."[66] What Ligon admired in the work of the conceptual artist David Hammons and jazz musician Sun Ra, according to a wonderful essay he wrote titled "Black Light," applies equally to his own work, that is, to employ a concern with "emptying the self as a critical strategy, one that has a particular resonance with people historically positioned at the margin of what was considered human."[67]

Take, for example, the best-known image from the series, *Hands* (figure 1). This image is taken from a newspaper photograph of the concluding moment in the Million Man March when the assembled men were asked to make a collective pledge to the cause of the family and male responsibility. Ligon takes this moment of public pledging and identification and turns it into a powerful but highly ambivalent image of collective affirmation unmoored from its original function or role. It could be a protest, but it could also be a roll call or a rock concert, a public assembly or a prayer meeting.[68] The openness of the hands contrasts sharply with the raised fist, which carries such powerful and perhaps overdetermined iconic status in the visual history of black representations, a status Ligon describes as the "trope of the expressive black hand."[69] Ligon's reframing of the image not only separates the action from its ritual function, but detaches the hands from the bodies to which they belong.

Ligon's sea of disembodied hands offers an affirmation of democratic equality in their collective but impersonal visibility—the hands float in anonymous equivalence, they are a mass without qualities, without predicates.

This equality seems founded on declassification rather than identity affirmation. The visual openness of the piece—like the openness of the hands themselves—does not transmit the univocal meaning of a collective pledge, the felicitous speech act, so much as it does the double bind of appearance that attempts to keep open its power and avoid the capture of identification, embodiment, or legibility. Ligon takes the march's concluding moment of collective articulation, and restages it as a moment of ambivalent, anonymous, but powerful resignification. "Why do we need to raise our hands in that symbolic space again and again and again to be present in this country?" Ligon asked in an interview.[70] The piece is not only about enforced invisibility but the strange requirement or imperative of visibility, and its distinction from the evanescence of appearance. This is, I think, also the point of Ligon's attempt to present what cannot be seen, that is the field of black that bisects the upper half of the canvas, drawing the viewer's eyes upward from the outstretched hands (rather than downward to the bodies to which they belong) as if to say what is not happening is at least as important as the scene of action itself.

A similar issue is at work in *We're Black and Strong* (figure 2). In this piece, Ligon took another newspaper clipping of the assembled crowd, and zoomed in on a large protest banner with the slogan of the work's title: "We're Black and Strong." Enlarging it to the point where the wording disappears entirely from the banner, the articulate expression, backed by the raised fists of several of the marchers themselves (backed, that is, by the "trope of the expressive black hand"), is converted into disarticulation, resistance into dissensus. The quiet pairing of the empty banner with the hazy Washington monument looming like a shadow in the background seems to attempt to bring into view a reigning distribution of the sensible with its dominant "modes of attending to the world" and correlation of bodily postures, while also short-circuiting its continued circulation. In Ligon's redeployment of the image and banner what is important is not so much *what* is said, as *that* something was said, not the object or identity made visible, but the process of appearance or staging itself. The result is another powerfully ambivalent image, one that elicits the affective intensity of the crowd scene, while inhibiting or suspending a full identification.

This pairing of protest sign and the symbolism of state power is duplicated in the third image from the series, *Screen* (figure 3). Here, however, instead of the protest banner and Washington Monument, we have

Figure 2. Glenn Ligon, *We're Black and Strong (I)*, 1996. Silkscreen ink and gesso on unstretched canvas, 120 × 84 in. (304.8 × 213.4 cm.). © Glenn Ligon; reproduced courtesy of the artist; Luhring Augustine, New York; Regen Projects, Los Angeles; and Thomas Dane Gallery, London.

Farrakhan's televised image provocatively juxtaposed with the head of the capital dome. The marcher-spectators have their backs to the viewer and seem equally transfixed by both images before them, although there is no way for the viewer to know whether it is Farrakhan or the capital dome that holds their gaze. In this piece, too, Ligon seems preoccupied with the visual life of power, and with the possibilities this visibility creates for resignification. I think *Screen* speaks in interesting ways to sensory mechanisms of captivation. Like the subjects so carefully drawn on the famous frontispiece to Hobbes's *Leviathan*, they stand enthralled, held together through their fixation on the head of the sovereign. Hobbes's transfixed subjects model the spectatorial passivity that Ligon then refuses in the

Figure 3. Glenn Ligon, *Screen*, 1996. Silkscreen ink and gesso on unstretched canvas, 84 × 144 in. (213.4 × 365.8 cm.). © Glenn Ligon; reproduced courtesy of the artist; Luhring Augustine, New York; Regen Projects, Los Angeles; and Thomas Dane Gallery, London. The Broad Art Foundation

relation that he establishes between his work and its viewer: in watching them watching him the enchantments of watching become more readily apparent. There is no doubt that there is something here to see, although its meaning remains obscure. I am not simply making the point that what Ligon presents us with is ambivalence, or that he leaves us with questions rather than answers. He instead tries to show a power or capacity that resides in illegibility, the promise of enactment that is not organized into a signifying content. The disruption of relations of sense and sense that distinguish Ligon's restaged photographs from their original source material (and the term "restaging" is one that he himself uses) do not take mobilization or politicization of their audience as their goal in any obvious way. But as a visual engagement with the complex mechanisms of visuality and power, they strike me as a powerful corrective to what is usually understood in terms of the politics of representation.

Let me conclude by noting that perhaps Ligon's single best-known work—*Untitled (I Am a Man)* from 1988 (figure 4)—also limns important issues raised by Rancière's theory of political subjectivization that bring it into conversation with the politics of the ordinary. Ligon painted on this canvas the slogan of a famous sanitation workers' strike in Memphis in 1968 (figure 5). What statement could be simpler? Subject, verb,

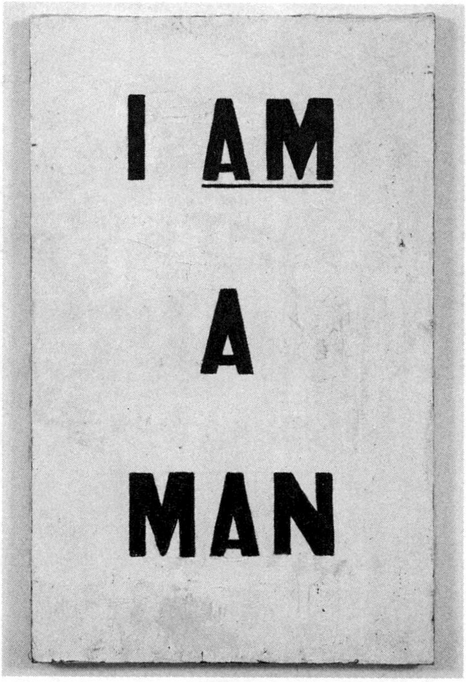

Figure 4. Glenn Ligon, *Untitled (I Am a Man)*, 1988. Oil and enamel on canvas, 40 × 25 in. (101.6 × 63.5 cm.). © Glenn Ligon; reproduced courtesy of the artist; Luhring Augustine, New York; Regen Projects, Los Angeles; and Thomas Dane Gallery, London.

predicate. Statement of fact. However, in the placards of the mostly black sanitation strikers this simple statement, opens up a clear dissensus that exposes a conflict—a wrong—deeper than those that appear over wages, hours, and benefits. This is not a question of "words alone" but "bears on the very situation in which the speaking parties find themselves." It is in other words not an argument or a claim, but "an opening up of the world where argument can be received and have an impact—argument about the very existence of such a world."[71] In attempting to monumentalize these placards in oil and acrylic, Ligon hints at the provisional and fleeting quality of such enactments that have been emphasized by some contemporary democratic theorists. Sheldon Wolin describes democratic action as inherently "fugitive," and Rancière considers "precariousness to

Figure 5. Ernest C. Withers, *I Am a Man, Sanitation Workers Strike, Memphis Tennessee*, 1968. Gelatin silver print; 22.2 × 37.9 cm. (image), 40.5 × 50.4 cm. (sheet). Library of Congress Prints and Photographs Division.

be one of its essential elements."[72] This would seem to be the counsel of a deep political pessimism. But Ligon's painting also seems to preserve the discreet simplicity or ordinariness of the worker's statement—I Am a Man—and charge it, unadorned, with extraordinary power. His painting suggests that when we are enthralled—terrified or entranced—by the dramatic logic of the exception, the event, and with emergency politics, by the gravity of the epochal events of a Revolution or a Founding, we become correspondingly deadened to how political capacities for refiguration emerge from within the simple fabric of our everyday lives. It is the anticipatory orientation toward these capacities to which any radical democratic politics of the ordinary must closely attend.

Notes

1. Jacques Rancière, "Does Democracy Mean Something?," in *Dissensus: On Politics and Aesthetics*, ed. and trans. Steven Corcoran, 45–61 (New York: Continuum, 2010), 50.

2. Jacques Rancière, "Thinking between Disciplines—an Aesthetics of Knowledge," *Parrhesia* 1, no. 1 (2006): 1–12.

3. See, for example, Samuel A. Chambers, *The Lessons of Rancière* (New York: Oxford University Press, 2012), and Davide Panagia, *Rancière's Sentiments* (Durham, N.C.: Duke University Press, 2018).

4. Rancière, "Does Democracy Mean Something?," 54.

5. See, for example, Jodi Dean, *Democracy and Other Neoliberal Fantasies: Communicative Capitalism and Left Politics* (Durham, N.C.: Duke University Press, 2009), 13–14.

6. Jacques Rancière, "The Method of Equality: An Answer to Some Questions," in *Jacques Rancière: History, Politics, Aesthetics*, ed. Gabriel Rockhill and Philip Watts, 273–88 (Durham, N.C.: Duke University Press, 2009), 288.

7. Todd May, *The Political Thought of Jacques Rancière: Creating Equality* (State College: Pennsylvania State University Press, 2008); Joseph J. Tanke, *Jacques Rancière: An Introduction* (New York: Continuum, 2011), 64; Peter Hallward, "Staging Equality," in Rockhill and Watts, *Jacques Rancière*, 140–57, 152; Slavoj Žižek, *The Ticklish Subject: The Absent Center of Political Ontology* (London: Verso, 2000), 128.

8. Jason Frank, "Logical Revolts: Jacques Rancière and Political Subjectivization," *Political Theory* 43, no. 2 (2015): 249–61.

9. Jacques Rancière, "Ten Theses on Politics," in *Dissensus*, 27–44, quotation on 43.

10. Jacques Rancière, *Disagreement: Politics and Philosophy* (Minneapolis: University of Minnesota Press, 1999), 17; Rancière, "Ten Theses on Politics," 35.

11. See Thomas Dumm, *A Politics of the Ordinary* (New York: New York University Press, 1999).

12. Jacques Rancière, "The Use of Distinctions," in *Dissensus*, 205–18, quotation on 217.

13. Jacques Rancière, "Democracies against Democracy," in *Democracy in What State?*, ed. Amy Allen, 76–81 (New York: Columbia University Press, 2011), 79–80.

14. Richard Wolin, *The Wind from the East: French Intellectuals, the Cultural Revolution, and the Legacy of the 1960s* (Princeton, N.J.: Princeton University Press, 2010); Kristin Ross, *May '68 and Its Afterlives* (Chicago: University of Chicago Press, 2014).

15. Kristin Ross, "Historicizing Untimeliness," in Rockhill and Watts, *Jacques Rancière*, 15–29, quotation on 19.

16. Jacques Rancière, *The Ignorant Schoolmaster: Five Lessons in Intellectual Emancipation* (Stanford, Calif.: Stanford University Press, 1991), 137.

17. Jacques Rancière, *The Philosopher and His Poor*, trans. John Drury, Corinne Oster, and Andrew Parker (Durham, N.C.: Duke University Press, 2004), 220.

18. Jacques Rancière, The Aesthetic Dimension," *Critical Inquiry* 36 (Autumn 2009), 16.

19. Davide Panagia, "'Partage du sensible': The Distribution of the Sensible," in *Jacques Rancière: Key Concepts*, ed. Jean-Philippe Deranty, 95–103 (Durham, N.C.: Acumen, 2010), quotation on 102.

20. Rancière, *Disagreement*, 100.

21. See Stephen White, *Sustaining Affirmation: The Strength of Weak Ontology in Political Theory* (Princeton, N.J.: Princeton University Press, 2000).

22. Rancière, *Disagreement*, xiii.

23. Rancière, *Disagreement*, 29.

24. Rancière, *Disagreement*, 132.

25. Rancière, "Ten Theses on Politics," 37.

26. Rancière, "Ten Theses on Politics," 33.

27. Rancière, "Ten Theses on Politics," 33.

28. Rancière, "Ten Theses on Politics," 33.

29. Rancière, "Ten Theses on Politics," 40; *Disagreement*, 99.

30. Rancière, *Disagreement*, 36.

31. Rancière, *Disagreement*, 99–100.

32. Rancière, "Does Democracy Mean Something?," 57.

33. Rancière, *Disagreement*, 41, 27.

34. Rancière, *Disagreement*, 23–26.

35. Rancière, *Disagreement*, 55–56.

36. Rancière, *Disagreement*, x.

37. Rancière, *Disagreement*, xi.

38. Rancière, *Disagreement*, 48.

39. Rancière, *The Philosopher and His Poor*, 226.

40. Jane Bennett, *Vibrant Matter: A Political Ecology of Things* (Durham, N.C.: Duke University Press, 2010), 105–7.

41. Rancière, *Disagreement*, xi.

42. Hallward, "Staging Equality," 142.

43. Hallward, "Staging Equality," 141.

44. Rancière, *Disagreement*, 41.

45. Rancière, *Disagreement*, 26.

46. Rancière, *Disagreement*, 55–56.

47. Rancière, "Ten Theses on Politics," 38.

48. Rancière "The Politics of Literature," in *Dissensus*, 152–68, quotation on 152.

49. Rancière, "Ten Theses on Politics," 36.

50. Rancière, *The Philosopher and His Poor*, 225.

51. Davide Panagia, *The Political Life of Sensation* (Durham, N.C.: Duke University Press, 2009), 42.

52. Panagia, *The Political Life of Sensation*, 3.

53. Rancière, "Art of the Possible."

54. Panagia, *The Political Life of Sensation*, 3.

55. Saidiya Hartman, "Will Answer to the Name Glenn," in *Glenn Ligon: America*, ed. Scott Rothkopf, 110–13 (New York: Whitney Museum of American Art, 2011), quotation on 112.

56. Ralph Ellison, *Invisible Man* (New York: Vintage, 1995), 581.

57. Robert Hughes, "A Festival of Whining," *Time*, March 23, 1993.

58. Jacques Rancière, *Emancipated Spectator* (New York: Verso, 2011).

59. Glenn Ligon, "Interview by David Drogan," *Museo* 14 (2010).

60. Tanke, *Jacques Rancière*, 82.

61. Rancière, *Emancipated Spectator*, 15.

62. Million Man March National Organizing Committee, "Million Man March Fact Sheet," in *Million Man March / Day of Absence: A Commemorative Anthology. Speeches, Commentary, Photography, Poetry, Illustrations, Documents*, ed. Haki R. Madhubuti, and Maulana Karenga (Chicago: Third World Press, 1995).

63. Million Man March National Organizing Committee, "Million Man March Fact Sheet."

64. Glenn Ligon, *Glenn Ligon: New Work* (San Francisco: San Francisco Museum of Modern Art, 1996).

65. Rancière, *Dissensus*, 2.

66. Rancière, *Politics of Aesthetics*, 40.

67. Glenn Ligon, "Black Light," in *Yourself in the World: Selected Writings and Interviews*, ed. Scott Rothkopf, 1–10 (New Haven, Conn.: Yale University Press, 2011), 9.

68. See Franklin Sirman's essay "Me and We" in Ligon, *America*, 166–69.

69. Ligon, "Interview by David Drogan."

70. Ligon, "Interview by David Drogan."

71. Rancière, *Disagreement*, xi, 56.

72. Sheldon Wolin, "Fugitive Democracy," in *Democracy and Difference: Contesting the Boundaries of the Political*, ed. Seyla Benhabib, 31–45 (Princeton, N.J.: Princeton University Press, 1996); Rancière, "Ten Theses on Politics," 43.

Fidelity to Disagreement: Jacques Rancière's Politics without Ontology

Benjamin Arditi

In the 1980s Jacques Rancière published two remarkable books. One was *The Nights of Labor*, the result of research in nineteenth-century French working-class archives. He found testimonies of workers who used part of their nights to study, write, act, sing, and other things. Rancière sees a subversive streak here: people living in misery and condemned to an anonymous existence ruled by the repetitive cycle of work and rest were not supposed to do those things. Yet they did. During those nights they were more than manual laborers, although not because they were ashamed of who they were. By using their resting time for other things, they were starting to experience a different way of being together. Says Rancière:

> The topic of this book is, first of all, the history of those nights snatched from the normal round of work and repose. A harmless and imperceptible interruption of the normal round, one might say, in which our characters prepare and dream and already live the impossible: the suspension of the ancestral hierarchy subordinating those dedicated to manual labor to those who have been given the privilege of thinking. Nights of studying, nights of boozing. Long days of hard labor prolonged to hear the message of the apostles or lessons from the instructors of the people, to learn or dream or debate or write.[1]

While they dreamed and began to live the impossible they anticipated something other to come: workers already acted as if they were equals to their bourgeois counterparts and could speak about the common like anyone else.

The other book, *The Ignorant Schoolmaster*,[2] examines the theses of Joseph Jacotot, a nineteenth-century educator who developed a method for intellectual emancipation. Instead of looking at the teacher-student relation as an opposition between knowledge and ignorance, Jacotot spoke of the equality of intelligences, showed that an ignorant person could teach another and that differences among people emerge only from their disposition to use that intelligence. Says Jacotot: "It's precisely because we are all equal by nature that we must all be unequal by circumstances."[3] The contingency of inequality puts into question its inevitability. Equality, though, is a presupposition. It doesn't conform to an *eidos* or foundation because it "is not given, nor is it claimed; it is practiced, it is verified."[4] This presupposition has no ontological consistency because it emerges through a polemical enactment. As a practice and not a future reward, intellectual emancipation (taking ourselves as equals) is a possibility of the here and now: emancipation starts to occur from the moment we act to make it come.

These books are forerunners of Rancière's theory of politics as emancipation. *Disagreement*[5] draws from the experience of proletarians who gave up part of their resting time to do something else. They were reconfiguring their lived world and changing who they were. A politics of emancipation emerges when people who don't count as much as others act as if they were their equals. Rancière calls this the process of equality or political subjectivization. The sequence begins when people say "Enough!" and affirm themselves as equals, even if the name "equality" is not yet applicable to them: they live it as a de facto label and experience. Gordon Allport presents a nice example in his study about prejudice: "A negro woman was a plaintiff in a case involving a restrictive covenant. The lawyer for the defense questioned her, 'What is your race?' 'The human race,' she replied. 'And what is your skin color?' 'Natural color,' she answered."[6] This exchange took place when racism was legal in many parts of the United States. The plaintiff acted as if she was equal to the defense lawyer even though she was aware that in a racist setting a black body occupied a subordinate position. She practiced her equality instead of yearning for its arrival.

Subjectivization involves this double move of decoupling oneself from what one is supposed to be and of practicing what you want to become. It does not describe a position but an interstitial region of movement: identities constitute themselves in the interval between the assigned name and a name to come. They are identities in transit. This has the telltale signs of Jacotot's process of equality, but instead of the equality of intelligences, Rancière speaks of the equality of all speaking subjects. Equality, the sole universal of politics, is configured casuistically through a polemical enactment. By saying "Equality remains the only reason for inequality,"[7] he can claim that inequality is actually a wronging of equality.

What follows is a discussion of the theory of politics developed in *Disagreement*. I use two reading criteria. One is that published work is not necessarily an author's last word on a given matter. Thinking, writing, and publishing take time, and people often reformulate their arguments in light of the events and polemics that frame their views. More than a body of work, we encounter work in progress. Rancière's intellectual itinerary is punctuated by the events of May 1968, racism and the consensus politics of the 1990s, by his disagreement with Hannah Arendt and other political theorists, and his reaction to his critics. He returns to familiar topics—subjectivization, verification of equality, wrong, demos, politics, police, and so on—and looks at them from slightly different angles. As work in progress, his writings are always exposed to the possibility of rewriting, whether by himself or others.

My second criterion is the role Rancière assigns to disagreement. He says: "Disagreement is not only an object of my theorization. It is also its method. Addressing an author or a concept first means to me setting the stage for a disagreement, testing an operator of difference. This also means that my theoretical operations are always aimed at reframing the configuration of a problem."[8] Disagreement is a speech situation in which one of the interlocutors understands and doesn't understand what the other is saying; it occurs "wherever contention over what speaking means constitutes the very rationality of the speech situation."[9] Disagreement functions as the human condition of politics and theory. It spares nothing, not even equality, which is not an a priori but a presupposition that has to be verified. If disagreement is the object and method of Rancière's political inquiry, then his own account of politics cannot enjoy an immunitarian privilege shielding it from the test of disagreement.

Submitting Rancière's arguments to the protocols he himself established is a way, perhaps the most honest one, of being faithful to the ethos of disagreement that reverberates through his political thought. This fidelity acknowledges the contingency of all foundations. It undoes the faith in masters and mastery, making good on Rancière's celebration of Jacotot's assumption of the equality of intelligences. And if Rancière says that "addressing an author or a concept" is "aimed at reframing the configuration of a problem," then the discussion of his political thought is also an invitation to reframe problems and explore possibilities that he didn't contemplate or didn't feel inclined to pursue.

I begin with Rancière's effort to flush ontology from his theory of politics. Then I look at his claim that police symbolizes the common as a partition without a supplement, which if taken literally leaves no room for dissensus. The other three sections are more contentious. I argue that politics has a double parasitic relation with police: it feeds off its themes and sets up its own partition of the sensible. I describe this with an oxymoron, the police of politics. Then I argue that the goal of politics is not to create a better, more inclusive police, because politics is a vanishing mediator. The final section introduces another oxymoron, the homeopathic politics of police as a possibility alongside Rancière's politics of emancipation.

Deontologizing Politics

Rancière sees politics as a name for the practice of emancipation or process of equality, "a set of practices guided by the supposition that everyone is equal and by the attempt to verify this supposition. The proper name for this set of practices remains *emancipation*."[10] He wants to strip his account of politics of all ontological dressings. This is a welcome respite in an interpretive field saturated by ontology. It sets the thinking of dissensus apart from many postfoundational theories of politics despite their shared belief in the contingency of all objectivity and the absence of transcendental signifieds. Advocates of postfoundationalism generally oscillate between the weak, negative, or quasi ontologies of excess and lack.[11] The inclination for one or the other depends on their proximity to the Nietzschean-like assumption of the world as pure becoming or to the Lacanian-inspired belief in an ineradicable void in Being. Both postfoundational lineages negotiate escape routes from the metaphysics of presence and deal with the absence of transcendental foundations. Those closer to a Nietzschean frame conceive the world as pure becoming: you can domesticate it, but something always escapes the grip of the best systemic drive. Those sympathetic to the psychoanalytical tradition reach similar conclusions by stating that the void in Being is a fault that can never be completely filled. Whether through excess or lack, Cartesian-like objectivity is jeopardized.

Among the Nietzscheans one finds people like William Connolly, whose ethos of pluralization[12] is built on the assumption that becoming prevents the closure of history, and Ernesto Laclau and Chantal Mouffe, whose theory of hegemony[13] states that no society ever manages to contain the infinitude of the social. Hegemony is a way of instituting finitude by means of a precarious suture. Slavoj Žižek[14] is an exponent of the ontology of lack. He discusses multiculturalism, subjectivity, and politics by reference to the Lacanian Real. Laclau's solo writings on politics, populism, and hegemony move in this direction. His reasoning borrows from Joan

Copjec's reading of Lacan. The *objet petit a* (shorthand for the cause of desire and for its unattainable object) seeks to negotiate the lack in Being by elevating the external object of the drive to the dignity of the Thing. Hegemony, Laclau adds, deals with the lack by making a particular assume the representation of the fullness of society, an ultimately impossible yet necessary object. His theory of populism takes the *objet petit a* as the main ontological category, only that the name for the absent fullness of community moves from hegemony to the people.

Rancière steps outside this system of alternatives. For him there are only limited forms of wrong, difference, and excess. Dissensus is always the dissensus resulting from a specific miscount, and excess is "inherent in any process of nomination: the arbitrariness of the relationships binding names and bodies together, the excess of names which makes them available to those who are not 'destined' to give names and speak about the common."[15] This is an argument of practical reason. If the relationship between names and bodies was necessary instead of arbitrary there would be no point in trying to challenge racist, patriarchal, or heterocentrist settings by linking black, female, or gay bodies with the name of equality. The rejection of the naturalness of subordination creates an opening for equality. Yet nothing guarantees that a challenge of one's place will follow from that opening, and if it does, there is no assurance that an act of refusal will bring change.

Addressing a wrong is a polemical exercise unencumbered by foundational narratives of equality. It doesn't seek to restore the spirit of the laws or enact the true principle of the community but to manifest the refusal of the uncounted to accept their lot. The practice of equality puts in motion an exodus from invisibility without any guarantee of reaching a promised land. There is no such thing as an egalitarian society because for Rancière all society wrongs equality. Equality is not an attribute of subjects. It is the nonpolitical supposition that every speaking subject is equal to every other speaking subject. Politics simply seeks to verify it:

> I don't have an irenic understanding of language as some sort of common patrimony which allows everyone to be equal. I'm just saying that language games, and especially language games that institute forms of dependence, presume minimal equality of competence in order that inequality itself can operate . . . I say this not to ground equality but to show, rather, how this equality only ever functions polemically. If this is a transcendental category, its only substance lies in the acts that make manifest its effectiveness.[16]

Readers of Rancière are acquainted with the example he uses to illustrate the supposition of minimal equality for inequality to operate:

> There is order in society because some people command and others obey, but in order to obey an order at least two things are required: you must understand the order and you must understand that you must obey it. And to do that, you must already be the equal of the person who is ordering you. It is this equality that gnaws away at any natural order. Doubtless inferiors obey 99 percent of the time; it remains that the social order is reduced thereby to its ultimate contingency. In the final analysis, inequality is only possible through equality.[17]

The contingency of equality and inequality trumps the suspicion that these terms may be endowed with ontological consistency. They are worldly practices whose status is not discernible outside a polemic.

Rancière's allergy to ontology reappears when he discusses politics as the practice of dissensus. Politics operates through demonstrations and verifications. It is casuistic. One has to put the universality of equality (or freedom, justice, etc.) to the test of disagreement because *knowing* that we are equal before the law doesn't guarantee that we will *be treated* as equals. Equality is not an *arkhē* or principle of all principles. It is a supposition to be verified. Without this verification there is no politics. This resembles his practice of philosophy, which he describes as follows:

> [It is] an-archical, in the sense that it traces back the specificity of disciplines and discursive competences to the "egalitarian" level of linguistic competence and poetic invention. This practice implies that I take philosophy as a specific battlefield, a field where the endeavor to disclose the *arkhē* of the *arkhē* simply leads to the contrary, that is, to disclosing the contingency or the poetic character of any *arkhē*.[18]

Rancière's postfoundationalism doesn't deny foundations but refuses to grant them the status of transcendental signifieds: all foundations are conventional. This is the meaning of the contingency of the *arkhē*. His view of philosophy as a battlefield matches his claim that disagreement is an object and a method of political inquiry. "An egalitarian practice of philosophy," he says, "is a practice that enacts the aporia of foundation, which is the necessity of a poetical act to constitute an *arkhē* of the *arkhē*, an authority of the authority."[19] He says that what sets him apart from the likes of Antonio Negri and Alain Badiou is his refusal to ontologize the aporia. Instead of seeing it as immanent, as derived from an excess that escapes a systemic drive, or as a proof of the ineradicable lack in being,

Rancière situates "the authority of authority" in a poetical act. So for him foundations are contingent, efforts to ascertain a principle of principles are always poetic acts, universals are polemical and only acquire consistency when they are singularized in cases, and ontology is basically a distraction for understanding politics.

All Police Is Always *n*–1 Police

Police basically means governing, the law or the status quo. Rancière uses other analogues like the partition of the sensible, configuration of the perceptible or distribution of shares where everyone has been accounted for and has a designated place and name. Police represents society as "made up of groups tied to specific modes of doing, to places in which these occupations are exercised, and to modes of being corresponding to these occupations and these places."[20]

Police resembles census data, classifying people according to their occupation, gender, ethnicity, age, education, and so on. This distribution of names, places, and bodies is not neutral. It is a symbolization of the common that distinguishes those who are entitled to speak about the common from those who are not really qualified to do so. Police wrongs equality by establishing a hierarchy of worth: "The logos is never simply speech, because it is always indissolubly the *account* that is made of this speech: the account by which a sonorous emission is understood as speech, capable of enunciating what is just, whereas some other emission is merely perceived as a noise signaling pleasure or pain, consent or revolt."[21] Eduardo Matte, a nineteenth-century Chilean banker and politician, expresses this view of the logos in the daily *El Pueblo* on March 19, 1892. He does so with the candor of someone utterly convinced that the rich have a natural command over the poor: "We, the owners of capital and land, are the owners of Chile. The rest is an impressionable mass that can be bought and sold. Their opinion and prestige carry no weight."[22] Matte does not dispute that rich and poor are fellow countrymen. He simply offers a computation of people's worth that creates an asymmetric common where everyone has been counted but some count less than others: there are those with land and capital and those whose "opinion and prestige carry no weight."

The question is whether the police count coincides with the whole or if something escapes its grip. For Rancière, there is no room for an uncounted remnant because the police signification of the common "is the principle of saturation; it is a mode of the partition of the sensible that recognizes neither lack nor supplement."[23] He is adamant about this: "The essence of police lies in a partition of the sensible that is characterized by the absence of void and of supplement."[24] He says something similar in his criticism of postdemocracy in the expert state. This state "eliminates *every* interval of appearance, of subjectivization, and of dispute in an *exact* concordance between the order of law and the order of facts," as politics ceases "wherever the whole of community is reduced to the sum of its parts with *nothing* left over."[25]

This leads to a strong conclusion: police symbolizes the common as a community of consent whose essence is the absence of a supplement. But is such a radical absence empirically possible? If we take Rancière's claims at face value, police resembles a metaphysical monster of plenitude or the fully realized fantasy of totalitarian and megalomaniac drives—a world where the inscription and the inscribed coincide, where the gap between norms and acts narrows down to such an extent that it is practically nonexistent. Augusto Pinochet expressed this possibility in no uncertain terms: "Not a leaf moves in this country if I'm not moving it. I want that to be clear!" In Pinochet's fantasy, the absence of a remainder leaves no room for disagreement, and thus for politics to challenge the status quo. It is the dream of a perfect police. Dissensus would be little more than residual noise in the system.

But for political inventiveness to emerge and deploy its disruptive effects there has to be a gap between laws and facts. Some interval of appearance must remain. So how should we understand the absence of a remainder? A first response is that police is a way of *symbolizing* order, not the actual rendition of the way it is structured. It symbolizes order *as if* there was an actual coincidence between norms and acts. This "as if" makes all the difference: it indicates that the police representation of itself as an order without remainder doesn't actually reach the factual *n* of plenitude. Every police is always of the *n*–1 kind.

Plato's allegory of the cave illustrates this. A man escapes from lifelong captivity in a cave and realizes that until then he had mistaken the shadows for true knowledge. Plato doesn't propose a simple passage from ignorance to knowledge. Opacity is immanent because caves are inside the world, which is why philosophy must remain vigilant to identify and destroy the pretenders that undermine the possibility of a transparent world. This is a Sisyphean task. Unable to banish all caves, philosophy has to settle for an imperfect or *n*–1 transparency. We can take as a general rule that every order must come to terms with its own impotence: it will never rule over everything and the fantasy of fullness expressed by Pinochet ("Not a leaf moves in this country if I'm not moving it") will remain a fantasy.

Rancière refers indirectly to this in his criticism of Althusser's theory of ideology as interpellation—the police hailing, "Hey, you there!" This, he says, is simply religious subjection; police is not about interpellating demonstrators but about breaking up protests. It "consists, before all else, in recalling the obviousness of what there is, or rather of what there is not, and its slogan is: 'Move along! There is nothing to see here!' " because "it asserts that the space for circulating is nothing but the space of circulation."[26] There is nothing to see precisely because there *is* something, but it should not be seen by those passing by or should be of no concern to them. If there were an exact concordance between norms and acts there would be no need to remind people to move along; traffic cops, the courts, tax collection agencies, and the rest of the paraphernalia of governing would be superfluous. These exist because the connection between the places allocated by the status quo and the bodies that occupy those places is not self-evident. People can deviate from the given *without* putting into question the given. They do so when they ignore a red light or cheat in their tax returns. Police is an ongoing effort to reproduce the communal space and doesn't have the luxury of a seventh day of rest.

This is true even if police manages to naturalize the difference between those who count and those who don't: a degraded presence pushed toward irrelevance (the mass of people whose "opinion and prestige carry no weight," as Matte put it) is not the same as its actual absence. The part without part has nowhere to go because it has no elsewhere at its disposal. Sometimes the no-part responds through the nonpolitical disorder of revolt, at others by means of processes of subjectivization whereby people disidentify with their place and resist efforts to make them invisible. So there's always an interval for the appearance of dissensus even if the latter appears seldom or never arises. Police remains in the vicinity of plenitude.

Moreover, police does *not* imply an absence of conflicts because nonpolitical conflicts—those that pit recognized and counted parts against one another—are a common fixture of police. But for Rancière there are conflicts and conflicts. Some disputes focus on distribution of public resources, others on power and prestige, or refer to the wrangling about policy among political parties, interest groups or movements. Many are about the accepted interpretation of norms. "A strike," he says, "is not political when it calls for reforms rather than a better deal or when it attacks the relationships of authority rather than the inadequacy of wages. It is political when it reconfigures the relationships that determine the workplace in its relation to the community."[27] Many labor disputes never cross the threshold that turns them into political events as Rancière understands them, yet still they short-circuit the presumed coincidence of norms and acts. The corollary is that the presence or absence of conflict is not a criterion to distinguish politics from police. Police is a site where those who want to govern confront those who resist being overcoded, even if they don't do so in the way Rancière understands politics.

So, police never rises above the n–1 threshold and the absence of a void doesn't refer to the elimination of the uncounted but to their condition as outcasts. They are an empirical part that has no real part because they count less than others. The police is haunted by the ghost of the uncounted: "What we call 'exclusion' refers to the one element that cannot be counted in a state system where everyone can supposedly be counted; where it is supposedly possible to quantify every element in the *polis*, their needs and their opinions. There is a remainder that has not been counted and cannot be counted."[28] The counting of the police is always already a miscount or symbolization of the common where the uncounted are included as the insignificant part. Such a miscount inscribes politics as a structural possibility (although not necessarily an actuality) of any order.

Politics as a Parasitic Practice and the Police of Politics

For Rancière conflicts that others call political—those between rich and poor or among interest groups—are not really so if they involve groups that are already counted and are therefore internal to police. These can become political when their practice generates a supernumerary part of the uncounted. Politics seeks to verify the supposition that everyone is equal to everyone else as opposed to police, which is concerned with governing or the creation of a community of consent.[29]

This doesn't mean that politics is so special that we can't mix it with other things. Rancière is no fan of purity. He is very clear about this: politics "has no objects or issues of its own. Its sole principle, equality, is not peculiar to it and is in no way in itself political. All equality does is lend politics reality in the form of specific cases to inscribe, in the form of litigation, confirmation of the equality at the heart of the police order."[30] "Politics acts on the police. It acts on the places and with the words that are common to both, even if it means reshaping those places and changing the status quo."[31] Finally, it "is never pure, never based on some essence proper to the community and the law."[32] These quotes confirm that police can thrive without politics but that politics does not enjoy this self-referential advantage. Politics feeds off the police—its rules, decisions, or prohibitions—and occurs in the territory of police because it has no space of its own.

Rancière confides that he wrote "Ten Theses on Politics" partly as a critique of Hannah Arendt and her strict separation of political and non-political life.[33] For Arendt, the polis is a way of life characterized by fierce agonistic competition among the *homoioi* or equals who want to stand out through their words and deeds. They seek greatness and transcendence because the memory of their accomplishment may offset the inevitability of death. In contrast, the private realm of the household, or *oikos*, is a unit of economic production that deals with activities required to maintain life. It is the invisible world of necessity characterized by despotic rule, violence, and the strictest inequality.[34] What Arendt describes as politics is an elitist view that depicts the doings of a few wealthy men unconcerned about the fate of the underclass. It takes the wronging of equality as a given: she doesn't seem troubled by the fact that the *homoioi* pursue transcendence while women and servants remain out of sight and inaudible in the *oikos*. Rancière dismisses a political life and people destined to it: there's only a political stage for the mise-en-scène of a quarrel about the common that is also a polemic about what counts as political and what doesn't.[35] Arendt, he says, takes for granted what she should have had to demonstrate: "The notion that politics can be deduced from a specific world of equals or free people, as opposed to a world of lived necessity, takes as its ground precisely the object of its litigation."[36]

Politics is thus parasitic of police. I don't mean it in a pejorative way. It is parasitic because it draws its themes from the given: "Politics has no 'proper' object" because "all its objects are blended with the objects of the police." It inscribes the democratic process—one of the names of politics, dissensus, and so on—"in the texts of the constitutions, the institutions of the states, the apparatuses of public opinion, the mainstream forms of enunciation, etc."[37]

This parasitism of politics has another face too. For Rancière, politics is a rare occurrence and domination, or police, is the norm. "If politics is the outline of a vanishing difference with respect to the distribution of social parts and shares, it follows that its existence is by no means necessary, but that it occurs as an always provisional accident within the history of the forms of domination."[38] This accident seeks to interrupt the normality of domination, a claim reminiscent of Walter Benjamin's view of revolution as an activity that makes the continuum of history explode.

His depiction of politics as vanishing, provisional, and accidental does not mean that the rarity of its occurrence also makes it an ephemeral and unexpected bolt of lightning in a blue sky, nor does it limit politics to moments of insurrection. "There is a historical dynamic of politics," says

Rancière, "a history of events that break the 'normal' course of time, a history of events, inscriptions and forms of subjectivization, of promises, memories, repetitions, anticipations and anachronisms."[39] He couldn't be clearer: the interruption of historical time has a history. It unfolds in the interval between an insurgency and the return of business as usual. History introduces duration into the polemic to reconfigure the world.

The effects of temporality are quite obvious. Politics must bind people together to do something in concert. It doesn't matter if they coalesce in a highly structured or a more informal manner: crafting a "we" requires a sustained effort over time. Consider the occupation of the Madrid square Plaza del Sol in May 2011. It detonated the mobilizations of the *indignados* (the outraged), a name that draws its inspiration from Stéphane Hessel's bestseller *Indignez-vous!* (*Time for Outrage!*). This event was political in Rancière's sense of the word. What came to be known as the 15M movement began when some forty people decided to spend the night in the square after a demonstration. They took their cue from the protests in Tahrir Square in Egypt earlier in 2011. The idea was to camp in the square for a week until the municipal elections. They ended up staying a month. During that time, they held countless meetings and formed committees to elaborate proposals that were later discussed in the general assembly. The initial occupants had no plans of what to do, but as time went by they started to imagine another world to come, and to figure out how to get there. The square evolved into a tent city where hundreds lived. People at Sol had to take care of practical issues like feeding themselves, making sure that sanitary facilities worked, providing medical assistance and day care, setting up broadcasting services, establishing mechanisms to solve controversies, and so on. That is, the occupation had to govern itself. It is hard to tell when a political act like the one spearheaded by the forty initial dwellers of Plaza del Sol morphs into police. There is no clear signpost to ascertain this passage. What we can say is that the makeshift city of the *indignados* bears the unmistakable signs of governance, that the practice of dissensus of those who participated in the occupation built its own ad hoc partition of the sensible. Shouldn't we call this by its name, a police of politics?

Rancière himself suggests this: "What do the plebs gathered on the Aventine do? They do not set up a fortified camp in the manner of the Scythian slaves. They do what would have been unthinkable for the latter: *they establish another order*, another partition of the perceptible, by constituting themselves not as warriors equal to other warriors but as speaking beings sharing the same properties as those who deny them these."[40] And again: "A demonstration is political not because it occurs in a particular place and bears upon a particular object but rather because its form is that of *a clash between two partitions of the sensible*."[41] There is an encounter of *two* partitions of the sensible—that is, the police distribution and the one that emerges through the practice of dissensus. This second partition is the police of politics.

I am not trying to neutralize Rancière's argument that politics and police are opposing ways of symbolizing the common. I just want to add another layer to the impurity of politics. For Rancière it is impure because of its parasitic relationship with police. For me politics also shares something of police logic. The Spanish *indignados* set up an ad hoc distribution of the sensible while they attempted to reshape the existing order because to sustain a practice of dissensus over time you need some kind of division of labor, mechanisms of accountability and redress, and so on. So politics is impure not only because it draws from the themes of police. It is also parasitic of police at the level of form: it creates its own distribution of the sensible, a police of politics.

Politics as a Vanishing Mediator

What does this parasitic practice of politics want? "Want" is obviously a misnomer because it endows politics with the human attribute of volition. I use "want" only as a rhetorical device to examine the specificity of politics.

We can begin by discarding the temptation of saying that politics wants to become police. There is some truth to this, for politics aims to redress exclusion. But a more inclusive and tolerant police is still police, so this would ground the specificity of politics in the desire to become order or consensus. Police is not the truth of politics or the goal to which it strives. It would also be wrong to claim that politics exhausts itself in the dissensus mounted by the demos to demonstrate that their equality has been wronged. This is because even a formal argument has to avoid the excesses of formalism. Unlike Carl Schmitt, who wanted to define the political in terms of friend-enemy relations alone—without invoking anything external to this relationship—Rancière has no problem in admitting that politics borrows something nonpolitical from which to take off. Equality is the "content" of politics. It is a supposition implicit in Plato and Aristotle: humans differ from beasts because they are in possession of the logos, which, by implication, establishes an egalitarian baseline for humanity. But equality can be wronged by the count and worth of people's speech. "I am far away from the Schmittian formalization of antagonism," says Rancière, because politics "has its own universal, its own measure that is equality. The measure never applies directly. It does so only through the enactment of a wrong."[42] It is a casuistic equality.

Yet people don't mount a quarrel about the exclusion of the uncounted to show that they have been wronged. Rather, they do so to address that wrong and make it right. The dispute has a triangular structure: A confronts B in order to get C, where C stands for the counting of the uncounted. To suppress the negativity of their exclusion you need to reconfigure the given, institute a new police. Wouldn't this contradict the claim that politics *doesn't* aim to become a better, more inclusive police? Not necessarily: Rancière finds a way around this. In an interview about art and the artistic experience he says, "Dissensus is a modification of the coordinates of the sensible, a spectacle or a tonality that replaces another."[43] An act is political if it disturbs (or tries to disturb) the partition of the sensible through "the demonstration of a possible world in which the argument could count as an argument . . . It is the construction of a paradoxical world that puts together two separate worlds."[44] Finally, politics is "not a world of competing interests or values but a world of competing worlds."[45]

These citations show that dissensus can avoid the problem of circularity through an object outside itself. I am not referring to the parasitism of politics vis-à-vis police, or to the verification of the nonpolitical supposition of the equality of all speakers. The object outside politics is the representations of worlds to come where the name "equality" could apply to bodies that until then didn't qualify for that label. This may entail a Kantian horizon, or not. Michelet provides a measure of levity to the Kantian option by saying that every epoch dreams the next. I interpret this to mean that those who embark in the processes of subjectivization characteristic of politics produce images of other worlds that could emerge through their actions. They do so from within the existing world. These images are surfaces of inscription of expectations and desires, not blueprints of the future police.

What happens if insurgents manage to shake the partition of the sensible sufficiently to trigger a change? They would start to build a new world, in which case they would cease to be the demos and would instead become counted groups within police. A successful politics would then seem to be "destined" to negate itself and become police, thus ceasing to be what it is: the practice of dissensus.

Rancière doesn't see it like this. Politics is "the tracing of a vanishing difference with respect to the distribution of social parts and shares."[46] It marks a *difference* vis-à-vis an existing distribution, it is not the architect of whatever distribution may follow, and it disappears as soon as one begins to allocate parts and shares:

> Do we not need to frame a specific temporality, a temporality of the "existence of the inexistent" in order to give sense to the process of political subjectivization? I prefer to reverse the argument by saying that the framing of a future happens in the wake of political invention rather than being its condition of possibility. Revolutionaries invented a "people" before inventing its future. Besides, in the context of the "ethicization of the political" that is ours, I think that we have to focus first on the specificity of the "aesthetics of politics," the specificity of political invention.[47]

Inventing a people before inventing its future seems counterintuitive because it inverts the usual sequence through which we think a politics of emancipation. Rancière's reasoning might be unusual but it is also impeccable. In the conventional narrative people get together to outline who they are and what they want, propose a plan for action, and then proceed to recruit followers. Rancière doesn't believe we need a program for people to do something. He is referring not to the disorder of revolt but to the process of emancipation. This process creates a people or part of the excluded-uncounted *before* anyone starts to think about the future society where those pariahs could name themselves as equals. Politics disturbs the given to show that another world is possible. Programs of what the future will look like can come in handy, but they are not a precondition for people to try to change the world. Programs and policies are assembled on the go.

Historical evidence is on Rancière's side. Insurgents always voiced their indignation and then began to think about what would follow. They often didn't even have demands, only goals, like the Spanish *indignados.* People camping in the square called for real democracy and an economic system that wouldn't reduce unemployment to a collateral damage of growth. They were not just fighting for a higher share of public resources but for a change in the way decisions about the allocation of shares are made. They started to figure out who they were and what they wanted as they built their tent city. Something similar happened in the Occupy Wall Street insurgency, which mobilized the U.S. *indignados* to fight for a world where the 99 percent could count. These experiences disturbed the given. Their aim was not to design a future society but to displace our cognitive maps and offer portals connecting the present to other, more egalitarian possibilities.

The role of politics as a connector brings Rancière's thinking close to what Fredric Jameson calls a vanishing mediator. Jameson coined this expression to describe the role that Max Weber assigns to the Protestant ethic in the development of capitalism. Protestantism, Jameson says, contributed to disseminate instrumental rationality and the means-ends relation required by capitalism. It functioned as a bridge connecting two eras, the Renaissance and capitalist modernity. Once capitalism had taken root, the Protestant ethic became redundant and could be jettisoned. Protestantism was a vanishing mediator of capitalism. Such a mediator, Jameson says, "serves as a bearer of change and social transformation, only to be forgotten once that change has ratified the reality of the institutions."[48] Jacobinism played a similar role in the birth of bourgeois society in France as the "guardian of revolutionary morality, of bourgeois universalistic and democratic ideals, a guardianship which may be done away with in Thermidor, when the practical victory of the bourgeoisie is assured and an explicitly monetary and market system can come into being."[49] Protestantism and Jacobinism were not a cause but a vanishing mediator of capitalism, its midwives rather than its parents.

Vanishing mediators overlap with Rancière's claim that politics is "the tracing of a vanishing difference with respect to the distribution of social parts and shares . . . [that] occurs as an always provisional accident within the history of forms of domination."[50] Their family resemblance doesn't lie in the shared adjective ("vanishing") but in their role as connectors: Jameson's mediators connect different modes of production or conceptual formations and subsequently fade away, whereas Rancière's politics is a provisional accident that connects different ways of symbolizing the common and then vanishes. When it actually succeeds, in the sense of opening the way to a different configuration of the given, things start to change, and police enters the scene to build and govern a new partition of the sensible.

Politics wants, wills, or desires nothing because it is a connector of worlds. Like the nocturnal activities of laborers described by Rancière, it interrupts "the normal round, one might say, in which our characters prepare and dream and already live the impossible." The uncounted "already live the impossible" because of the performative dimension of politics: when they connect the existing world with another one, as in Allport's example of the black plaintiff, people don't wait for the arrival of the many Godots of equality, justice, or freedom because they have already begun to experience what they strive for. This is the public secret of Jacotot's intellectual emancipation and Rancière's process of equality: they are always an enactment. Even if politics fails to trigger a change, this doesn't mean that it achieves nothing. It experiments with different ways of organizing the common that leave behind the memory of ways of being together that change participants as well as a trove of ideas and experiences that function as a toolbox for other insurgencies.

So, the specificity of politics is to open up possibilities, not to become police. It resembles the rabbit hole in *Alice in Wonderland,* except that it doesn't link a conventional adult world with a fantastic one: dissensus puts into contact an existing world that is unbearable for the uncounted and another in which they might find a fit. There will have been politics even if the passageway it opens fails to take us to other worlds. Politics is not the engineer that designs and builds the world in which those other possibilities of being together may flourish. Designing, organizing, and governing are what the police order does.

The Politics of Police as a Homeopathic Process

The last question I examine is another oxymoron, the politics of police. The expression seems incongruous because it squares off the practice of dissensus with the pursuit of consensus. I want to show that it isn't.

My starting point is Amador Fernández-Savater's depiction of police and politics as two different visions of politics, one literal and the other literary. He uses a passage in Count Joseph de Maistre's *Considerations on France* to illustrate the literal or police view. Says de Maistre: "The Constitution of 1795, like its predecessors, was made for *man*. But there is no such thing as *man* in the world. In my lifetime I have seen Frenchmen, Italians, Russians, etc.; thanks to Montesquieu, I even know that *one can be Persian*. But as for *man*, I declare that I have never in my life met him; if he exists, he is unknown to me."[51] De Maistre wants something more substantive, says Fernández-Savater, people classified "according to their position at birth within the Ancien Régime (royalty, nobility, the peasantry), all of this conforming to natural laws 'about which nothing can be said except that they exist because they exist.'" Equality is not one of those things that "exist because they exist." It is simply a fiction, or abstraction. What is real for de Maistre is people's position at birth, and their nationalities.

The former British Prime Minister Margaret Thatcher mirrored this reasoning in an interview where she famously stated, "There is no such thing as society." She expands this in another passage: "I think we have gone through a period when too many children and people have been given to understand 'I have a problem, it is the government's job to cope with it' . . . And so they are casting their problems on society, and who is society? There is no such thing! There are individual men and women and there are families."[52] Thatcher says that society doesn't exist, or is an abstraction, in order to displace the burden of responsibility for inequality onto the individuals and their families, who must then deal with their lot as best they can. De Maistre doesn't see man, and man as citizen, because he refuses to come to terms with the subject of rights championed by the rebels of 1789.

Both narratives fall under what Fernández-Savater describes as a literal vision of politics, one that occurs within the parameters of the given. But how literal is this literality? In *S/Z*, his study of Balzac's novel *Sarrazine*, Roland Barthes demonstrated that nothing is strictly literal, not even realist novels that pretend to be so through their use of denotative language. This is because denotation is not a nomenclature of the real but an attempt to present language as nature. As Barthes puts it, "Denotation is not the first meaning, but pretends to be so; under this illusion, it is ultimately no more than the *last* of the connotations (the one which seems both to establish and to close the reading), the superior myth by which the text pretends to return to the nature of language, to language as nature."[53]

Similarly, de Maistre's symbolization of the common is not a rendition of reality but a narrative that celebrates a stratified partition of the common. His units of analysis—the nation and, therefore, Italian, British, and other nationalities—are creations of modernity and not empirically given entities drawn from the nature of things. Thatcher's individuals are as abstract as the market individualism that functions as a backdrop for her tirade about the nonexistence of society. But their literality wavers as all politics, even the literal kind, turns out to be literary. When Fernández-Savater calls de Maistre's narrative "literal politics," he means simply to indicate that it presents itself *as if* it were a description of the world rather than what it really is, a set of judgments about the meaning of the lived world.

Politics, in contrast, is a fiction whose generative force unsettles the given and seeks to renew it. Political fiction counts the uncounted, invents narratives that construe the uncounted as visible and speaking subjects. So when de Maistre says, "As for *man*, I declare that I have never in my life met him," he is probably telling the truth. He hasn't met him because man falls outside his symbolization of the common. "If de Maistre sees *nothing*," says Fernández-Savater, "it is because revolutionary fiction invents a space that didn't exist before; it interrupts the order of classifications that define reality by questioning the necessity of the necessary and suspending the injunction that commands subjectivities to be what they are." De Maistre isn't interested in inventing another world. He wants to thwart the emergence of a new one, and even go back to the Ancien Régime. Politics for Rancière is clearly literary: it disputes "the necessity of the necessary" to show something that didn't seem to exist, and for this you have to imagine a world different from the one defined by the status quo.

But we've seen that literality is not simply literal. De Maistre is aware that "man" creates a baseline for humanity—that is, something we all share. This challenges the stratified image of the world he expounds, so he wants to counter it with a narrative that highlights the national differences within humankind. This is why he says that there are only flesh-and-bone men like the Italians or the French. But his real goal is to change the world backward by undoing what the revolutionaries of 1789 achieved. This means that a literal politics that seeks to neutralize changes that improve the lot of the excluded is never purely literal. It also has a literary-fictional dimension that celebrates the past (and sometimes glorifies the present) and construes inequality as a result of heritage, chance, laziness, and so on. In de Maistre's literal-literary politics, the contingency of one's lot is a matter of necessity: he describes as natural what is really a stratagem of verisimilitude like the one Barthes identifies in the realist novel.

This invites us to reassess Fernández-Savater's view of police as literal politics. A *literal* politics might be his analogue of police, but if it is also a literal *politics*, then police can't simply be literal. It has a fictional dimension too, like politics. This makes all the difference. Fernández-Savater subverts Rancière's schema, perhaps without realizing it. He grants police the attributes of politics. I call this a *politics of police*. To think this through, one has to work both with Rancière—by positioning oneself in the speech situation he calls disagreement—and against him. I do so by interrogating the relationship between politics and the verification of equality. I argue that politics has two modes of being, both of them literary: the politics Rancière identifies with emancipation and the politics of police, which seeks to modify the status quo without necessarily riding the Siamese twins of equality and emancipation.

Samuel Chambers was the first to talk about a politics of police, in an article aptly titled "The Politics of Police."[54] Like Rancière, he avoids the temptation of dissing police in the name of the higher calling of politics. Politics is always entangled with the themes and rules of police. Similarly, if Rancière sees democracy as the institution of politics and not as a political regime, Chambers is right to say that democracy is not a promise of something in waiting. We will *never* live in a democracy because democracy is the paradoxical condition of politics and not a type of regime. To speak of a democratic government would be a misnomer. But we can make life more bearable by intervening in the partition of the sensible. As he says, "We must remain committed to and concerned with the politics of the police in the sense of changing, transforming, and improving our police orders."[55] This is an invitation to "cultivate a democratic politics more not less attendant to the possibility of transforming the police order."[56]

By stating the desirability of a better police (because it is more inclusive, not because it controls us better), Chambers builds on Rancière's refusal to grant a normative preference to politics over police. His politics of police also introduces something different from politics and police: Rancière sees politics as emancipation (it redraws the given) and Chambers chooses to use the same name, politics, to designate emancipation *as well as* the activity of improving the status quo. Hence the trilogy: police, politics, and the option Chambers adds, the politics of police. His distinction between politics as a project of redrawing the field of experience and a politics of police intent on "changing, transforming, and improving" police echoes the opposition between revolutionary and reformist politics, whose archetypical proper names are Rosa Luxemburg and Eduard Bernstein, correspondingly. Rancière himself flirts with this distinction when he says that a strike for wages (reform) can make things better but is not political unless it seeks to reconfigure the given (revolution). Politics and the politics of police reopen the polemic about how to differentiate between reform and revolution.

Rancière believes that there are better and worse varieties of police too. The Scythian would be less desirable because they "customarily put out the eyes of those they reduced to slavery, the better to restrict them to their task as slaves, which was to milk the livestock."[57] Rancière doesn't specify what makes a police more or less desirable. He lets the brutality of the Scythian practice do the argumentative legwork. Saying "There is a worse and a better police" and "One kind of police may be infinitely preferable to another"[58] involves a tacit normative assumption about what is desirable in police matters. It also means that Chambers's call for an improvement of police is not outside Rancière's conceptual framework.

Chambers pegs the politics of police to the consequences of our actions on the status quo—that is, to whether they will improve or redraw the given. This is a perfectly legitimate option, but for me a politics of police is inherent to the police-politics relation, and shows the structural impurity of these two terms. This impurity opens the door for understanding the politics of police as a homeopathic practice of counted groups: they are part of the police yet seek to reconfigure the given. I am not referring to the becoming-politics of a police occurrence, for Rancière himself contemplates this in his example of the workers' strike. My point is that named groups can modify the given without embarking in a process of subjectivization. Grounding the politics of police on the impurity of its terms means *both* terms, politics as well as police. Rancière addresses the impurity of politics. I want to add the impurity of police.

I begin by reiterating that conflicts are part of the police. The very obviousness of what can be said, heard, seen, and done by whom, when, and where is anything but obvious. Nobody really knows for sure the limits of the place she occupies. Courts and governmental agencies would be redundant if we all knew the norms, understood their meaning, and adjusted our behavior to their dictates. Streets are meant for circulating, but they are also places where people assemble to protest, run marathons, hold public festivals, argue with one another, and so on. We quarrel about when they can be used for circulation and when for other purposes. This kind of polemic is a police affair, not the manifestation of political dissensus in the sense Rancière gives to that word. Interpretive conflicts highlight that the consensus that characterizes police is not all that consensual.

But counted groups also subvert the stability of a governable space. These are parts of the status quo and can generate effects that resemble the dislocations Rancière associates with politics. They are homeopathic in the usual sense that like can cure like. I take this idea from Carlo Donolo. He speaks of allopathic politics as shorthand for the politics of political parties that intervene on society from the political system. Homeopathic politics, by contrast, refers to social movements that want to cure society from within the social.[59] Donolo's distinction is pertinent even if his topology of spaces as well as the debate about parties versus social movements is a bit dated. Homeopathy serves as a counterpoint to Rancière's view of the political as the encounter of two heterogeneous processes—governing, or police, and equality, or politics as the effort to verify the supposition that everyone is equal.[60] A politics of police is not an encounter of radically different processes but a homeopathic one where like changes like. It happens when counted parts, whether individuals or groups, act on the existing field of experience to reconfigure it. This politics taps on the generative force of counted parts and the multiple conflicts they generate inside police.

These groups sidestep political subjectivization. I mentioned subjectivization when I spoke of identities in transit. Rancière describes it as "a disidentification, removal from *the naturalness of a place*, the opening up of a subject space where anyone can be counted since it is the space where those of no account are counted, where a connection is made between having a part and having no part."[61] The meaning of this quote depends on how we understand "the naturalness of a place." I interpret it as something less than natural: if the subject identifies with an assigned place to the extent that she lives it as natural (as if there were no gap between the place and its occupant), it wouldn't be a subject but a substance, or the fantasy of a literal world. A full identity with what one is supposed to be is rare. Torturers can develop empathy for people whom they have just waterboarded. People who clean toilets in slums would prefer to do anything other than what they do. And Rancière himself reminds us that at night many proletarians chose to study or join theater groups rather than rest.

There is no shortage of examples. If there is no straightforward relation between bodies and places, or if their relation is open to discussion, then disidentification is not the first step in breaking from the assigned place because every subject position is already exposed to uncertainty. This is either because people don't quite know who they are supposed to be or because they negotiate what can and cannot be said, seen, or done within the place they find themselves. The way people represent their relationship with the places they occupy is always a matter of debate because there is a gap between their identification with a place and the place as such.

This gap won't disappear through police correctives—something like infinite variations of the "Move along!" that Rancière invokes as exemplary of police activity. The presence of the uniformed police in the streets is a reminder that the actions and places occupied by agents never quite coincide. The gap is a feature of the changing nexus between places, names, and bodies. Our metastable identities are defined by this nexus. So if identification with a place is always already subverted by the distance between the representation of a place and the body associated with it, then the certainty of who we are is something less than certain and the stability of frontiers between police identification and political disidentification can never be a sure thing.

This complicates matters. Rancière says that a practice counts as political if it puts into question the partition of the sensible. Yet the instability of frontiers between identification and disidentification makes it difficult to make a priori judgments on whether actions undertaken by counted groups reshuffle the deck or reshape the status quo by changing the parts, the rules, or the playing field. This is reminiscent of the polemic about reform and revolution. How can we tell if the decriminalization of abortion is a police process—a change brought about by pressure groups, advocates of reproductive rights, and legislators—or a game-changing event in gender relations?

The question is: What counts as putting the given into question? How different does another experience of being together have to be before we can say it has become something other than what it was? Focusing on quantity and intensity won't take us far due to the notorious difficulty of measuring the intensity and numerical magnitude of a difference. The threshold between police reform and political innovation is never clear. But, again, Rancière sees disagreement as an object and method of his theorization, so there is a way to address the difference between retouching and transforming the given. It consists of submitting the statement "putting into question" to the test of disagreement. Rancière does this in his critique of Arendt. Her clear-cut separation of polis and *oikos* works only if you take for granted that there is a political life with people destined to such life, as opposed to the prepolitical life of those who have to endure inequality and oppression for the good of the polis. Rancière rejects this reasoning because the separation between political and nonpolitical is not the foundation but the object of politics. He is right: politics is an operator of difference, a practice that disputes what is and isn't political. But this also applies to Rancière: why should we accept a clear demarcation between politics and police, and between subjectivization and the identification with the subject positions we occupy? These are objects of dispute because the naturalness of frontiers is not natural. It is the contingent outcome of the practice of disagreement.

Let us assume that there is no gap between a place and its occupier. This hypothetical case of individuals who identify happily with the places they are allotted wouldn't change the fact that frontiers are fuzzy. Senators, councillors, and other figures of representative democracy are quintessential agents of constituted power. They have no reason to disidentify from the place popular suffrage assigned them. All they want to be is what they already are, professional politicians. The in-between or interval between identities and political subjectivization is not even a remote possibility. But representatives *can* dislocate the existing order by amending the constitution, making laws to abolish sexist or racist discrimination in the workplace, raising the legal age to purchase drinks, and so on. Some might see this as an adjustment within police. Maybe it is, but how can we tell? It can't be settled by fiat. It has to be submitted to the protocols of disagreement. Yet even then we could agree that elected officials have a reservoir of constituent power. Their subject positions have a generative force that can be mobilized to make a difference without them ever having to disidentify from their designated places.

The point is that frontiers between social groups and processes of political subjectivization are a matter of dispute. The politics of police feeds off this possibility. It shows that counted parts can generate the disruptive effects of dissensus analogous to those Rancière associates with political subjectivization. They embark on a homeopathic politics of police.

Rancière might wonder why we make such a fuss about the instability of frontiers if he himself says that the doings of groups can morph into political acts. This is true, but, again, I am not referring to the sequence whereby an identity ceases to be what it is through a process of subjectivization. This is not the birth of a place of enunciation that had not been perceived within the existing field of experience. The politics of police describes counted groups that act *as* social groups and still manage to modify the given. Put differently, it is not a matter of how a subject transforms herself but how counted parts reconfigure the given without inserting themselves into a sequence of subjectivization. The homeopathic politics of police is a politics whose subjects are not in-between names and places. Better still, all subject positions are metastable, or in transit: police identities also undergo changes, but without passing through the emancipatory narrative of subjectivization. This gives us yet another reason to polemicize about how natural the naturalness of place is, and how to discern if (or when) a conflict has crossed the threshold of a census-like category and become political.

A homeopathic politics of police highlights the impurity of police because practices that are internal to it can also reconfigure the given. This is why I argue that Rancière's police exhibits some of the traits of politics. A politics of police names the transformative practices triggered by counted groups. It identifies the homeopathic interplay between the institution and the instituted within the instituted and through transformative practices triggered by counted groups.

Notes

1. Jacques Rancière, *The Nights of Labor: The Worker's Dream in Nineteenth-Century France* (Philadelphia: Temple University Press, 1989), viii.

2. Jacques Rancière, *The Ignorant Schoolmaster: Five Lessons in Intellectual Emancipation* (Stanford, Calif.: Stanford University Press, 1991).

3. Joseph Jacotot quoted in Rancière, *The Ignorant Schoolmaster,* 88.

4. Rancière, *The Ignorant Schoolmaster,* 137.

5. Jacques Rancière, *Disagreement: Politics and Philosophy* (Minneapolis: University of Minnesota Press, 1998).

6. Gordon Allport, *The Nature of Prejudice* (1954; reprint, Cambridge, Mass.: Perseus, 1979), 135.

7. Rancière, *The Ignorant Schoolmaster,* 88.

8. Jacques Rancière, "The Thinking of Dissensus: Politics and Aesthetics," in *Reading Rancière,* ed. Paul Bowman and Richard Stamp (London: Continuum, 2011), 2.

9. Rancière, *Disagreement,* xi.

10. Jacques Rancière, "Politics, Identification, and Subjectivization," *October* 61 (1992): 58.

11. There is a third option: immanence without transcendence, like the one we find in the theory of the multitude of Michael Hardt and Antonio Negri, which draws from the work of Gilles Deleuze and Spinoza. Rancière is not very sympathetic to this perspective. He says: "The concept of the multitude manifests a phobia of the negative, of any politics that defines itself 'against.'" Jacques Rancière, "The People or the Multitude?," in *Dissensus: On Politics and Aesthetics,*

ed. and trans. Steven Corcoran (New York: Continuum, 2010), 86. The multitude differs from his own concept of the people because it is predicated on "an ontological claim that substantializes the egalitarian presupposition": the multitude is a political subject that "ought to express the multiple insofar as the multiple is the very law of being" (*Dissensus*, 86). Rancière is opposed to any law of being.

12. William Connolly, *The Ethos of Pluralization* (Minneapolis: University of Minnesota Press, 1995).

13. Ernesto Laclau and Chantal Mouffe, *Hegemony and Socialist Strategy: Towards a Radical Democratic Politics*, trans. Winston Moore and Paul Cammack (London: Verso, 1985).

14. Slavoj Žižek, *The Sublime Object of Ideology* (London: Verso, 1989), and "Schlagend, aber nicht Treffend!," *Critical Inquiry* 33 (2006): 194ff.

15. Rancière, "The Thinking of Dissensus," 12.

16. Jacques Rancière, "Politics and Aesthetics: An Interview," *Angelaki* 8, no. 2 (2003): 198.

17. Rancière, *Disagreement*, 16–17.

18. Rancière, "The Thinking of Dissensus," 15.

19. Rancière, "The Thinking of Dissensus," 15.

20. Jacques Rancière, "Ten Theses on Politics," in *Dissensus*, 36. See also Jacques Rancière, "Introducing Disagreement," *Angelaki* 9, no. 3 (2004): 6.

21. Rancière, *Disagreement*, 22–23.

22. Eduardo Matte quoted in Claudio Vázquez Lazo, "Los dueños de Chile," *El Mostrador*, 2015, http://www.elmostrador.cl/noticias/opinion/2015/11/09/los-duenos-de-chile/, 2015. I thank Jorge Arditi for telling me about this article. If the count of one's speech is more relevant than access to it, then one could reexamine Gayatri Spivak's celebrated article about subalternity. The question wouldn't be so much "Can the Subaltern Speak?," for they can speak with or without their academic interpreters, but whether their speech *counts* or not, or if it counts as much as the speech of intellectuals, government employees, politicians, businesspeople, and so on. The shift from speech to the count of that speech makes the subaltern a part of the no-part, the part of the uncounted. See Gayatri Chakravorty Spivak, "Can the Subaltern Speak?," in *Marxism and the Interpretation of Culture*, ed. Cary Nelson and Lawrence Grossberg, 271–313 (Urbana: University of Illinois Press, 1988).

23. Rancière, "Dissenting Words," 124.

24. Rancière, "Ten Theses," 36.

25. Rancière, *Disagreement*, 112, 123, my italics.

26. Rancière, "Ten Theses," 37.

27. Rancière, *Disagreement*, 32.

28. Jacques Rancière, "Democracy Means Equality," *Radical Philosophy* 82 (1997): 32.

29. Rancière, "Politics, Identification, and Subjectivization," 58. See also "Post-Democracy, Politics and Philosophy: An Interview with Jacques Rancière," *Angelaki* 1, no. 3 (1994): 173.

30. Rancière, *Disagreement*, 31–32.

31. Rancière, *Disagreement*, 33.

32. Rancière, *Disagreement*, 61.

33. Rancière, "The Thinking of Dissensus," 3.

34. Hannah Arendt, *The Human Condition* (Chicago: University of Chicago Press, 1974), 27–33, 33, 28–29, 43–51, 57–58, 65, 177–78, 197–99.

35. Rancière, "The Thinking of Dissensus," 4.

36. Rancière, "Ten Theses," 39.

37. Rancière, "The Thinking of Dissensus," 5.

38. Rancière, "Ten Theses," 35.

39. Rancière, "The Thinking of Dissensus," 5; see also Jacques Rancière, "Comments and Responses," *Theory and Event* 6, no. 4 (2003), https://muse.jhu.edu/article/44787.

40. Rancière, *Disagreement*, 24, my italics.

41. Rancière, "Ten Theses," 39, my italics.

42. Rancière, "The Thinking of Dissensus," 4.

43. Jacques Rancière, "Art of the Possible: Fulvia Carnevale and John Kelsey in Conversation with Jacques Rancière," *Artforum International.* 45, no. 7 (2007): 259, http://artforum.com/inprint/issue=200703&id=12843&pagenum=0.

44. Rancière, "Ten Theses," 39.

45. Rancière, "The Thinking of Dissensus," 7.

46. Rancière, "Ten Theses," 35.

47. Rancière, "The Thinking of Dissensus," 13.

48. Fredric Jameson, "The Vanishing Mediator: Narrative Structure in Max Weber," *New German Critique* 1 (1973): 80.

49. Jameson, "The Vanishing Mediator," 78.

50. Rancière, "Ten Theses," 35.

51. Count Joseph de Maistre, *Considerations on France*, quoted in Amador Fernández-Savater, "Política literal y política literaria (sobre ficciones políticas y 15M)," 2012, http://www.eldiario.es/interferencias/ficcion-politica-15-M_6_71452864.html.

52. Margaret Thatcher, "AIDS, Education and the Year 2000!," interview with Douglas Keay, *Woman's Own*, September 23, 1987, 8–10.

53. Roland Barthes, *S/Z* (Oxford: Blackwell, 1972), 9.

54. Samuel Chambers, "The Politics of Police," in Bowman and Stamp, *Reading Rancière.*

55. Chambers, "The Politics of Police," 36.

56. Chambers, "The Politics of Police," 37.

57. Rancière, *Disagreement*, 12.

58. Rancière, *Disagreement*, 30–31.

59. Carlo Donolo, "Algo más sobre el autoritarismo político y social," in *Los límites de la democracia*, vol. 2, ed. Mario R. Dos Santos (Buenos Aires: CLACSO, 1985), 56–59.

60. Rancière, "Politics, Identification, and Subjectivization," 58.

61. Rancière, *Disagreement*, 36, my italics.

Which Politics of Aesthetics?

Joseph J. Tanke

What is once again open for debate in contemporary Continental philosophy is the meaning and significance of the aesthetic, that intellectual-perceptual space carved out, as distinct from the cognitive and the moral dimensions of human experience, by the texts of German idealism. Much of the credit for reopening this debate is owed to Jacques Rancière, a thinker who is largely responsible for revitalizing aesthetics in the European philosophical tradition. Rancière's contribution consists of offering a compelling series of arguments about the continued relevance of aesthetics for understanding contemporary visual art, as well as an interesting, if at times strained, argument that classical German aesthetics can be viewed as giving rise to a meaningful experience of equality, and not just to the instances of freedom described by thinkers such as Kant, Schiller, and Hegel.

This attempt to clarify the egalitarian kernel of aesthetics can be viewed as in keeping with Rancière's project more generally, which he envisions most generally as giving sustenance to those working on behalf of human emancipation. Throughout the 1980s and '90s, Rancière did much to revise our understanding of democracy, describing it as the disruption of hierarchical and exclusionary forms of community. Hierarchical forms of community are what Rancière calls the police. Punning on the sense in which "police" sounds like "polis," Rancière describes the police as an inegalitarian arrangement of the community, one which claims, falsely, the community is representative, and that no one of any significance has been excluded from taking part in its affairs. Politics, for Rancière, is the process of actively challenging the account of the city or the community offered by the police. Politics occurs whenever the hierarchical allocations of the police are questioned in the name of equality. Rancière's idea is that in order for politics to break with the police's "distribution of the sensible [*partage du sensible*]"—his concept for the general allocation of bodies, voices, roles, and capacities at work within a given community—it must find or invent a value that is foreign to it. Rancière argues that equality is the only supposition capable of radically contesting the distributions defined by the police. As an initial axiom, equality supplies thought, action, and political organization with a fundamentally different starting point than that of the police. This new starting point thus helps to ensure that politics does not stumble and become a mere shuffling of the sensible, as opposed to an actual redistribution of it, and guards against the possibility of inadvertently reinscribing hierarchy somewhere along the way. Central, then, to Rancière's conception of democracy—the countering of the police's idea of community with an alternative premised on the equality of all—is the supposition, polemical affirmation, and demonstration of equality. This is why Rancière describes politics as dissensus, or as being about the creation of a conflict between two worlds. Politics is the process of confronting the world defined by the police, a world of hierarchy, with the one outlined by democracy and its supposition of equality.

After this brief reminder about Rancière's basic political assumptions, we can better understand the impetus for attempting to find and preserve some idea of equality in the texts of philosophical aesthetics. If Rancière can isolate instances of equality in the texts of classical philosophical aesthetics, then he can argue that they have, to some degree, been misunderstood, and make the case for aesthetics as the discourse that preserves the relationship between art and politics. Artistic practices can be described as political inasmuch as they redistribute the allotment of roles, capacities, and bodies at work in a given community, or at least change the meanings assigned to these roles, capacities, and bodies, and thus initiate a more explicitly political process of redistribution. As has been explained, in order for a practice, a discourse, a process, or an action to be truly political, it must maintain some relationship with equality. Thus, in order for artistic practices to amount to something more than an apolitical shuffling of the sensible, they too must be premised on equality.

Rancière's *Aesthetics and Its Discontents* offers readers a brief yet incisive reading of classical German aesthetics as well as a series of interesting commentaries on his relationships with some of his contemporaries, notably Jean-François Lyotard and Alain Badiou. It is a singular book whose polemical force sometimes overshadows the subtle movement that it tries to carry out, namely the project of reinterpreting the aesthetic experience—often described as an instance of the mind's freedom—in terms of equality. For many reasons, I am inclined to see Rancière's rightly celebrated accounts of the political capacities of art and aesthetics, as well as his highly illuminative accounts of contemporary practices, as stemming from this novel insight into classical German aesthetics. Throughout *Aesthetics and Its Discontents*, the development of this idea of the aesthetic experience relies on Rancière's ability to distinguish his political reading of aesthetics—which is what we see in his comments on

Kant and Schiller—as well as his ability to prevent the political problematic from being confused with various other readings of the aesthetic. In this respect, one can view the engagements with Badiou and Lyotard as designed to prevent the political account of aesthetics developed in the first essay, "Aesthetics as Politics," from lapsing into an ethical account of the aesthetic experience. For Rancière, the ethical readings carried out by Lyotard and others are problematic to the extent that they drop the connection between the aesthetic experience and equality, thereby replacing a narrative of capacity with one of incapacity. These frameworks, in Rancière's view, deprive art of its ability to redistribute the sensible.

As I read it, a large portion of *Aesthetics and Its Discontents* revolves around Rancière's idea that Kant's account of the aesthetic judgment can be read as an instance of equality. This is undoubtedly an idea that Rancière derived from his encounter with Schiller, one of the first thinkers to read Kant's aesthetics as a political allegory. Specifically, Rancière points to the difference between the cognitive faculties as they exist in cognition, and as they relate to one another when encountering something beautiful. For Rancière, the famous "free play" of the imagination, and the understanding that Kant sees as providing the transcendental conditions for our experiences with the beautiful, can and should be understood as the suspension of the hierarchies that normally obtain between the cognitive faculties. Whereas cognition subordinates the imagination to the understanding, the aesthetic allows for their free and equal resolution. Rancière explains that we should understand the free play of the cognitive faculties not only as the key to understanding how aesthetic judgments are possible, but also as the political promise that animates aesthetics. In this respect, the free play of the cognitive faculties should be read, simultaneously, as an account of the mind as it enters into aesthetic contemplation, and as a political proposition. Rancière: "What the aesthetic free appearance and free play challenge is the distribution of the sensible that identifies the order of domination with the differences between two humanities."[1] If cognition is a world wherein reason dominates sense, the aesthetic is the place where they reach an accord. Indeed, in a number of places, Rancière describes the aesthetic experience as "a liberty and an equality of sensing" that anyone and everyone can appropriate in order to carry out a demonstration of equality.[2] This means that, for Rancière, the texts of philosophical aesthetics have managed to identify an experience of equality, one that can be construed as a reminder that social hierarchies are arbitrary and easily overturned by adopting a simple, if somewhat exceptional, point of view. Further, these texts indicate not only that equality is possible, but also that it is in some sense actual inasmuch as it can be detected in our encounters with art and nature.

While I am sympathetic to Rancière's analyses of the political aspects of aesthetics, I think it is necessary to complicate his picture by attending more fully to some of the more disquieting aspects of aesthetics. It is in part correct to say that the aesthetic experience *can* be read as the cancellation of a world divided between two different types of humanities; however, I think that this is only part of the story and that one can also see in the history of post-Kantian aesthetics the gradual, and often inadvertent, restoration of hierarchies based on sensible and intellectual dispositions. In contrast with Rancière, I see the aesthetic as a metastable phenomenon that oscillates between, on the one hand, the intimation and promise of equality, and, on the other, the division of the community of spectators and readers into those capable of grasping the true nature of the aesthetic experience and those on whom it will be lost. Not long after Schiller, Schelling, for example, would explain that the purpose of aesthetics is to put an end to the "literary peasant wars" that obscure everything in art and literature that is truly elevating.[3] Indeed, as an almost point-by-point reversal of the egalitarian tendency that Rancière reads out of Kant and Schiller, Schelling will define aesthetics as the attempt to reintroduce rank and order into a world that is losing its way. Schelling not only distinguishes the true philosophy of art, that is, aesthetics, from so many literary theories, he positions the aesthetic itself as an experience that retraces the dividing line between "noble" and "crude" natures.[4] And while membership in this elect is no longer determined by birth, Schelling nevertheless estimates that only a few will be capable of seeing the absolute at work in individual works.

Such changes have less to do with the specific political positions of individual authors than they do with the nature of the aesthetic phenomenon itself, an unstable mode of sensuous apprehension capable of sustaining a number of different and sometimes contradictory social, political, and ethical concerns. If Rancière is inclined to see the discourse of aesthetics as reflective of the democratic revolutions that convulsed Europe, we should also see in it the vestiges of the aristocratic worldview. Rather than lending itself to an uncomplicated democratic appropriation, these texts articulate the experience of a withdrawal from a world of preestablished meanings, providing the ground for both the democratic sensibility Rancière points to *and* the more reactionary theories of human nature that proliferated in European literature and philosophy throughout the second half of the nineteenth century.

However desirable the goal of a democratic aesthetics may be, we should remember that the aesthetic is an intoxicating vertigo, one that emboldens the cognitive faculties and convinces them of their superiority over the rest of nature. Before long, within the very tradition inaugurated by Kant, the aesthetic will come to carry the name of Dionysus. While Schiller is perhaps right to find in Kant's account of the free play of the mental faculties a political allegory that may be useful for imagining a more egalitarian social order, we must remember that this idea of a disinterested pleasure separated from the domains of cognition and morality also supplies the perceptual-intellectual soil for Baudelaire's Dandy and Nietzsche's Overman, two figures at odds with the democratic conception of aesthetics.

It is only after we have grappled with these different strands that we can take sides with one tendency within the tradition in order to battle against the tradition itself. I attempt to do this in the final section of this essay. After pinpointing the ways in which I find Rancière's account of the history of aesthetics to be at points strained, I will explore some of the resources that exist within his thought for redescribing the nature of the aesthetic experience. I contend that Rancière's recent revitalization of spectatorship constitutes a more promising route for a democratic theory of aesthetics than does his allegorical reading of classical German aesthetics. These accounts of spectatorship will allow us to specify the ways in which artistic practices revolve around a presupposition of equality between the artist and the spectator. I argue that this understanding of spectatorship can be viewed as a corrective to some of the more common descriptions of the aesthetic experience and that this contrast allows for us to better gauge the novelty of Rancière's position. Thus, despite contesting Rancière's idea that the texts of classical philosophical aesthetics articulated that experience in terms of equality, I do think that one can claim both that certain forms of artistic communication revolve around equality and that Rancière's account of spectatorship allows us to become more sensitive to the role that equality plays in our appreciation of art. The true significance of this position, however, emerges only when we contrast this emancipated form of spectatorship, premised on a notion of equality, with the standard view that the aesthetic experience is an instance of the mind's freedom.

Equality or Freedom?

For those interested in the question of art today, Rancière's central idea is that art is not autonomous from other aspects of existence, as so many misleading theories of modernism have held. Its practices redefine what can be seen and said, as well as the implicit estimations placed on members of our communities. It is important to stress, however, that the intertwining of art and politics that Rancière hopes to re-create is not the same as the customary thesis about the blurring of the boundaries between art and life. For Rancière, art's power is contained in its difference from the everyday, not its identification with it. Art harbors propositions for other ways of life, and thus has a type of political agency, inasmuch as it refuses to be directly inserted into everyday systems of meaning, that is, inasmuch as it refuses to be explicitly political.

A large part of Rancière's efforts have gone into creating a taxonomy and loose historical structure for taking account of the different ways in which art and politics meet. This historical-philosophical account of art depends on his distinction between three different "regimes of art."[5] For Rancière, a regime is not a strict chronological marker, even though certain movements, thinkers, and historical moments have been central to the formation of each. Rather, a regime is a series of axioms that defines what art is, and assigns it a position in relation to other practices more generally. A regime imposes sense on the sensible productions of art and, in so doing, determines what, if any, political significance it can have.

The first such regime that Rancière discuses is the "ethical regime of images." Within his discussions of art, it is employed the least for the simple reason that, within the ethical regime of images, art, understood as an autonomous or semiautonomous sphere of practices distinct from the broader domain of daily practices, does not exist. This regime finds its inspiration in Plato's critique of imitation, a problematic that prevents art from emerging from the ways of doing and making specific to a given community. As Rancière explains, the problem is not that Plato places art under the watchful eye of politics; it is that he recognized no such distinction. For Plato, practices either support or undermine the order that resides in the soul or the polis.[6]

Extrapolating from Plato, we can say that there is an ethical relationship with images whenever a discourse, practice, arrangement, or conception of art subordinates its ways of doing (*technai*), the ways of doing specific to art, to the *arkhē* (principle) of community. An ethical regime conceives of "art" as a means of establishing or reinforcing the ethos of a given community. Its primary concern is to determine what effects are created by a given form or practice, and, in some instances, to contain or defuse them.

The "representative regime of art" was developed from the principles found in Aristotle's *Poetics* and in response to some of Plato's concerns regarding the dangers of imitative art. At the heart of the representative regime is the idea that even though art is essentially imitative, not all of its images are harmful simulacra. Indeed, Aristotle's conception of *mimēsis* can be understood as responding to Plato's concerns about *technai* unfettered from the *arkhē* of community. The representative conception of art grants art some autonomy from the ethos of the community, while making concessions to the ethical concerns expressed by Plato.[7]

Historically speaking, this regime corresponds roughly with what Foucault called the Classical age, the period of European culture that extends from the seventeenth century through the end of the eighteenth. For Rancière, the representative regime includes primarily *les belles letters* and *les beaux-arts,* although it can be taken to refer to any normative system of artistic production that posits a direct relationship between the artistic cause and its effect on the spectator. For Rancière, the representative regime is essentially a system of normativity according to which there is a causal relationship between the *poiēsis* of art, that which is produced, and its *aisthēsis,* the effects on viewers.[8] Concretely, what this means is that within the representative regime there are very precise rules for performing artistic labors, rules which are thought to result in very definite affective responses. The representative regime is at bottom the belief in a strict pairing of the causes of art and the effects experienced by viewers.

From a political point of view, the major problem with this regime—even though neoclassicism was responsible for many beautiful things—is that it relies on and reinforces a hierarchical model of community. And although this is a point that will come into greater relief when we analyze the differences with the aesthetic regime, one can nevertheless see an example of this hierarchical distribution of the sensible at work in the idea of creativity supplied by the representative regime. To create, according to this model, is to create fictions through the active imposition of form on matter. These fictions are determined by a rule-based system of poetics that specifies in advance how a given subject matter should be treated, as well as how it should be judged by spectators. The representative regime of the arts thus implies that there are those who are active in the composition of these fictions, and those who are its passive recipients. Thus, throughout the representative regime we find a series of divisions and hierarchies that revolve around a distinction between activity and passivity. It is precisely this activity/passivity schema that Rancière's conception of spectatorship will call into question.

The majority of Rancière's recent work has been an attempt to clarify what he calls the "aesthetic regime of art."[9] For our purposes here, the aesthetic regime should be understood as introducing two essential changes into the nature of art and the experience that surrounds it. In the first instance, the aesthetic regime gives rise to an unprecedented form of equality in the production and appreciation of art. And, second, this newfound experience of equality means that the art of the aesthetic age will be the bearer of the promise of political emancipation.

Rancière understands this experience of equality as stemming from the sundering of the representative regime that was carried out by various arts at the start of the nineteenth century. This transformation at the level of art's being is so profound, that Rancière describes this event as the "aesthetic revolution."[10] This revolution includes a diverse array of artistic currents—realism, Romanticism, abstraction in painting, the supposed intransitivity of modern literature, and even the development of the social sciences—many of which are rarely thought of as sharing a common set of concerns. For Rancière, what unites these disparate endeavors is their elimination of the representative regime's rules for pairing a given subject with a specific mode of presentation. Outside the representative framework, the idea that there is a single form appropriate to a given subject matter collapses. The cumulative effect of the aesthetic regime is the positing of new forms of relation between the arts themselves, the subjects they depict, and the manner in which they relate to their audiences. In the aesthetic regime there are no longer any rules prescribing how the subjects of art should be handled or for rigorously determining in advance what can be the subject of art.[11] The aesthetic regime of the arts is thus, at the most fundamental level, the abolition of the representative regime's normativity. *Poiēsis* (the productions of art) and *aisthēsis* (art's effects considered from the vantage point of the spectator) remain linked *only* in the sense that works continue to produce responses in viewers; however, these responses are no longer guaranteed by ideas of human or social nature, or indeed by the treatises that once specified how a particular artistic cause should be received.[12] Henceforth, the relationship between the productions of art—or the sense that art produces—and its effects on the viewer—the sense given to the sensuous productions of art—is indeterminate.

Strictly speaking, it is only with the advent of the aesthetic regime that we can rightly speak of art as engendering an "aesthetic experience." With the collapse of the representative regime's rule-based poetics, the significance of each work must be established on a case-by-case basis through analysis, reflection, and judgment. Aesthetics' investigations into the significance of feeling, for example, are premised on the realization that it is no longer possible, as it once had been, to provide a conceptual account of how and why certain presentations are appropriate to a given subject matter, while others are not. The audiences of the aesthetic age no longer passively absorb the artist's fable, as they had throughout the age of representation. Now they must consider whether or not the subject matter and its means of expression are properly suited to one another, and indeed consider whether or not the resulting production is art.

Essential for understanding how this new idea of art comes to carry the promise of political emancipation is a recognition of the aesthetic experience's essential difference from the everyday status of the mind. In cognition—Kant's name for the relationship between the mental faculties as we try to make sense of the world—the imagination is subordinated to the understanding.[13] The understanding supplies concepts, or—sticking with the political allegory—imposes an order on that which appears before the senses. In cognition, the rational component of the human being has the final world, with understanding determining the essential meaning of experience. In the aesthetic experience, on the other hand, the imagination and the understanding—or, for Schiller, sense and reason—meet one another freely.

With respect to an art object, one can understand the process like this: because of its form—part sensible, part intelligible—the work of art blocks the habitual functioning of the mind. The "living form," as Schiller described the work of art, opens a space between sense and reason, allowing for the two sides of the human person to enter into a type of reciprocal play.[14] In the "free play" of the cognitive faculties, the imagination and understanding solicit each other to continually reengage a given presentation. The faculties prompt one another, without producing a definitive thought. Kant described this experience as a "quickening" in order to indicate that in these experiences the mind flourishes, discovering a type of satisfaction denied by other quarters of experience. Schiller saw the aesthetic as something of an anthropological revolution, one that would liberate the sensuous side of the human person from a historically conditioned overgrowth of reason. Aesthetics, Schiller thought, could teach us how to balance the two sides of our nature, and even how to synthesize them into a more perfect unity. Even after the damage wrought by the division of labor, art offers us the opportunity to curb the excesses of reason, and to build a society more compatible with the needs and desires of the human person. As the opening line of the *Letters* attests, the aesthetic is an essential moment in the political development of Western societies, inasmuch as they contain a necessary lesson in how to negotiate our freedom.

Following Schiller, Rancière draws what he thinks is an obvious political conclusion about the nature of aesthetic art. However, whereas for Schiller the political capacity of art was tied to respect that it showed for the sensuous component of our nature, its ability to serve as a counter to the division of labor, and the vital lesson in freedom that it is said to provide, Rancière shifts the terms of the equation, grounding the politics of aesthetics in the egalitarian promise he detects in the relationship between the cognitive faculties. These experiences, Rancière claims, provide those who undergo them with a sensible model of a world no longer divisible into two, and thus a glimpse of emancipation. Here is how

Rancière describes this idealized form of aesthetic experience: "The fabricating activity and the sensible emotion [*l'émotion sensible*] meet each other 'freely,' *like* two pieces of nature which no longer testify to any hierarchy of the active intelligence on the sensible passivity [*la passivité sensible*]."[15] The mind, when engaged in the aesthetic experience, is dramatically at odds with the order of the faculties required by cognition. In the aesthetic experience, sense and reason meet each other without rivalry, thereby canceling the customary privilege of reason over sense. Therefore, in contrast with the everyday condition of the mind, the aesthetic offers us a glimpse of emancipation. The aesthetic relationship between sense and reason is thus politically significant inasmuch as it is the intimation of a world without hierarchy. It is, for Rancière, a distribution of sense that refutes the distribution of the sensible in which hierarchies are justified by the supposedly inevitable differences in mental capacity.

Whereas for Schiller the heterogeneity of the aesthetic experience stemmed from the indeterminacy imported by the art object and the ensuing freedom of the mental faculties, for Rancière that heterogeneity is interpreted as the intimation of a world without hierarchy. This interpretation, however, runs the risk of cancelling the initial impetus for the experience itself, namely the indeterminacy on which the aesthetic reflection was founded. It assigns a meaning, namely that of equality, to that which the tradition placed beyond the domain of signification. And, as such, Rancière's reading threatens to render determinate, and thus to defuse, the productive rupturing of sense discovered by thinkers like Kant and Schiller.

While I think Rancière well describes the situation accompanying the breakdown of representational poetics and provides an enormously useful framework for displacing many of the clichés about modernism and postmodernism, his presentation of the texts of classical philosophical aesthetics is at points strained by the desire to make the aesthetic experience function as a manifestation of equality. This reading of the aesthetic experience is perhaps employed in order to escape from the fact that the texts of the aesthetic regime are hardly uniform on the question equality. One need simply undertake a genealogy of the concept of taste or recall the names Edmund Burke and Friedrich Nietzsche in order to see that aesthetics too has at points divided the world in two. Likewise, and closer to Rancière's own concerns, one could cite the problem of Schiller himself, a thinker who was more deeply marked by Christian Martin Wieland's concept of the *Schöne Seele* (beautiful or noble soul) than his democratic readers would like.[16] Schiller, ostensibly the most democratic of the post-Kantian aesthetic thinkers, claims that those who are suited for "subordinate occupations"—as opposed to those who are destined for "distinguished roles in life"—are incapable of the holistic contemplation required by aesthetic phenomena.[17] And in the last of his letters, Schiller seemingly backtracks on some of the more radical aspects of his own project when he confesses that an aesthetic education is probably best suited for the "select circles" of an aesthetic aristocracy that he likens to a "pure Church."[18]

Importantly, and perhaps more immediately, it remains to be seen how in terms of the texts cited by Rancière, the primary lesson is that of equality, and not, as Kant, Schiller, Schelling, and Hegel would have it, freedom. Schiller is clear on this point: people are fully human when they play, precisely because it is the first time they are not *compelled* by the sense and form impulses. He describes beauty as annulling both compulsions, to "set man free both physically and morally."[19] Schiller writes, "As our nature finds itself, in the contemplation of the Beautiful, in a happy midway point between law and exigency, so, just because it is divided between the two, it is withdrawn from the constraint of both alike."[20] In Rancière's reading, however, freedom is too quickly assimilated to the ideal of a world no longer divisible in terms of mental capacities.

The point I am making is not that the politics of these authors are in conflict with the politics of aesthetics. It is that there are divisions in the aesthetic texts themselves at odds with Rancière's project of reading aesthetics as the announcement of equality. In terms of the theoretical texts that make up the aesthetic regime of art, it is difficult to argue that the primary import of such an experience is equality. The experience laid out by the foundational texts of aesthetics cuts many ways. It is a disruption of cognition that can be understood as an expression of the mind's freedom with respect to nature; the promise of a new humanity that will no longer be subject to the ancien régime; *and* it is the indication that one belongs to that class of humanity that possesses taste and is sensitive to the mysteries of nature.

It seems to me, then, that aesthetics is best described as having defined a radically ambiguous experience of withdrawal from the world of meaning, one to which it is possible to assign any number of significations. Rancière can be seen as battling against the grain of the tradition in order to make this sensuous disruption of cognition serve the idea of equality. In order to know whether or not such a project is even coherent, we would first have to determine whether it is possible to state, unequivocally, the meaning of the aesthetic experience, without thereby closing down on the indeterminacy that generated it. I suspect that it is not, which is why I prefer to speak as empirically as possible about how the aesthetic experience has been understood and used historically, rather than what it means absolutely.

It will nevertheless be important to pinpoint where equality can and cannot be located within the texts of the aesthetic regime, as well as to gauge to what extent it is preferable to freedom for describing the aesthetic experience. And it is certainly possible that, with a more concerted effort, one could direct our understanding of those experiences away from the vertiginous experience of freedom, toward the emancipating idea of equality. To do so, one would need to demonstrate that equality is implicit in many artistic practices, although it has often been obscured by the tradition's conceptualization of the aesthetic experience. This, as I will now show, is the exciting avenue opened up by Rancière's account of emancipated spectatorship.

Reconfiguring Aesthetics

Nowhere is the originality of Rancière's approach more evident, and the connections between equality and aesthetic experience more credible, than in the veritable transfiguration of spectatorship that he proposes in books like *The Emancipated Spectator*.[21] As he explains, his goal in revisiting the question of spectatorship is "to define a way of looking that doesn't preempt the gaze of the spectator."[22] Emancipated spectatorship requires that we challenge the idea that literary, visual, and material arrangements carry responses that follow directly from the artist's intentions, that is, that we insist on treating them aesthetically, according to the breakdown of the strict and direct connections between *poiēsis* and *aisthēsis* caused by the onset of the aesthetic regime of the arts. Artistic works inaugurate a more indeterminate space-time, wherein the meanings of sensible productions are not immediately apparent. They are a breach between the sense or meaning habitually given to sense. It is this gap between sense and meaning that enables viewers to become active, and to participate in a process of aesthetic cocreation.

In this respect, artistic works have much in common with the pedagogical method elaborated by the ignorant schoolmaster, Joseph Jacotot, the radical nineteenth-century pedagogue whose thought serves Rancière as a touchstone.[23] Jacotot developed a method for teaching what he did not know, opposing what he termed "universal teaching," a form of instruction premised on the idea that all intelligences are equal, to the forms of stultification found in traditional methods, such as explication. Whereas explication sustains a relationship between two intelligences such that the student's intelligence will always be deemed inferior, the ignorant master exercises his will on the student's will in order to allow the student to discover his own intellectual capacities. This distinction between a stultifying pedagogical relationship in which the instructor's *intelligence* acts on the student's *intelligence*, and an emancipated relationship in which the teacher's *will* acts on the student's *will*, is essential for grasping the radical gesture at work in Rancière's account of spectatorship. In particular, it will allow us to articulate the difference between ordinary communication and poetic communication. Poetic forms of communication are those that respect an audience's intelligence, while exercising their will.[24]

In his celebration of Jacotot's method, Rancière stresses that Jacotot worked to prevent his intelligence from subordinating those of others. Jacotot did not explicate texts or tell students what they needed know; he exercised his will on those of his students, forcing them to venture forth, make connections, articulate discoveries, and to develop their own mental capacities. Despite his faith in the equality of intelligences, Jacotot was not so naive as to believe that all expressions would be of like quality, or that his students would learn at the same rate. Thus, in order to maintain his belief in the equality of intelligences, despite what looks like overwhelming empirical evidence to the contrary, Jacotot argues that thought precedes language, and that disparities of expression result from a poorly focused will. For Jacotot and Rancière, this distinction between thought and its expression enables us to continue with the assumption that intelligence is equal, even as we note disparities of expression.[25]

From this vantage point, Jacotot and Rancière will understand learning, writing, and communicating as poetic processes. They involve creating expressions for the experiences, feelings, and thoughts one has regarding the facts one finds in the world. In the first instance, communication is an activity of translating immaterial thoughts into material signs. One gains facility with this process through the repeated and strenuous exercise of the will; an ignorant master can therefore still be a taskmaster, applying his or her will to our own in order to allow us to discover our own intelligences. The products resulting from the translation of thought into material signs in turn require a counter-translation by others back into thought, in order for the scattered signs to become meaningful. Understanding results from applying one's will to the traces left by another.[26] One might thus even claim that communication is a process of cocreation in that any initial messages would be meaningless without the addressee undertaking to retranslate them back into the immaterial realm of thought. As such, Jacotot and Rancière credit most forms of *genuine* communication—as opposed to thinly veiled attempts to instantiate hierarchy—as operating in good faith, that is, on the belief that others can navigate our signs, and, more importantly, that there are not two different types of mental substances. Generally speaking, communication is not simply the transmission of thought; it is a process that draws from one of two different worlds: the one in which we assume that we will be understood because our minds are fundamentally alike, or the one in which we condemn ourselves to never being understood because we suppose ourselves to be surrounded by inferiors.

Artistic forms continually rediscover this experience of intellectual equality when they credit their audiences with possessing this ability to re-create the words of the poet or work of the artist. In this sense, the poet's lesson is opposed to that of the stultifying master's, and indeed to all those forces in the world today that perfect our political and intellectual tutelage under the pretense of attempting to abolish it.[27] Explication posits a dissymmetry between two intelligences, making the student dependent on the master for advancement. The poet or artist, on the other hand, creates a community of equals when he or she speaks. What she offers is simply one translation into words of the primary poem of experience in which everyone shares. Jacotot and Rancière credit the playwright Racine, good Cartesian that he was, with having hit on this insight. "Like all creators, Racine instinctively applied the method . . . of universal teaching. He knew that there are no men of *great thoughts*, only men of *great expressions*."[28] Believing his audiences already in possession of great insights, Racine could dispense with the didactic tendencies of art. Instead, he would channel his efforts into finding the expressions that solicit the work of cocreation.

From the *Ignorant Schoolmaster* and its remarks about poetry, we can deduce that the equality of persons is not a goal that will be advanced by the lobbying of art; rather, it is a principle that is either verified or denied by our cultural practices. *The Emancipated Spectator* is an important extension of this line of thought. The book once again marshals the ideas of Jacotot, this time to challenge the consensus that has recently ensnared the art world. *The Emancipated Spectator* serves as a critique of the well-intentioned forms of art and theory that want to liberate us, but end up reproducing the logic of stultification. The book is directed at the various positions—significantly, those fashioned in response to Debord's "society of the spectacle"—that construe spectatorship as fundamentally passive and thus something to be overcome by the heroic agency of art.[29]

Aesthetic stultification, as we might call it, is discernible in much of what passes today for "political art." These are arrangements that attempt to transmit certain knowledge, political opinions, or—as is most often the case—the sentiment of indignation. Across Rancière's writings on contemporary art, one can witness a distinctive, though never fully articulated, preference for art that contains a subtle, as opposed to overt, political sensibility. This taste in art likely follows from Jacotot's critique of explication/stultification. Art that attempts to make viewers understand at any cost subordinates their consciousness to art, thereby confirming the division of labor and the police's estimation of capacities. Without distance, without a space for translation and counter-translation, there is little to distinguish art from the forms of communication that attempt to divide the world into two. Such forms of art, one might say, short-circuit the poetic processes of translation and counter-translation at the heart of communication. They thereby subordinate the audience's liberation to the wisdom of the artist.

One of the central challenges for art aspiring to be truly critical is to refuse didactic means of expression. Here one sees the import of Jacotot's ideas regarding the essentially poetic nature of communication. They offer us the possibility of reconfiguring our understanding of the aesthetic experience and describing it as an active form of viewership. By Rancière's account, the spectator is already active inasmuch as a work of art requires of us the work of counter-translation in order to be understood. Rancière: "This is a crucial point: spectators see, feel and understand something in as much as they compose their own poem, as . . . do actors or playwrights, directors, dancers or performers."[30] In Rancière's analysis, viewers constantly interpret, select, and navigate their way through a given arrangement, in a sense recompleting it each time.

This position allows us to dismiss distributions in which there are inevitably those who are active and those who remain passive. "Emancipation," Rancière explains, "begins when we challenge the opposition between viewing and acting . . . It begins when we understand that viewing is also an action that confirms or transforms this distribution of positions."[31] Spectatorship is a form of inhabiting the world that follows traces, draws connections, and offers interpretations. It is essentially the activity of establishing new relationships between seeing, doing, and thinking—that is, of redistributing the sensible.

Conclusion

Articulating a coherent politics of aesthetics requires that we identify the ways in which spectators are already active, and then juxtapose that active model of communication against those distributions in which passivity serves as grounds for hierarchy. In this respect, when we locate, describe, and sustain the activity of spectators, we will also be sustaining the postulate of equality. It is an open question to what extent the tradition of aesthetic philosophy has recognized and then denied this experience of equality, which as we have seen is central to the creation and reception of certain works of art. And even though a more methodical account is wanting, Rancière's contribution consists of offering an initial redescription of these experiences in terms of their possible opening toward equality.

This idea of spectatorship may well serve as a dramatic new point of departure in the development of aesthetics. If this idea of an active spectatorship sounds somewhat paradoxical to us today, it is no doubt because emphasis has been placed on the passive dimension of aesthetics for far too long. The challenge, as I see it, will be to build on Rancière's account of spectatorship in order to recover the emancipatory potential at work in notions such as "reflection," "judgment," and "critique."

Of course, we cannot expect art or aesthetic philosophy to carry the weight of our politics, which as I indicated consists of presupposing, verifying, and inscribing equality into arrangements and institutions set up to deny it. Rancière himself has explained that despite the congruence he analyzes, art and politics are distinguishable in that the former alters the framework of what is perceptible, while the latter is a struggle for the constitution of a collective subject that fundamentally changes the distribution of roles, capacities, and forms of participation in a given community.[32] While the two endeavors sustain one another, they are not synonymous. Politics attempts to extend equality in a world hostile to it. Art is the reminder of what we struggle for.

Notes

1. Jacques Rancière, *Malaise dans l'esthétique* (Paris: Éditions Galilée, 2004), 47. Unless otherwise indicated, all translations are my own.

2. See, for example, Rancière's reading of Stendhal's *The Red and the Black* in Jacques Rancière, *Aisthesis: Scènes du régime esthétique de l'art* (Paris: Éditions Galilée, 2011), 61–77. According to Rancière's reading, Julien Sorel triumphs not through his scheming and social climbing, but at "the moment when . . . he ceases to struggle [*combattre*], where he simply shares [*partage*] . . . the pure equality of an emotion" (67).

3. F. W. J. Schelling, *The Philosophy of Art*, trans. Douglas W. Stott (Minneapolis: University of Minnesota Press, 1989), 11. Schelling: "A serious study of art based on ideas is even more necessary in this age of literary peasant wars, wars conducted against all that is sublime, great, or ideal, indeed against beauty itself in poesy and art, an age in which the frivolous, the sensually provocative, or nobly base are the idols to which the greatest reverence is paid."

4. Schelling, *The Philosophy of Art*, 9.

5. Jacques Rancière, *The Politics of Aesthetics: The Distribution of the Sensible*, trans. Gabriel Rockhill (London: Continuum, 2004), 20–30.

6. Rancière, *The Politics of Aesthetics*, 21.

7. Rancière, *The Politics of Aesthetics*, 21–22.

8. Rancière, *Malaise*, 16.

9. See, for example, his most important and comprehensive work to date in the field of aesthetics, *Aisthesis*.

10. Jacques Rancière, "The Aesthetic Revolution and Its Outcomes," *New Left Review* 14 (March/April 2002).

11. Rancière, *Politics of Aesthetics*, 23, 25, 32–33.

12. Rancière, *Malaise*, 17.

13. In *On the Aesthetic Education of Man*, Schiller uses "sense" and "reason" in an attempt to expand Kant's faculties of the imagination and the understanding. For the purposes of the contrast that I am drawing in this paragraph, the specific terminology need not overly concern us. The point is that cognition entails an antagonism between the sensuous and rational sides of the human being, while aesthetic reflection relies on their reciprocal play and postulates their reconciliation. Friedrich Schiller, *On the Aesthetic Education of Man*, trans. Reginald Snell (London: Dover, 2004).

14. Schiller, *On the Aesthetic Education of Man*, 76, translation modified.

15. Rancière, *Malaise*, 24.

16. Regarding Wieland's influence on Schiller, see Frederick Beiser, *Schiller as Philosopher: A Re-Examination* (Oxford: Oxford University Press, 2005), 93–94. My suggestion is that some of the aristocratic tendencies in Schiller, such as his discussions of grace, nobility, and the noble soul, are attributable to the influence of Wieland and his revival of the Greek ideal of *kalokagathia*.

17. Schiller, *Aesthetic Education*, 102. The passage cited is from Schiller's footnote to the Twenty-Second Letter.

18. Schiller, *Aesthetic Education*, 140.

19. Schiller, *Aesthetic Education*, 74.

20. Schiller, *Aesthetic Education*, 78.

21. Jacques Rancière, *The Emancipated Spectator* (New York: Verso, 2009).

22. Jacques Rancière, "Art of the Possible: Fulvia Carnevale and John Kelsey in Conversation with Jacques Rancière," *Artforum* 45, no. 7 (March 2007): 267.

23. Jacques Rancière, *The Ignorant Schoolmaster: Five Lessons in Intellectual Emancipation*, trans. Kristin Ross (Stanford, Calif.: Stanford University Press, 1991).

24. Rancière, *The Ignorant Schoolmaster*, 4–15.

25. Rancière, *The Ignorant Schoolmaster*, 50–65.

26. Rancière, *The Ignorant Schoolmaster*, 60–65.

27. Rancière, *The Ignorant Schoolmaster*, 65–73.

28. Rancière, *The Ignorant Schoolmaster*, 69, italics in the original.

29. Rancière, *The Emancipated Spectator*, 5–7.

30. Rancière, *The Emancipated Spectator*, 13.

31. Rancière, *The Emancipated Spectator.*

32. Jacques Rancière, "The Aesthetic Dimension," plenary lecture at the annual meeting of the Society for Phenomenological and Existential Philosophy, October 31, 2009.

"Equality Must Be Defended!" Cinephilia and Democracy

Codruţa Morari

"I have always tried to live in an ivory tower, but a tide of shit is beating at its walls, threatening to undermine it," wrote Flaubert to Turgenev on November 13, 1872. "It is not a question of politics, but of the *mental state* of France. Never have things of the spirit counted for so little. Never has hatred for everything great been so manifest—disdain for Beauty, execration of literature."[1] The opposition between the elite and the hoi polloi inherent in the metaphor of the ivory tower becomes more dramatic as Flaubert invokes the implied aspiration of the masses to challenge relations of power, the desire of the tide to undermine the tower. The fragility intimated by Flaubert surely deviates from the conventional understanding of the "dominant" elite espoused by contemporary defenders of democracy.[2] Indeed, the elitism of the ivory tower has often been questioned and denounced in the name of democracy and egalitarianism. While professing his renewed patriotic feelings as France entered the Third Republic, Flaubert deplored the state of the people, the "overwhelming stupidity of the public," and its "hatred for anything great." Only faith in art and beauty, maintained Flaubert, can ensure the stability of the ivory tower and the promise of democracy. Such a faith does so, however, at the expense of democracy itself, for it widens the gap between the elite and the masses. In this way the metaphor of the ivory tower, as evoked by Flaubert, enacts, with compelling suggestiveness, the strained relationship between art and democracy.

The Postulate of Equality

In the discussions that try to settle the opposition between the elitism of the ivory tower and the voice of the people, Jacques Rancière emphatically stresses the egalitarian promise of the aesthetic experience: "It is true that we don't know that men are equal. We are saying that they *might* be. This is our opinion, and we are trying, along with those who think as we do, to verify it. But we know that this *might* is the very thing that makes a society of humans possible."[3] Equality is a promissory structure that abides in every man's right to articulate speech. In principle, everyone can verify the presupposition of equality. Autonomous voice is the equivalent of political action that leads to emancipation. Unlike commentators who reveal the political triggers of the work of art, Rancière seeks to uncover the aesthetic values of emancipation, which for him are central to a truly democratic politics. Contrary to sociological methods that posit the elite against the masses, Rancière's approach postulates equality, going beyond the assumption of an adversarial relation that can only be resolved by abolishing inequities.

This seemingly simple proposition is alluring when we think about cinema. For all the consensual discussions about the universal access to the movies and the new culture of the "pillow-film,"[4] spectatorial equality still must contend with the argument of quality. The tension between an authorized, and thus privileged, access to film art and the popular entertainment of movie culture remains very much in place.[5] The history of this tension, in fact, can be traced to the early days of film spectatorship. If Le Club de Treize, a cinephilic organization that gathered the most prestigious members of 1920s French film culture and industry only met once, it was because of conflicts among its membership about the equality of spectators and the status of film as a popular form. The members all swore to "love and defend a great cinema, a cinema of quality,"[6] but Ricciotto Canudo and Louis Delluc disagreed on what would become a major point of contention. While Canudo[7] was debating the place of cinema among the established arts, Delluc spoke of "cinema as popular art."[8] Originally hailed as a popular practice, cinema soon underwent the complex process of social legitimization that would lead to its elevation to the rank of an art form in its own right. The history of subsequent discussions about cinema will continually return to this impasse: is film a privileged art or an industrialized mode of packaging narratives?

In Rancière's promissory egalitarianism, this tension between the visual power of an art form and the attraction of storytelling receives more conciliatory treatment. "Cinema, the pre-eminently modern art," he observes, "experiences more than any other art the conflict of these two poetics, though it is, by the same token, the art that most attempts to combine them."[9] Cinema as an art form does not oppose the unfolding of a story and the recording of this process; it combines them. Film illustrates in an unrivaled way the potential to engineer a face-off between these two dimensions, what he calls the representative and the aesthetic regime of art, concepts that are essential in his aesthetics. His film writings, in this way, need to be understood within the larger context of his reflections on aesthetics.

Within Rancière's deliberations on aesthetics and politics, the postulate of equality aims to explain not only how aesthetic judgments are performed by viewers, but also how these aesthetic judgments bring viewers together—that is, how they constitute and function within communities. Assuming equality among viewers, Rancière shifts focus from the celebration of film as an artistic experience that maintains a rarefied approach to artistic objects and communities, but also avoids the traps of populist denunciations of elitist discourses. For all its constructive resolve and desire to reposition the terms of the debate, to withdraw them from the consensual reduction of problems, the proposition has met with considerable reticence. It is an "illusory" approach, signals Bourdieu in *The Distinction*,[10] for political and intellectual disparities are embodied in the social order. Despite its undeniable sensitivity to discord and tension, Rancière's equality is criticized as a consensual reduction. To these objections, one might add a more general skepticism regarding the invocation of democracy and egalitarianism, categories whose meanings have come to seem empty.[11] And there is the additional concern that democracy cannot work outside the sphere of politics and policies. Even if the egalitarian objective is a noble aspiration in the political sphere, it seems to be misplaced and futile in the sphere of art and spirit, for neither beauty nor intelligence nor love is democratic.[12]

Whether art can fulfill a democratic promise is not disputed by either Flaubert or Rancière. Both suggest that art and aesthetic experience play a key role in the political emancipation of a community. While the former sees art, beauty, and literature as potentially edifying and political, the latter views things in reverse. For Rancière, the expression of equality is the prerequisite of emancipation and, as such, involves an aesthetic component. Men who *express* their right to equality *act* politically. Political action is always a form of address, an allocution, a speech addressed to another. This is the case even if this other refuses to or cannot recognize it as articulated discourse. In this way, speech constitutes a "reconfiguration of the sensible"; it affirms the equality of all speaking men, an equality that is otherwise denied or concealed by social hierarchy. Such speech makes audible the voices of those who were otherwise thought to be voiceless and dismissed as mute bodies. There are substantial stakes in this transgressive act of speech-enablement: it makes something that could not be seen visible, it makes speech audible where before there was only mumbling, grunting and inarticulate chatter. For Rancière, transgressive speech redefines the sensible, makes visible what the previous distribution of functions concealed, and in so doing *creates a community.*

The question whether art can fulfill a democratic promise can be answered in two ways that involve quite different understandings—indeed, two competing forms of equality. In the paradigm represented by Flaubert, aesthetics entails a politics of its own; political freedom lies at the top, and the citizen of the Republic could access it by partaking of beauty and art and literature. For Rancière, politics permeates the *autonomous* work (literature, cinema, speech, etc.) with a promise of political freedom.

Cinema Set Adrift: The Intervals of Cinema

Aesthetics was born, argues Rancière, at the time of the French Revolution, and as such it meant "the dismissal of the hierarchies of subject matters, genres and forms of expressions separating objects worthy or unworthy of entering in the realm of art."[13] This aesthetic equality went along with the end of French monarchy and the sovereignty of the people. On the other hand, aesthetic equality meant relinquishing the superiority of the power of the high classes and educated senses over the low classes and the raw senses. This implied a nonhierarchical relation between the intellectual and the sensorial faculties, between objects of knowledge and objects of desire.

In his introduction to *The Intervals of Cinema*, his second book dedicated to the seventh art, Rancière probes the existence of what is sought under the name of "film theory," that is, "the unity between an art, a form of emotion and a coherent vision of the world."[14] No theory of cinema was able to provide the means to resolve Rancière's recurring puzzles as he watched, again and again, movies that fueled his writing. Indeed, he questions the use value of film theory in principle; maybe cinema escapes theory because it exists "precisely in the form of a system of unbridgeable gaps [*écarts*] between things that have the same name without being parts of the same body."[15] Making his discontent productive, Rancière seeks to account for cinema in his own "rather singular"[16] way, trusting his relation with cinema, an object with which he engages not as a philosopher or as a critic, but as a cinephile: "My relationship with it is a play of encounters and distances which can be discerned through these three memories. They summarize the three types of distance through which I have tried to talk about cinema: between cinema and art, between cinema and politics, between cinema and theory."[17]

This play of chance encounters, however, is not a disinterested, accidental form of engagement with movies. The "detractor of theory" is accompanied by the "amateur," and affected by his "theoretical and political position that challenges the authority of experts by re-examining the way in which the limits of their domains are drawn at the junction of experience and knowledge."[18] The amateur defends cinema as a common territory: everyone, equally, can follow a singular path that ultimately "adds to the world of cinema and our understanding of it."[19]

Reprinted from an issue of *Trafic*[20] from 2004, the introduction to *The Intervals of Cinema* echoes the concerns of *Aesthetics and Its Discontents*, which Rancière was completing at the time. It would not be unfair to say that his reflections on cinema continue a line of thought aimed at revealing the confusion and malaise in the realm of aesthetics. In 2005, *Cahiers du cinéma* announced Rancière's new book in an interview titled "Le destin du cinéma comme art" and chronicled the story of cinema in relationship with "the impossibility to define an art by a proper essence, technique or medium."[21] The discontent that affects the understanding of cinema as art—that is, the rift between cinema and art—is negotiated in terms of cinephilia. The object of many current debates, cinephilia is typically defined as "a kind of an intense loving relationship with cinema,"[22] a fetishism of cinema,[23] or an artistic culture.[24] For Rancière, cinephilia is a passionate engagement with movies and, as such, the sign of a rupture between cinema and the other "arts," between cinema and Art. In other words, the moviegoing experience both reflects and resists the wish for cinema's artistic legitimacy.

Rancière's attempt to account for cinema as an aesthetic experience is at odds with existent theories (or simply theory) that would define cinema as a savoir faire rather than a practice within a community of senses. Even when concerned with particular case studies (e.g., a group of viewers watching a film in a specific theater, or spectators in different venues viewing the same episode of a television show), Rancière examines these formations as "communities of senses," communities that are brought together by a sense of the common. A spectatorial community in Rancière's understanding is not "a collectivity shaped by some common feeling." Rather, it is a "frame" that enables specific practices, values, and forms of visibility "under the same meaning, which shapes thereby a certain sense of community."[25] In other words, a group of spectators sharing a quality, for example an interest in the work of David Lynch, will not coalesce into a community; communities of senses come together by dint of a shared practice that bestows on them the sense of community.

For Rancière, cinephilia allows for such a sense of the common. In light of such a definition, theory fails on two levels: it rationally (rather than passionately) drags cinema into the realm of art, and it overlooks the multilayered relationship between cinema and politics. Where theory fails, cinephilia might succeed, suggests Rancière. By recognizing theory's limitations in accounting for cinema, cinephilia reveals the gap between cinema and politics. This gap is very much in keeping with the one encountered in the discussion about the paradox of equality. Because theory affirms the superiority of understanding over the raw pleasure of the senses within the cinephilic encounter, it perpetuates a hierarchal order and as such defeats the requirements of aesthetic equality. The only egalitarian encounter with cinema is that of cinephilia.

As it is often the case with Rancière, this chronicle of rifts concludes in a perfect isomorphism. Cinephilia, the name for the gap between cinema and art, also provides a bridge. In addition, cinephilia reframes the distance between film and theory. Most importantly, Rancière argues, cinephilia fosters the democratization of cinema: it "links the cult of art to the democracy of entertainment and emotions by challenging the criteria for the induction of cinema into high culture."[26] Cinephilia thus takes recourse to a tradition that opposes "minor arts" to already constituted cultural legitimacies.

Understood as a judgment of taste, cinephilia is already difficult to rationalize, and even more so when caught in the great theoretical upheaval of structuralism that claimed to renew the paradigms of thought, science, and art. The 1960s present a particularly rich situation for the analysis of cinephilic behavior; here the cultural practice of cinephilia coincided with the desire to unify everything under a general theory that would fit the political effervescence of the time, with the anti-imperialist and decolonization movements. These cinephiles ventured to manage the rift between theory, politics, and art "by filling it with the simple notion of *mise-en-scène* that tried to dissimulate the heterogeneity of the filmic object and to tie it to a singular artistic will. Inversely, the consciousness of this gap could indeed harbor a practice very different from 'theory,' a practice whose object is grasped in the encounter of heterogeneous logics."[27]

Classical Cinephilia

In France of the 1950s and 1960s, a group of Parisian young men of a certain generation came together and gave rise to a new strong voice, that of a New Wave. They began as film critics, pursuing a profession that emerged from their practice of watching films all day and discussing them into the night. They criticized "a certain French tradition"[28] and instead turned to Hollywood and especially American B-movies. They passionately loved cinema, albeit a certain cinema, and transformed cinephilia into a legitimate cultural praxis. Appearing in the monthly journal *Cahiers du cinéma*, their articles eschewed academic discourse and instead lingered on memorable scenes and privileged moments: "If you read the early Cahiers stuff that Truffaut and Godard were writing," observed British film scholar Paul Willemen, "you see that they were responding to films. They were not doing criticism but were doing written responses to films . . . What they were writing at that time was a highly impressionistic account; in T. S. Eliot's terms, an 'evocative equivalent' of moments which, when encountered in a film, spark something which then produced the energy and the desire to write."[29]

Cinephilia (which subsequently became known as "classical cinephilia") was a "way of looking" that, as the French film historian Antoine De Baecque puts it, transforms "images, as if snatched by the reappropriation of a few spectators" into "fragments of intimate life."[30] This way of looking, this vision, had to be *learned*, and learning how to "see" meant "to create a representation of the world that already reflects the filmmaker's volition and praxis."[31] The learning of this vision implied a double invention: cinephilia "invented," in the sense that it discovered, a cinema that the Young Turks loved passionately and defended blindly—the cinema of auteurs; of Hitchcock and Hawks; of Renoir, Rossellini, and Visconti; of Nicholas Ray; of Bergman; of Vigo and Bresson. In the same process, cinephilia invented its own cinema, the Nouvelle Vague, which is to say that these cinephiles—Truffaut, Godard, Rohmer, Rivette, *les copains*—invented themselves. In De Baecque's eloquent words, "These inventions took shape in the vision exercised by the films they loved. Cinephilia has thus watched films about watching; it learned to see films that themselves learned how to see through their characters. And learning from this learning, it learned how to see in return, how to make movies."[32]

Under the tutelage of auteurs invested with an authoritative and militant power, cinephiles took their place in a community ruled by a judgment of taste. For the *Cahiers* critics, the cult of the auteurs went hand in hand with the glorification of the mise-en-scène: "The originality of the auteur lies not in the subject matter he chooses, but in the techniques he employs, i.e. the mise-en-scène, through which everything is expressed on the screen."[33] They did not hesitate to compare mise-en-scène to literary style:

> As Sartre said: "One is not a writer for having chosen to say certain things, but for having chosen to say them in a certain way." Why should it be any different for cinema? . . . The thought of a *cinéaste* appears through his mise-en-scène. What matters in the film is the desire for order, composition, harmony, the placing of actors and objects, the movements within the frame, the capturing of a movement or a look; in short,

> the intellectual operation which has put an initial emotion and a general idea to work. Mise-en-scène is nothing other than the technique invented by each director to express the idea and establish the specific quality of his work.[34]

Christian Keathley insightfully points out in his pathbreaking book on cinephilia that mise-en-scène was what led the auteurs to issues of cinematic language (framing, editing, etc.) and ultimately to issues of cinema itself: that is, to ontological questions.[35]

Resurgent scholarship on cinephilia violently criticized the *Cahiers* model, especially because it was so dominant and exclusionary. Noël Burch, participant to the *Cahiers* movement that celebrated cinephilia, put forward one of the most acerbic exercises in critique and revisionism. He lamented "the establishment of a pantheon as proof for the artistic legitimacy of cinema, the cult of films [*oeuvres*] removed from socio-historical contingencies," claiming that these features "institute cinephilia as a cultural practice that is masculine, individualist and elitist."[36] Classical cinephilia enjoys the status of an idea type and an idealized praxis; to this day it is still defended by a number of French and Anglo-American intellectuals.[37]

In 2009, Laurent Jullier, one of the most virulent French detractors and an advocate of a more inclusive, "postmodern" cinephilia, waged a renewed attack against the dominance of the *Cahiers* practice.[38] He sought to rekindle awareness that "there is still the cult of Great Men (the *auteurs*), esotericism, aestheticism, sexism and especially 'a disgust for the taste of others' in the words of Pierre Bourdieu."[39] In his petition to support the *Cahiers du cinéma* during the journal's acute financial crisis, Jean Douchet wrote that "the cinema concerns us all in a pressing way: artists, philosophers, writers, filmmakers, critics, actors, directors of festivals." Jullier was not amused. The petition, he replied, "lacks only one category of people: those who are not part of this 'little world,' that is to say, common mortals!" He went on to say that "one sees it clearly when one talks to a Parisian critic: they conform still to the Baudelairian model of *the one who knows* (how to appreciate Modernity), above the *vulgar taste* of the public." And voilà, we are back to the metaphor of the ivory tower.

A Passionate Affair

A private pleasure evoking the postulate of sensorial equality gets quickly caught in a discourse of dominance, distinction, and reproduction. Although recent scholarship has insisted that this is just one form of cinephilia, it either defended or reprehended it as the dominant one, and, as such, the one being *reproduced.* Cinephilia is one of these rare objects able to animate both the populist ideology of mass entertainment and the discourse of connoisseurs and experts. Negotiated between film industry and the mass consumers it created, cinephilia appears to be the immediate gratification of desire. Cinephilia can gather anyone. But mostly, though in the name of a democratic promise, cinephilia advocates for cinema's artistic status and remains a highly eclectic arrangement, a sort of a court society with strict rituals, ruled by connoisseurs who transmit their wisdom.

However opposed their practices, both the cognoscenti and the mass audiences form "communities." Both the eulogistic and the accusatory accounts of classical cinephilia recognize the mise-en-scène as a touchstone of value. As a matter of taste, cinephilia is difficult to rationalize and connect either to the history of cinematic representation or to contemporary practices and technologies. Thomas Elsaesser, for example, argues in favor of "the preference of contemporary media culture for the extreme close-up, the motion blur, wide or pan, and the horizon-less image altogether." Although "the image today does not seek to engage the focusing gaze," and instead fascinates the viewer in a more haptic way, cinephilia still remains a matter of passion. "How to manage the emotions of being up close, of burning with passion, of how to find the right measure, the right spatial parameters for the pleasures, but also for the rituals of cinephilia, which allow them to be shared, communicated, and put into words of discourse?"[40] How does cinephilic passion engineer community? And to what extent can this community be a democratic one?

At this point let us return to Rancière and to his triad of intervals. Rancière has often been criticized for his unhistorical approach, mainly due to the apodictic tone of his analysis and his idealistic faith in the egalitarian promise of art. However, he acknowledges in an interview about *The Intervals of Cinema* that his relationship to movies was a generational effect and that it should be contextualized as such, rather than crystallized into some absolute truth about film spectatorship.[41] His cinephilic behavior and reflections fall into the classical model practiced at the *Cahiers.* The French philosopher acknowledges the journal's crucial importance for his intellectual career: he wrote regular contributions beginning in 1977.[42] In a way, Rancière's first collection of essays on cinema, *Film Fables,* is his own cinephilic diary. There he argues against the need for film theory, the only encounter with cinema taking place as an "enlightened" form of cinephilia. How to reconcile his absolute faith in the democratic promise of cinema as art with his eclectic cinephilic practice?

The elucidation of this paradox might start from his notes on cinephilia in *The Intervals of Cinema.* In thinking about cinephilia, suggests

Rancière in the introduction, one is bound to think about the relationship between cinema and politics. This consensual parallelism points to different levels at which one might consider the political meaning of cinephilia. First, there is the recurrent view of cinephilia as democratization of cinema, in terms of both its spatial and its symbolic distribution. Linking ciné-clubs that "preserved the memory of art" to neighborhood cinemas that screened "disparaged Hollywood films," cinephilia joined "the cult of art to the democracy of entertainment and emotions."[43] Second, defining cinema as art has a political component, argues Rancière. As a passionate affair, cinephilia challenges the dominant categories of thinking about art; blurring the accepted views, it leads to a new account of cinema itself. To the question of how cinephilia accounts for its passion and for the object of its love, Rancière gives a vague reply: "By relying on the blunt phenomenology of the mise-en-scène as the inauguration of a relationship with the world."[44]

Writing in *Film Fables* on Fritz Lang's *Moonfleet* (1955), Rancière reiterates the well-known tale of *Cahiers* cinephilia: the film's story of a gaze is doubled by the mise-en-scène of the director and thus empowers the spectator whose eye returns the gaze to its origin and enables the continuation of the fable. But *Moonfleet* is not only a fortunate example of what these cinephiles meant by mise-en-scène. *Moonfleet* is the story of a stubborn child on a mission. The fanatic Young Turks had a lot to learn from this boy who does not stray from his goal: "John, for his part, is as deaf to double meaning as he is to any sentence telling him that what he sees hides what it is. He makes his way through the studios of the hidden truth imposing his own gaze and storyboarding the shots for his script, that of the letter that sent him off in search of someone who has no choice but to be his friend." The boy's negotiation of the story has a "childlike simplicity," setting up an exchange between two characters, and inverting the logic of the script where he is constantly being told not to believe what he is being told. " 'Not words, deeds,' declare the wise in their wisdom, and the child's mise-en-scène follows suit. He responds to the speeches telling him not to put any stock in words with the deaf tranquility of gestures that hear and yet don't hear, gestures that extract a different truth from the words. The child, though, does not speak or laugh, he just looks, greets, smiles."[45] Rancière argues that the play of mise-en-scène produces an excess of meaning that cannot be accounted for in a "theoretical" reading. Theory could not enable him "to decide which political message was conceived by an arrangement of bodies in a shot or a cut between two shots."[46]

The experience of a meaningful world where smiles and gestures take on the power of words makes Rancière wonder, in *The Intervals*, "what relation . . . a student first discovering Marxism in the early 1960s [could] see between the struggle against social inequality and the form of equality that the smile and the gaze of little John Mohune in *Moonfleet* reestablishes within the machinations of his false friend Jeremy Fox."[47] A gap has opened between the response to the interplay of storytelling and the form given by the mise-en-scène, and the vision of the world these cinephiles had at the time. Rancière expected film theory to enable us to close the gap, to "conceive the equation between the pleasures we take in the shadows that are projected onto the screen, the intelligence of an art, and that of a vision of the world."[48] Cinephilia brought new light to an enigma that theory could not fathom.

A Theoretical Matter After All

Mise-en-scène reconciles the tension between "form" and "matter," between intelligence and sensation. It offers to the cinephile an intuitive tool to access an inviting world. As it was understood and expanded by the *Cahiers* critics, mise-en-scène was bound historically and conceptually to the sociopolitical changes that came after the war. For Rancière, who draws on the analytical framework provided by Schiller's reading of Kantian aesthetics, mise-en-scène resembles the concept of "free play of the faculties." This "blunt phenomenology of the mise-en-scène" in a way corresponds to the universality of aesthetic judgment. Although the impossibility to ground today's cinephilia in the mise-en-scène is obvious, Rancière's claims are poignant precisely because he recognizes the ontological quality of the mise-en-scène for the *Cahiers* critics. As argued in *Film Fables*,[49] central to his analysis of film "is the idea that its characteristics as an art form pre-existed the development of its particular technological apparatus and were already an established part of the meaning of the artwork in the age of aesthetics."[50]

This interpretation of mise-en-scène as a judgment of taste central to a cinephilic community is in keeping with Rancière's aesthetic project, in which cinema is not one of the arts. Rather, cinema must be apprehended under what Rancière defines as the aesthetic regime of art. An object of sense experience, cinema is part of the world, which has been transformed by being invested with thought in a singular way. The mise-en-scène is precisely this, a way to "extricate a portion of the sensory realm (*ce sensible*) from its ordinary connections and inhabit it by a heterogeneous power"[51] that will suspend the dualities of ordinary sense experience. At stake here are the separations not only "between appearance and reality, but also between form and matter, between activity and passivity, understanding and sensibility."[52] Invested with the power to dismiss these hierarchies, mise-en-scène exemplifies cinema as art, or cinema under the aesthetic regime, and confirms cinephilia's status as the frame or "thought of the new disorder."[53]

However persuasive his demonstrations, Rancière remains under critical scrutiny for defending the universality of aesthetic judgment,[54] a point of contention in his polemics with Bourdieu and their exchanges concerning the post-Kantian European philosophical inheritance. Critics of cinephilia who take a Bourdieusian approach[55] object to building a cultural practice on such universalistic grounds. Rancière's defense (or rather offense) starts from the fact that aesthetic judgments are universal because we make them for everyone capable of cognition without exception and on an equal basis, undeterred by distinctions of wealth, sex, height, education, nationality, and so on. There is then something *egalitarian* about the capacity for aesthetic judgment in Kant's account and in the tradition of philosophical aesthetics it founded; this *egalitarian* universalism is what Rancière seeks to defend.

Although in the debate with Bourdieu Rancière stays with Kant, it should not be forgotten the extent to which his rethinking of aesthetics, and the elaboration between aesthetics and democracy, offers a challenge to this inheritance. Rather than denouncing the promise of equality as "illusory," Rancière firmly believes that artists and spectators together should endeavor to deliver on this promise. Rancière's aesthetic theory is an attempt to spell out more clearly how such a promise of equality might be articulated.

Bourdieu argues in response that the appeal to universality is a philosophical fiction that not only disavows social inequities but also serves to perpetuate them. The characterization of aesthetic experience by the Kantian legacy of philosophical aesthetics sustains the aristocratic regimen of the court. Conducted in the realms of philosophy and politics, the Rancière-Bourdieu disagreement frames the debate on cinephilia. The classical model of cinephilia, seen through Bourdieu's prism, perpetuates an oligarchic form of power. Inaugurating the domination of the focusing gaze, the mise-en-scène seals the hegemonic power of classical cinephilia. There is nothing democratic about this community, Bourdieu might argue, for it is founded on the ability to appreciate art and express judgments of taste, qualities that reinforce a social dynamic in which the power of ruling elites remains intact. Classical cinephilia, in such an understanding, legitimates and perpetuates elitist hegemony. In light of Bourdieu's sociology, the plural in Jullier and Leveratto's *Cinephiles and cinephilias* is an attempt to challenge the universality of the aesthetic judgment.

The optimistic promise of equality is what makes Rancière's theory so strong and at the same time so vulnerable. Much turns on the definition of cinephilia as a matter of passion that enables the autonomous voice and the fervent discourse it articulates. The refusal to accept the alternative of the *amateur* reveals indeed the vulnerable side of this approach. Bourdieu's *Questions de sociologie*, for example, responds avant la lettre to the cinephilic defense of mise-en-scène as an intuitive relationship with the world: "Intellectuals spontaneously understand the relationship to a work of art as a mystical participation in a common good, without rarity. My entire book [*The Distinction*] argues that access to a work of art requires instruments that are not universally distributed."[56] In other words, Bourdieu states that no encounter with a work of art, cinema in this instance, takes place outside a system of predefined, embodied codes that only reveal the act of "dispossession."

Unlike Bourdieu, Rancière prefers to start from the premise of equality. Cinema constitutes the ideal art to explore the consequences of such a postulate: "Precisely because cinema is not a language, because it does not define an object of knowledge belonging to a systematic order of reason, learning it suits particularly well the application of the method of intellectual emancipation—'to learn something and to relate it to all the rest by this principle'[57]—We *learn* cinema by widening our circle of perceptions of affects and of significations organized around several films."[58] Cinephilia is to be understood as such a form of intellectual emancipation. *Moonfleet* exemplifies beautifully this thesis, for little John Mohune will experiment with his own way of learning, in a form of rebellion against the master, but especially against the lesson. As cinephiles of sorts, we follow "the artist's emancipatory lesson, opposed on every count to the professor's stultifying lesson. Each one of us is an artist to the extent that he carries out a double process; he is not content to be a mere journeyman but wants to make all work a means of expression, and he is not content to feel something but tries to impart it to others. The artist needs equality as the explicator needs inequality."[59]

The argument for the artist's singular visionary sensibility is seen in a new light. The auteur is not so much a master as an enabler of a learning situation. The singularity of films and auteurs that constitute a cinephile's arsenal has, according to Rancière, no hierarchical weight. Rather, it is a circumscribed learning situation. The auteur's lesson is not an explanation, but an invitation to a learning situation, and the testing of a new method, as proved by the inverted logic of John Mohune's mise-en-scène. As he did in *The Philosopher and His Poor*, Rancière does not argue that the sociologist's analyses of oppression are incorrect, but rather that they are paralyzing and self-serving.[60] Dethroning the auteurs and declining the "ordinary" spectators' access to their films does not offer a hope for a better future, for cinephiles or for citizens. Instead, there is only "the mediocre hope of a future in which 'dumbed-down' cultural products are more equitably distributed."[61] With the reassertion of the political potential inherent in the aesthetic revolution, by the dismissal of the hierarchy between noble and popular taste, Rancière offers an alternative to the sociologist's battle of legitimization of what are repeatedly called "vulgar" pleasures.

The Mise-en-scène of the Straw Man

The detractors of the *Cahiers* cinephilia took aim at its eclecticism, its club culture, and its hegemonic status. The democratic distribution of cinephilic pleasure becomes a matter of a rebellion. Noël Burch suggests that one should eradicate "cinephilia"; Laurent Jullier, by contrast, wishes to multiply its forms, and Thomas Elsaesser calls for the evidence of "disenchantment."[62] One could argue that the club culture inherent in cinephilic practices is indeed present in all forms of cinephilia. The "proto-cinephilic" clubs in France in 1920s cultivated a circle of followers that belonged to an upper-middle-class category. The fees imposed on the club members in order to sustain the bourgeois habits of the clubs (for example, serving tea or dinner) and encourage the patronage of important figures in the social community, speak volumes about cinema's admittedly popular status. These early cinephilic manifestations practiced in fact a highly eclectic discourse. From the infatuation with the American cinema expressed by Louis Delluc at the screening of Cecil B. DeMille's *The Cheat* to the "reenactment" of this classic by France's Marcel L'Herbier and to the aesthetic turn that filmmakers like L'Herbier or René Clair will stir in the British cinephilic context,[63] everything testifies to the "salon" atmosphere surrounding early cinephilia. Ciné-clubs belonged to specialized journals that fostered a specialized discourse about movies.[64] The exclusive quality of classical cinephilia is not different in essence from such proto-cinephilic manifestations. Ironically, classical cinephiles turned against "eclectic" films and put their faith and passion in a popular cinema that would become part of a cultivated elite. The inner contradiction between "the will to account for cinema as a popular culture and the desire to legitimate it as lawful part of the erudite culture"[65] became part of its legacy.

Breaking with this tradition, new waves of cinephiles challenge the hegemonic status of classical cinephilia. Borrowing Jullier's term, I will refer to these groups and practices as postmodern cinephilia. It mainly aims to provide recognition for all cinephiles, not only the forgotten ones, but like the soldiers the unknown ones too.[66] Based on "ordinary competence" or "cultism,"[67] postmodern cinephilia is an attempt to stabilize "a situation of collective expertise, rather than a professional discourse or organized community."[68] Its advocates claim to have replaced the "elevated taste" with the "conjugation of disparate tastes."[69] Most importantly, they wish to stop the essentialist battles of drawing the borders of cinephilia, and rather attempt to edify a "community of interpretation" where everyone can "build his own cinephilic capital by assimilating the expertise of the other."[70]

In postmodern cinephilic practices, the club culture persists as a form of sociability. Their discourse suits the speed and intertext of the web space, but it remains an essentially discursive enterprise, that of the "*parole cinéphile*."[71] Snippets of film, sounds, images are traded as fans engage with one another; this engagement, however, is a display of individual perception, incidentally caught in the attempt to construct a collective perception that will legitimate them as a group. The insistence on the cinephilic capital of the individual[72] lends to opportunistic strategies to join a constituted community. The main debate is always with the *academy*, with reenacted forms of classical cinephilia.[73]

The fervent exchanges between clans, clubs, and generations reveal the core of the disagreement. At the heart of the debate there is the issue of the "ivory tower," with its consequences in the emancipation and legitimization of cinephiles. In other words, the debate still gravitates around the hierarchy in the field of cinephilia and the hegemony of the *Cahiers* model. If it holds the reins of power, it is because the myth of a common enemy or a tutelary power still endures. The metaphor of the ivory tower captures the tensions and disparities of today's cinephilia, as its multiple manifestations strive to undermine what started as a contestatory movement and became the official one. If classical cinephilia was a lover's discourse, postmodern cinephilia is a culture of war. Flaubert's striking implementation of the trope from the end of the Second Empire has enjoyed a long, effective history, and it remains relevant for contemporary discussions.[74]

Representative Cinephilia

Postmodern cinephilia proclaims its fundamental concern with the "democratization of the cinephilic judgment,"[75] an initiative that is deemed unsustainable within the classical model based on connoisseurship. Classical cinephilia is the dominant position, edified on the basis of a form of consumption reserved to a small number of individuals able to dedicate themselves to film viewing for reasons both spatial (access to the technical equipment of Parisian theaters) and social (including distinctions of class and gender). Democratization means universal access, that is, domestication.[76] Enjoying the full approval of Jullier's and Leveratto's study, one of these emancipated postmodern cinephiles writes: "Instead of building a common history of cinema, cinephiles are staying home to build each their own personal one."[77]

While proclaiming the end of the hegemonic regime of classical cinephilia and hailing a new cinephilic democracy, Jullier and company think to affirm "the reign of many,"[78] or, better, "the regime of multiple accommodations."[79] Their position, in defense of democracy, coincides with the one that an "adversary of democracy, Plato, mocked in Book VIII of the *Republic*, describing equality as conceived by the democratic man as the incapacity to prioritize, to choose between the necessary and the superfluous, the equal and the unequal. The democratic man, for Plato, wants equality in everything, even in the unequal."[80] Postmodern cinephilia democratized cinema by domesticating it, by investing a private practice with the virtues of a public one. In this sense, it inverted the classical model in which private pleasure became a shared experience. In the form acquired in France in the 1950s and 1960s, cinephilia was a vision that brought life and cinema into an undistinguishable communion. It suppressed the difference between private and public as well, but in a contrasting way.

Hatred of Democracy takes issue, among other things, with the strained relationship between private and public. Placed in dialogue with his idea of democracy, Rancière's notion of cinephilia grows stronger—and more strongly in opposition to the classical cinephilia of the *Cahiers*. Rancière's comments on pedagogy and egalitarianism from *On the Shores of Politics* resonate soundly here: cinephilia has become "the theater of a fundamental symbolic violence which is nothing else but the very illusion of equality."[81] "The term democracy," Rancière maintains, "does not strictly designate either a form of society or a form of government. 'Democratic society' is never anything but an imaginary portrayal designed to support this or that principle of good government. Societies, today as yesterday, are organized by the play of oligarchies."[82] In *Hatred of Democracy*, Rancière lingers on the distinction between "direct democracy" and "representative democracy."[83] Representative democracy, he claims, is a mixed form; "although initially founded on the privilege of so-called 'natural' elites, its formation of the state took shape, little by little, through democratic struggle."[84]

Rancière's distinction between "representative democracy" and "direct democracy" is essential to the understanding of his cinephilic aesthetics. As he considers exemplary case studies that reflect his own cinephilic revelations (Rossellini, Godard, Murnau), Rancière positions his personal predilections within the context of a "representative" cinephilia. In this sense, the elective representatives in a democracy resemble the relationship between cinephilia and its critical elite. Cinephilia is similar to the representative democracy in more than one way. It is true that the cult of the Great Men, the auteurs, animates cinephilia's critical elite. But cinephilia also enables the circulation of values, the displacement of one tradition and the inauguration of another. In this way, cinephilia reinforces the democratic struggle.

The advocates of postmodern cinephilia are concerned with the existence of inequality between the hegemonic elite and the "dispossessed" cinephiles. The perpetual reproduction of Bourdieu's "distinction" keeps the gap wide open and delays the reduction of inequality. Rancière responds to this claim with the argument of community. It is not believable for Rancière that a man could forget that he is a man, that he could exclude himself willingly from the category of men.[85] If this happens, it is less because of an inferiority complex, than by virtue of a judgment of his peers. The dispossessed cinephile would act similarly, looking for an accepting community. The idea of community is essential to emancipation not because it transmits knowledge, but because the sense of belonging to a community rekindles in the individual the awareness of his status, awareness that leads to emancipation. Cinephilia is democratic only if, as a practice of the individual within a community, it leads to emancipation. When "applied" to art, democracy should be conceived of as a form of power that is neither quantitative nor centered on control. It should rather be understood as potentiality or predisposition for emancipation: the capability of the ordinary people to discover modes and ways of action to settle the common affairs of the public sphere. Rancière thus restores the original, wider, and more evocative meaning of "democracy," which is the people's capability to act, and thus to access the sensible world.

Cinephilia as rift opens up a space of equality. In this way, Rancière's notion of a contestatory democracy problematizes the elitist exclusionism of classical cinephilia. "Far from being the form of life individuals dedicated to their private pleasure," cinephilia, assessed within Rancière's inquiry in democracy, involves "a process of struggle against this privatization, the process of enlarging this sphere."[86] Put in different terms, Rancière's cinephilia holds the utopian promise of a more inclusive access to the sensible world, both to the public sphere and the world of cinema.

Notes

1. Gustave Flaubert, *The Letters of Gustave Flaubert 1830–1880*, trans. and ed. Francis Steegmullert (London: Picador, 2001), 572.

2. See particularly Pierre Bourdieu, *The Distinction: A Social Critique of the Judgment of Taste* (London: Routledge & Kegan Paul, 1986); Pierre Bourdieu and Jean-Claude Passeron, *Reproduction in Education, Society and Culture* (London: Sage, 1977); Pierre Bourdieu and Jean-Claude Passeron, *The Inheritors: French Students and Their Relation to Culture* (Chicago: University of Chicago Press, 1979).

3. Jacques Rancière, *The Ignorant Schoolmaster: Five Lessons in Intellectual Emancipation* (Stanford, Calif.: Stanford University Press, 1991), 73.

4. Laurent Jullier and Jean-Marc Leveratto, *Cinéphiles et cinéphilies: Une histoire de la qualité cinématographique* (Paris: Armand Colin, 2010), 162. Unless otherwise indicated, the translations are mine.

5. See Adam Sternberg, "What Was, Is and Will Be Popular: The Driving Force of Pop Culture," *New York Times Magazine*, September 8, 2013, 23: "From all this chaos, though, one truism about popularity apparently survives: if something is popular, it can't also be good."

6. Christophe Gauthier, *La passion du cinéma: Cinéphiles, ciné-clubs et salles spécialisées à Paris de 1920 à 1929* (Paris: AFRHC, 1999), 58, my translation.

7. Ricciotto Canudo, "Manifeste des sept arts," *Gazette des Sept Arts*, no. 2 (January 23, 1923) (reprinted in *L'usine aux images* [Paris: Séguier, 1995], 161–64), and "La naissance d'un sixième art: Essai sur le cinématographe," *Entretiens Idéalistes* 10, no. 61 (October 25, 1911): 169–79 (reprinted in *L'usine aux images* [Paris: Séguier, 1995], 32–40).

8. Louis Delluc, "Le cinéma, art populaire" (1921), in Louis Delluc, *Le cinéma au quotidien: Écrits cinématographiques* (Paris: Cinémathèque Française–Cahiers du cinéma, 1990), 279–88, my translation.

9. Jacques Rancière, *Film Fables*, trans. Emiliano Battista (Oxford: Berg, 2006), 161.

10. Bourdieu, *The Distinction*, 493–94.

11. See *Democracy in What State?*, ed. Giorgio Agamben, trans. William McCuaig (New York: Columbia University Press, 2011), particularly the essays by Wendy Brown, "We Are All Democrats Now . . . ," 44–57, and Kristin Ross, "Democracy for Sale," 82–99.

12. See Simon Leys, *Le studio de l'inutilité: Essai* (Paris: Flammarion, 2012), 289.

13. Jacques Rancière, "Contemporary Art and the Politics of Aesthetics," in *Communities of Sense: Rethinking Aesthetics and Politics*, ed. Beth Hinderliter, William Kaizen, Vered Maimon, Jaleh Mansoor, and Seth McCormick (Durham, N.C.: Duke University Press, 2009), 36.

14. Jacques Rancière, *Les écarts du cinéma* (Paris: La Fabrique, 2011), 11. Unless otherwise indicated, the translations are mine.

15. Rancière, *Les écarts du cinéma*, 11..

16. Rancière, *Les écarts du cinéma*, 8.

17. Rancière, *Les écarts du cinéma*, 8; Jacques Rancière, *The Intervals of Cinema*, trans. John Howe (New York: Verso, 2014), 1–2.

18. Rancière, *Les écarts du cinéma*, 14.

19. Rancière, *Les écarts du cinéma*, 14.

20. Jacques Rancière, "Les écarts du cinéma," *Trafic* 50 (Summer 2004).

21. "Le destin du cinéma comme art: Entretien avec Jacques Rancière à la parution de *Malaise en esthétique*, par Emmanuel Burdeau et Jean-Michel Frodon," *Cahiers du cinéma* 598 (February 2005): 64–67.

22. Christian Keathley, *Cinephilia and History, or, The Wind in the Trees* (Bloomington: Indiana University Press, 2006), 2.

23. Jullier and Leveratto, *Cinéphiles et cinéphilies*, 9–33.

24. Antoine de Baecque, *La cinéphilie: Invention d'un regard, histoire d'une culture—1944–1968* (Fayard, France: Hachette Littératures, 2003).

25. Rancière, "Contemporary Art and the Politics of Aesthetics," 31: "A community of sense is a certain cutting out of space and time that binds together practices, forms of visibility, and patterns of intelligibility. I call this cutting out and this linkage a partition of the sensible."

26. Rancière, *Les écarts du cinéma*, 8.

27. Jacques Rancière, "Questions for Jacques Rancière around his book *Les écarts du cinéma*: Interview conducted with Susan Nascimento Duarte," *Cinema: Journal of Philosophy and the Moving Image* 2 (2011): 200–201.

28. François Truffaut, "Une certaine tendance du cinéma français," *Cahiers du cinéma* 31 (1954). See also "La tradition de la qualité," in *Sept ans du cinéma* (Paris: Edition du Cerf, 1953).

29. Paul Willemen, *Looks and Frictions* (Bloomington: Indiana University Press, 1994), 235.

30. De Baecque, *La cinéphilie*, 14. Unless otherwise indicated, the translations are mine.

31. De Baecque, *La cinéphilie*, 24.

32. De Baecque, *La cinéphilie*, 25, my translation.

33. Fereydoun Hoveyda, "Sunspots," in *Cahiers du Cinéma, the 1960s: New Wave, New Cinema, Reevaluating Hollywood*, ed. Jim Hillier (Cambridge, Mass.: Harvard University Press, 1986), 142.

34. Hoveyda, "Sunspots," 142.

35. Keathley, *Cinephilia and History*, 28.

36. Noël Burch, "Cinéphilie et masculinité," in *De la beauté des latrines: Pour réhabiliter le sens au cinéma et ailleurs* (Paris: L'Harmattan, 2007), 86.

37. See Susan Sontag, "The Decay of Cinema," *New York Times Magazine*, February 25, 1996; David Denby, "The Moviegoers: Why Don't People Like the Right Movies Anymore?," *New Yorker*, April 6, 1998, 95; Stanley Kauffmann, "A Lost Love," *New Republic*, September 8 and 15, 1997, 28.

38. Jullier refers to "classical cinephilia" as "modern cinephilia," in opposition to "postmodern cinephilia." See Jullier and Leveratto, *Cinéphiles et cinéphilies*.

39. Laurent Jullier, "Philistines and Cinephiles: The New Deal," *Framework* 50, nos. 1 and 2 (Spring and Fall 2009): 202.

40. Thomas Elsaesser, "Cinephilia or the Uses of Disenchantment," in *Cinephilia: Movies, Love and Memory*, ed. Marijke de Valk and Malte Hagener (Amsterdam: Amsterdam University Press, 2005), 38.

41. Rancière, "Questions for Jacques Rancière around His Book *Les écarts du cinéma*," 196–97.

42. He had his own column, "La Chronique de Jacques Rancière."

43. Rancière, *Les écarts du cinéma*, 8.

44. Rancière, *Les écarts du cinéma*, 8.

45. Rancière, *Film Fables*, 65.

46. Rancière, *Les écarts du cinéma*, 11.

47. Rancière, *Les écarts du cinéma*, 9.

48. Rancière, *Les écarts du cinéma*, 12.

49. Rancière, *Film Fables*, 6.

50. Oliver Davis, *Jacques Rancière* (Cambridge: Polity, 2010), 141: "The same tension between the unfolding of the fable and the suspensive moments which frustrate that process is found in literature with Flaubert, in the theatre of Maeterlinck, etc."

51. Jacques Rancière, *The Politics of Aesthetics: The Distribution of the Sensible* (London: Continuum, 2004), 24.

52. Jacques Rancière, *Aesthetic and Its Discontents* (Cambridge: Polity, 2009), 30.

53. Rancière, *Aesthetics and Its Discontents*, 13: "Aesthetics is the thought of the new disorder."

54. See Jacques Rancière, *The Philosopher and His Poor*, trans. John Drury, Corinne Oster, and Andrew Parker (Durham, N.C.: Duke University Press, 2004); Bourdieu, *The Distinction*. See also Charlotte Nordmann, *Bourdieu/Rancière: La politique entre sociologie et philosophie* (Paris: Editions Amsterdam, 2006).

55. See particularly Jullier and Leveratto, *Cinéphiles et cinéphilies*. See also Burch, "Cinéphilie et masculinité."

56. Pierre Bourdieu, *Sociology in Question* (London: Sage, 1993), 2.

57. Rancière, *The Ignorant Schoolmaster*, 18.

58. Rancière, in "Questions for Jacques Rancière around His Book *Les écarts du cinéma*," 210, my translation: "Précisément parce que le cinéma n'est pas un langage, qu'il ne définit pas un objet de savoir relevant d'un ordre systématique de raison, son apprentissage se prête particulièrement à l'application de la méthode d'émancipation intellectuelle: 'apprendre quelque chose et y rapporter tout le reste.' On 'apprend' le cinéma en élargissant le cercle des perceptions d'affects et de significations construit autour de quelques films."

59. Rancière, *The Ignorant Schoolmaster*, 70–71.

60. Rancière, *The Philosopher and His Poor.*

61. Davis, *Jacques Rancière*, 133.

62. See Noël Burch, "Cinéphilie et Politique," in *De la beauté des latrines*, 65–76; Jullier and Leveratto, *Cinéphiles et cinéphilies*; Elsaesser, "Cinephilia or the Uses of Disenchantment"; Gauthier, *La passion du cinéma.*

63. French cinema was used on the British scene to counter the massive distribution of Hollywood movies. Ciné-clubs and specialized film journals turn

to the French example in order to transform the cinema's artistic status and potential. See, for example, Anne Friedberg, "Reading *Close Up* 1927–1933," in *Close Up 1927–1933: Cinema and Modernism,* ed. James Donald, Anne Friedberg, and Laura Marcus, 1–26 (London: Cassell, 1998). See also Lucy Mazdon and Catherine Wheatley, eds., *French Film in Britain: Sex, Art and Cinephilia* (New York: Berghahn, 2013).

64. See Gauthier, *La passion du cinéma.*

65. Burch, *De la beauté des latrines,* 84.

66. Jullier and Leveratto, *Cinéphiles et cinéphilies,* 30.

67. "Cultism" is defined as an attitude attached to the defense of marginal work, usually belonging to popular culture. See Greg Taylor, *Artists in the Audience: Cults, Camp, and American Film Criticism* (Princeton, N.J.: Princeton University Press, 2001), and Jeffrey Sconce, "Movies: A Century of Failures," in *Sleaze Artists: Cinema at the Margins of Taste, Style, and Politics,* ed. Jeffrey Sconce (Durham, N.C.: Duke University Press, 2007).

68. Jullier and Leveratto, *Cinéphiles et cinéphilies,* 31.

69. Jullier and Leveratto, *Cinéphiles et cinéphilies,* 173.

70. Jullier and Leveratto, *Cinéphiles et cinéphilies,* 188.

71. Jullier and Leveratto, *Cinéphiles et cinéphilies,* 28–31.

72. See Olivier Donnat, *Les pratiques culturelles des Français à l'ère numérique, enquête 2008* (Paris: La Découverte, 2009); Gilles Renouard, *Paris cinéphile* (Paris: Guide Parigramme, 2006); Kevin Murphy, *A Year at the Movies: One Man's Filmgoing Odyssey* (New York: HarperCollins, 2002).

73. Jeffrey Sconce, "Trashing the Academy: Taste, Excess, and an Emerging Politics of Cinematic Style," *Screen* 36, no. 4 (Winter 1995).

74. See Steven Shapin, "The Ivory Tower: The History of a Figure of Speech and Its Cultural Uses," *British Journal for the History of Science* 45, no. 1 (March 2012): 1–27.

75. Jullier and Leveratto, *Cinéphiles et cinéphilies,* 160.

76. Jullier and Leveratto, *Cinéphiles et cinéphilies,* 155–79.

77. Gauthier Jurgensen, *J'ai grandi dans des salles obscures* (Paris: J.-Cl. Lattès, 2008).

78. Jacques Rancière, *On the Shores of Politics,* trans. Liz Heron (London: Verso, 1995), 40.

79. Rancière, *On the Shores of Politics,* 42.

80. Rancière, *On the Shores of Politics,* 41.

81. Rancière, *On the Shores of Politics,* 53.

82. Jacques Rancière, *Hatred of Democracy* (London: Verso, 2006), 13.

83. Rancière, *Hatred of Democracy,* 52.

84. Rancière, *Hatred of Democracy,* 54.

85. Rancière, *The Ignorant Schoolmaster,* 71–73.

86. Rancière, *Hatred of Democracy,* 55.

The Aesthetics of Displacement: Dissonance and Dissensus in Adorno and Rancière

Sudeep Dasgupta

> Art, far from foundering upon these intrusions of the prose of the world, ceaselessly redefined itself . . . building its own domain by blurring the specificities that define the arts and the boundaries that separate them from the prosaic world.
>
> —Jacques Rancière

> The worst calamity for a theory is when nothing resists it.
>
> —Jacques Rancière

> Under patient contemplation artworks begin to move.
>
> —Theodor Adorno

Writing of the practice of the cultural critic, Theodor Adorno avers, "By making culture his object, he objectifies it once more. Its very meaning, however, is the *suspension* of objectification."[1] Culture remains itself by paradoxically exceeding the boundaries that separate it from society. Adorno's critique of cultural critics who "help to weave the veil" concealing "the objectivity of the ruling mind" is premised on thinking culture's excess.[2] In *Aesthetic Theory*, he goes on to elaborate on how the aesthetic experience of artworks harbors the potential to rend the veil that hides both the objectivity of the ruling mind and the compartmentalized objectification of culture. As the epigraph from *Aesthesis* demonstrates, Jacques Rancière too rejects a simple assertion of art's autonomy, albeit in a different language from Adorno's. The excessive character of art lies precisely in its undoing of the simple opposition between art's autonomy and heteronomy. Rancière understands art's specificity precisely in its blurring of the boundaries between the arts, and between them and the prosaic world. In *Les écarts du cinéma*, Rancière, the cinéphile, argues that the power of cinema does not reside in anything solely specific to it, or to those who discipline it as an object of study. The power of cinema relies in thinking its *internal* distance from itself, in the ways in which it produces yet spans the gaps (*écarts*) between cinema, philosophy, and politics. This specific form of cinema's nonspecificity enables it to help us "lose the thread"[3] that weaves narratives stitched together with words, images, and sounds.

Rancière's displacement of disciplinary boundaries, and his errant redrawing of the landscapes through which he arrives at the terms "politics" and "aesthetics," have received considerable attention. In this essay, the displacing logic in his work will be approached through the productive tensions inherent to *aesthetic experience* in order to construct what is termed the *aesthetics of displacement.* By focusing on specific articulations of the term "aesthetics" in his writings, and linking the specificity of these articulations to the centrality of sensorial experience's destabilizing potential, an understanding of the aesthetics of displacement will be developed. Adorno's writings on aesthetics accompany this construction of Rancière's aesthetics of displacement. Specifically, the inherent tension within aesthetic experience between the subject of experience and the sense-object, crucial to Adorno's deployment of the aesthetic as a critical field of experience, is woven into the aesthetics of displacement in Rancière's work.[4] The purpose of this intertwining is twofold: first, the moving back and forth between Rancière and Adorno brings into relief both an understanding of aesthetics as *sensorial experience* and its destabilizing potential for both the subject and the social world it inhabits. Neither have developed a "theory" of the subject. Their hesitation to offer full-blown theories of the subject is precisely a function of the instability inherent to aesthetic experience. The potential of displacement continually traces and retraces the centrality of aesthetic experience for an understanding of subjectivity; second, Rancière's construction of the aesthetic has been perceived by many (though not all) as a productive provocation for thinking *both* political struggle and art practice. In Adorno, on the other hand, the aesthetic has often been seen as a refuge into which the subject flees from the evisceration of the hope of political struggle. By focusing on the emphasis on destabilizing and dissonant aesthetic experiences in both writers, the essay elaborates on the specific forms of mediation through which aesthetic experience's political dimensions become perceptible.

The Kantian legacy in aesthetics receives very specific articulations in Rancière and Adorno. Their particular readings of Kant, when thought together, blur the boundary between the optimistic and pessimistic evaluations of their work. The thinking together of Rancière and Adorno's particular debt to Kant operates in the background of the trajectory the essay constructs. The value of this debt resides in centralizing *sensorial experience* for understanding the aesthetics of displacement.

Between cultural critique as a weaving of the veil and the power of the aesthetic as a way of losing the thread, Adorno and Rancière produce an *aesthetics of displacement.* The dissonances and dissemblances of aesthetic experience set into play the relationship between sensory experience and meaning. Aesthetic experience's derangement of the fit between sensory experience and meaning, as developed by Adorno and Rancière's specific readings of Kant, constitute the focus of the first section. In the second section, their readings of specific artworks are analyzed to explore the destabilizing consequences of the aesthetics of displacement for the divisions between the arts. Returning to specific readings of artworks in the long third section, and supplementing them with a more recent example, the aesthetics of displacement's consequences for disciplinary thinking are argued for. My argument develops by moving continually between the general, particular and expansive dimensions of aesthetic experience across the three sections, reframing the aesthetics of displacement from the perspectives of philosophy, aesthetic analysis, and the critique of disciplinarity.

Sensorial experience functions as the "point of intelligibility" for the construction of what I term the aesthetics of displacement. By tying specific knots between the writings of Rancière and Adorno, the essay seeks to begin the task of constructing a landscape through which this point may be approached. To borrow from Rancière "to find the point of intelligibility . . . you have to blur the borders and reshape the territory." The construction of a specific relation between the two authors through the intertwining of their writings helps find this point of intelligibility. This point—the aesthetics of displacement—has to be constructed.

Aesthetic Experience in Rancière and Adorno

Describing his intervention in Marxist historiography in "From Politics to Aesthetics?" Rancière states, "I mean here 'aesthetic' in a sense close to the Kantian idea of 'a priori forms of sensibility': it is not a matter of art and taste; it is, first of all, a matter of time and space. But my research [here] does not deal with time and space as forms of presentation of the objects of knowledge. It deals with time and space as forms of configuration of our 'place' in society, forms of distribution of the common and the private, and of assignation to everybody of his or her own part."[5] The sensorial experience under the name "aesthetic" transforms the subject of experience (the worker) and the world it inhabits, restaging the latter and displacing the former. Rancière's reading of Kant in this passage redirects the Kantian a priori away from the Analytic of the Beautiful toward the wrong kind of subjectivity exercising a displacement of social configurations. This displaced subject, produced by dissensual aesthetic experience, becomes other to itself, just as the coordinates of the world it constructs displaces the staging of the social order. Expanding on this displacement by revisiting Schiller, Rancière observes, "Primitive man gradually learns to cast an aesthetic gaze on his arms and tools or on his own body, to separate the pleasure of appearance from the functionality of objects. Aesthetic play thus becomes a work of aestheticization."[6] Displacing the assigned function of a tool (the hand or the eye) and employing it to indiscriminately wander through space or read the wrong words, the worker engages in an aestheticization which produces a disturbance and reorientation of the subject of experience and their position within it. That is why Rancière argues, "Emancipation does not hinge on the power of words as such. It hinges on the power of the relation with the book."[7] The "power of relation" reorients the phrase "relations of power," substituting a power-driven grid-like stabilization with the displacing potential of aesthetic experience.

"Aesthetic experience," Rancière argues elsewhere, "is that of an unprecedented sensorium in which the hierarchies are abolished that structured sensory experience."[8] Rancière refigures the aesthetic as the entire domain of "sensibility" by undoing the narrowly circumscribed link between aesthetics and art and introducing a social dimension. The aesthetic comprises the experience of a city's spatial ordering, for example, as much as the apprehension of a painting and the encountering of moving images on a television screen. Further, the capacity for aesthetic experience disturbs the proper distribution of people and places, of times and spaces. Just as the broad understanding of the aesthetic as a sensible experience (the Kantian "a priori forms of sensibility") disrupts any specific link to only art, the aesthetic, as Rancière insists, calls into doubt the configuration of places and times in society.

The a priori coordinates of sensory experience are the starting point for thinking the "idea of a sensible element torn from the sensible, of a *dissensual* sensual element."[9] Threading Deleuze and Kant together, Rancière writes, "When Deleuze speaks to us of the work that tears the percept from the perception, and the affect from affection, he is expressing, in his own way, the original formula of aesthetic discourse . . . encapsulated by the Kantian analytic of the beautiful: aesthetic experience is of a sensory weave [*un sensible*] that is itself doubly disconnected. It is disconnected with respect to the law of understanding which subordinates sensory perception to its own categories [of understanding], and also with respect to the law of desire, which subordinates our affections to the search for a good."[10] By disconnecting aesthetic experience from an interested "search for a good," Kantian disinterestedness does not mean, *pace* Bourdieu, an Olympian distance of contemplation which masks social privilege. Instead, the disinterestedness of aesthetic experience is a radical *indifference* to the alignment of capacities with bodies ordered in social space. An aesthetics of displacement reconfigures this social space through the exercise of disinterested and undisciplined capacities for aestheticization.

In "Keeping One's Distance," an obvious allusion to Kant, Adorno argues that "every thought resembles play . . . The unbarbaric side of philosophy is its tacit awareness of the element of irresponsibility, of blitheness springing from the volatility of thought."[11] He goes on, "If it [thought] tried to claim its distance as a privilege," it would fail to comprehend that "distance is not a safety-zone but a field of tension . . . manifested not in relaxing the claims of ideas to truth, but in delicacy and fragility of thinking."[12] Keeping one's distance enables the exploitation of the "field of tension" for engaging in a contingent and fragile exercise of thinking. The barbaric side of philosophy closes the gap between thought and sense object by converting the distance between both into a proximity where play is abolished. Adorno's philosophical critique of philosophy from the side of thought is linked to Rancière's understanding of the aesthetic experience's disconnection from the laws of understanding. Both Adorno and Rancière undermine the primacy of thought, the former by emphasizing the internal fragility of thought's tentative engagement with the empirical, the latter by emphasizing the disconnection from codified understanding precipitated by sensory experience.

It is in *Aesthetic Theory* that Adorno confronts philosophy from the specific perspective of aesthetic experience. Thinking Rancière's argument about dissensual sensory experience and its disconnect from "the law of understanding," with Adorno's interrogation of the artwork's provocation to thought in this book are revealing. Adorno claims, "Artworks are, as synthesis, analogous to judgement; in artworks, however, synthesis does not result in judgement; of no artwork is it possible to determine its judgement or what its so-called message is. It is therefore questionable whether artworks can possibly be *engagé*, even when they emphasize their *engagement*."[13] Leaving aside for now both Rancière's and Adorno's rejection of so-called political art based on the transparent communication of meaning, why is it that Adorno claims the artwork cannot arrive at a judgment except analogically? "Artworks share with enigmas," Adorno asserts, "the duality of being both determinate and indeterminate. They are question marks, not univocal even through synthesis."[14]

Their lack of univocality is registered at the level of *sensory experience.* In his dialectical reading of the enigma Adorno argues, "For the experience of artworks . . . is as Kant himself described it, necessarily immanent and transparent right into its most sublime nuance . . . However, as soon as the experience of artworks flags, they present their enigma as a grimace. Incessantly, the experience of artworks is threatened by their enigmaticalness [which when it] . . . disappears completely from the experience, if the experience supposes that it has become completely immanent to the object, the enigma's gaze suddenly appears again."[15] This grimacing of the artwork necessitates "the concept of tension" as an integral element in the formal analysis of specific artworks, a tension which "by pointing up dissonant experiences or antinomical relations in the work" names "the element of 'form.'"[16] The formal dissonance in the artwork is "at once the quintessence of relations of tension and the attempt to dissolve them."[17] This play between dissonance and dissolution is experienced as an "aesthetic shudder" in the subject of experience. Formal dissonance and the subjectively experienced shudder register both thought's fragility (conceptual understanding) and art's displacing potential.

The sensory experience of the enigmatic quality of the object prevents the artwork from being subsumed to purely determinate judgment. In Rancière's terms, the dissensual sensible element disconnects aesthetic experience from the law of understanding, the transparency of the message and the immanence of meaning. Adorno's relating of the dual enigmatic quality of the artwork to Kant's aesthetic "experience" parallels Rancière's Kantian understanding of the aesthetic as "a priori forms of sensibility." The "doubly-disconnected" "sensory weave" that forms "aesthetic experience" in Rancière, and the enigmatic character of the artwork's duality registered in sensory experience in Adorno, are coupled in a specific way. For Rancière, this aesthetic experience is also the displacement of hierarchies of social order. In the examples above regarding workers' practice of aestheticization, Rancière is far more explicit about the consequences for the social order of this displacement; for Adorno too, aesthetic experience comes to unweave the veil of "objectivity" that sequestrates "culture" from society. He comes to this through an exploration of the artwork's resistant enigmaticalness, with consequences for cultural criticism and philosophy. But the exploration of the aesthetic in Adorno is not without social implications. The aesthetic for Adorno harbors the potential for upstaging sedimented social imaginaries through the sensory (dis)configuration of experience. Aesthetic experience, Adorno argues, enables the subject to become "aware of the world, which is his own, and that isolates him . . . in the same instant that he jettisons the conventions of the world."[18] This subjective awareness of the world triggered by "the advances of dissonance" in the form of the artwork by which "nature slips through the conceptual net of this aesthetics"[19] displaces the individual's relation to his place in the world, making him simultaneously aware of this place and displacing it. That is why Adorno argues that the dissonance within an artwork "originates in empirical layers of life" which the artwork registers but which cannot be conceptually captured. Although "artworks offer themselves to observation, they at the same time disorient the observer," producing the "aesthetic shudder" by which the subject "convulsed by art, has real experiences."[20] Formal dissonance and social displacement are linked. Adorno links aesthetic experience here to the social world, paralleling Rancière's Kantian rereading of the aesthetic as a question of space and time. Dissonances, antinomies, and tension felt at the sensory and cognitive levels in aesthetic experience both undermine conceptual certitude and emphasize a movement or displacement in the subject of experience. This experience isolates the subject, separating it from the social order as it jettisons or emancipates it from social conventions.

Given that the aesthetic is understood in terms of *experience*, and the effects of displacement it produces are registered at the level of thought and the social order, how precisely can one understand aesthetic experience in relation to the specificity of artworks? What displacements occur within artworks, and how are they registered at the level of the sensory?

Formal Dissonance and Aesthetic Displacement within and between the Arts

For Kant and Adorno, as we have seen, the aesthetic throws doubt on the possibilities of judgment because it evades conceptual capture and logical justification. Writing of the specificity of the image, Adorno translates his reading of Kant by separating (in Deleuzian terms) the percept from perception. In the short entry "Picturebook without Pictures" in *Minima Moralia*, Adorno posits such a paradoxical book precisely because in such books, images only illustrate, offer only perception but no percept. The pictures tell and explain rather than accompany and interrupt—"What was once called intellect is superseded by illustrations . . . One is supposed, schooled by countless precedents, to see what is 'going on' more quickly than the moments of significance in the situation can unfold."[21] The power "to imagine" and the "freedom of the mind" is dissipated when pictures function as illustrations, replacing aesthetic experience with information transfer and communication.[22] Adorno's counterreading of the picture as an image introduces a gap internal to the image that simultaneously opens another gap between it and the subject. He argues, "The perceptual image does indeed contain concepts and judgements. [But] Between the actual object and the individual sense datum, between inner and outer, yawns an abyss which the subject must bridge at its own peril."[23] The gap between the perceptual image and its other side, "the individual sense datum," provokes a tension, a dissonance in the subject of aesthetic experience. The image is divided, and its effect is loosened from the drive for conceptual mastery. The image then, is not an object, but a provocation, an operator of dissonance in the subject. That is why Adorno argues that "transcendence in artworks" is "their eloquence, their script, but it is a script without meaning, or more precisely, a script with broken or veiled meaning."[24] Artworks are the combination or "nexus of their elements" whose broken meaning produces a dissonance—"nothing is so full of expression as what flickers out—that tone that disengages itself starkly from the dense musical texture."[25] This element that disengages itself from the artwork it forms a part of is not dissimilar to the dissensual sensual element torn from the fabric of the sensible in Rancière. Reading Hölderlin's *An Hoffnung* in his essay "On Epic Naiveté," Adorno fastens on the sheer objective registering of concrete sensorial experience, characterized by some as "*Urdummheit*" (primal stupidity) within the poem.[26] This coexistence within the same artwork of different language uses is not a mark of Hölderlin's naïveté. It is a trace of that which has been extinguished in the transformation of language's function from registration of experience to transfer of meaning through communication. Hölderlin's poem combines two potentials of language: comprehension through linguistic communication, and registration of pure sensorial experience by using words which interrupt sense-making narratives with non-sense. This Homeric stupidity, which indexes the concrete particularity of experience through language, interrupts the logical progression of narrative by converting the temptation to quickly grasp "what is going on" into an experience of interruption and displacement ("losing the thread" of the plot, in Rancière's words). The disengaging, separating tone which weaves away from the densely woven texture of the artwork, and the anachronistic presence of epic naïveté in lyric poetry, like the dissensual sensual element in Rancière, converts the artwork from a coherent whole of transparent meaning into a series of elements that provoke dissonance and dissensus. The Kantian undermining of reason's capacity for judgment is manifested in the aesthetic experience of displacement, where proper language use for one art form, lyric poetry, is interrupted by the eruption of another, the epic. This conjunction of a philosophical insight and an aesthetic analysis is captured in Adorno's reading of Hölderlin:

"The attempt to emancipate representation from reflective reason is language's attempt, futile from the outset, to recover from the negativity of its intentionality, the conceptual manipulation of objects, by carrying the defining intention to the extreme and allowing what is real to emerge in pure form, undistorted by the violence of classificatory ordering."[27] In this reading of a poem, the specific knot between Adorno and Rancière can be glimpsed in their deployment of Kant. Where for Rancière the aesthetic marks the disturbance of the subject's bodily relation to the object and disorders the proper apportioning of places and times in the social order, in Adorno's Kantian reading, language attempts to escape the classifying imperative of conceptual thought by provoking a disorder in the artwork's intention to communicate.

The image, communication, and sensoriality are also brought into relation in Rancière. In *The Future of the Image*, he dissects the movement of images in time, analyzing them as operations rather than manifestations either of the real or of imitations of the real. For him "images of art are operations that produce a discrepancy, a dissemblance . . . Visible forms yield a meaning *to be construed* or subtract it. A camera movement anticipates one spectacle and discloses a different one."[28] Viewing the opening sequence of Bresson's *Au hasard Balthazar*, Rancière argues, "The images . . . are . . . operations: relations between a whole and parts; between a visibility and a power of signification and affect associated with it; between expectations and what happens to meet them."[29] The nexus of elements in this sequence are neither manifestations of the real nor specific to the medium of film. They operate by constructing joinings and producing gaps through time, whose subjective apprehension driven by expectation encounters *whatever happens to meet them*. The contingency, indeed errancy, of the flow of images, just like the dissonant tone that disengages from the musical text(ure) in Adorno, makes the aesthetic experience of an artwork into an occasion for a wandering, a splitting, an anticipating. The specificity of an artwork is neither its medium nor its faithfulness to what it imitates—for the artwork's eloquence is precisely the in*script*ion of broken meaning through the production of unanticipated turnings and contradictions.

Dissonance, dissemblance, and separation in artworks are understood in the relation between the whole and parts. The fragmentation within an artwork does not simply undermine meaning; it plays between meaning and sense, an interplay between production and retraction, eloquence and fading out, perception and percept, affection and affect. This setting into play within an artwork, for Rancière and in a different way for Adorno, is not limited to a specific medium. The internal displacement in an artwork is related to an external displacement *between* artworks. It is here that the unprecedented sensorium of aesthetic experience must be thought in the *power of relation*, now between artworks and not just the subject and its experience of them. Rancière concludes from his reading of the opening sequence of *Au hasard Balthazar*, "By compressing the action into a sequence of perceptions and movements, and short-circuiting any explanation of the reasons . . . it forms part of the novelistic tradition begun by Flaubert: an ambivalence in which the same procedures create and retract meaning, ensure and undo the link between perceptions, actions and affects. The wordless immediacy of the visible doubtless radicalizes its effects, but this radicalism itself works through the operation of the power which separates cinema from the plastic arts and makes it approximate to literature."[30] This quote compresses an aesthetics of displacement by linking the radical (unrooted) power of the image to a separation from one medium (cinema) and relating it to its proximity to another (literature). The play between meaning and "wordless immediacy" turns cinema into a picturebook *with* pictures. That is why anticipation and displacement are perversely coupled in the flow of images—"the power of anticipating an effect *the better to displace or contradict it.*"[31] The radical power of a medium resides precisely in manifesting a "wordless immediacy" whose own power transports it into the space of another. That is why "images of art are, as such, dissemblances" and "the image is not exclusive to the visible."[32] The destructive dimension of what Rancière calls the "aesthetic regime" cuts the link between the different registers of sensory perception captured in his notion of the "phrase-image"[33]—"In the aesthetic regime there is a transformation . . . the aesthetic work is first considered a kind of destructive intervention creating a difference between levels of sensory experience."[34] The phrase-image is the conjunction of conjunction and disjunction. The phrase, or what he calls the phrastic function is one of semantic organization, that is the construction of transparent meaning, similar to Adorno's understanding of the perfect overlap between concept and referred object or referent. This phrastic function, which stabilizes meaning by ordering the senses, is undercut by a cut or a gap (*écart*), which is also an extension. The cut disrupts the semantic stability of the phrase by conjoining the conjunctive power of the phrase with the disjunctive power of the image. The image intervenes by destroying the phrastic function of communication. (Both "phrase" and "image" are to be understood not in terms of writing and the visual, but as forms of inscription.) This dissensual and dissonant experience of an artwork is a function of both the production of a gap between different levels of sensory experience, between sense and meaning, and a displacement of the perspective from which an art form's power is recognized by acknowledging its relation with other arts.

The analysis of images in both, as we have seen, is related to the power of words. The movement between these two forms of inscription displaces the specificity of the arts, and this displacement redraws the topography between politics and inscription, exposing where precisely the politics of inscription resides. Reviewing Sartre's critique of Flaubert's use of writing, Rancière argues in the essay "The Politics of Literature,"

> He [Sartre] had to pursue outside of literature a political commitment of literature, which he had first purported to ground on its own linguistic specificity. It is not a casual or a personal failure. In fact, the identification of literature with a specific state or use of language has no real linguistic relevance, and it cannot ground any specificity of literature or its political involvement. Moreover, it proves very ambiguous in its practical use, and we have to deal with this ambiguity if we want to move forward in understanding literature as a new system of the art of writing, as well as its relationship to the political partition of the sensible.[35]

When the essay reappears in revised form in *The Politics of Literature*, Rancière rewrites the ambiguity between language use and literary form thus:

> This vicious circle [Sartre looking inside but having to move outside language use to identify Flaubert's politics] is not some individual mistake. It is connected to the desire to connect the specificity of literature *in language* . . . The [modernist] paradigm tries to anchor the autonomy of the arts in their own materiality. It thereby requires the claim of a material specificity for literary language. But this material specificity proves impossible to find. The communicational functions and the poetic functions actually never cease to overlap, as much in communicational language which is crawling with tropes, as in poetic practice, which is able to turn perfectly transparent language to its advantage.[36]

The coexistence of the troping and communicative functions of language within the same form, literature, makes the determination of the politics of a medium through the identification of its material specificity indeterminate. The *use* of the material in a form (literature) and the politics of literature cannot be defined by identifying the specificity of material use. This argument is the reappearance in a different form of the precise knot that binds aesthetics to politics in Rancière's *Proletarian Nights* and the essays of *Staging the People*. The use of the eyes and hands of the worker cannot be determined. Their deployment outside the humdrum of authorized employment refunctionalizes the material elements of the worker's body just as the composite form of literary language breaks through any specific language use that literature must deploy. The displacement of language use in literature and body-part function in the worker's body both tie a specific knot between aesthetics and politics. At a third level, then, the aesthetics of displacement not only disturbs the integrity of an artwork, and its separation from other art forms, but also undoes the link between politics as a message to be transmitted and the artwork as its communicative medium.

Writing in a very different context, Gayatri Spivak in *The Aesthetic Education in the Era of Globalization* argues, "I employ the word 'figure' . . . from the word 'figurative' as opposed to the 'literal.' When a piece of prose reasonably argues a point, we understand this as its literal *message.* When it advances this point through its *form,* through images, metaphors, and indeed its general rhetoricity we call it figuration or figuring-forth. Rhetoric is . . . not mere *alamkara* (ornamentation). The literal and the figurative depend on each other even as they *interrupt each other* . . . they make each other *operate.*"[37]

The analyses of specific artworks in both authors details the specifics of aesthetic experience in three ways. First, the internal tensions and contradiction between the elements of an artwork disturb the link between sense and sense-making. These disturbances are characterized as dissonances and dissemblances produced by the splitting away of specific elements of the artwork from the "violence of classificatory ordering." Second, this displacement or splitting between part and whole within an artwork displaces the artwork's own integrity by revealing borrowing from another medium—cinema from literature, the lyric poem from the epic. The displacement within and across artworks in aesthetic experience, finally, circles back to the politics of place-holding and space-making with which the previous section opened. The link between aesthetics and politics there, lay in the displacement of the aesthetic from a specific domain (art) to characterize the sensorial restaging of the subject and its world. The reading of artworks here deranges their specificity as particular mediums and produces an aesthetics of displacement within and between artworks, undermining thought's capacity to grasp the object.

The term "aesthetic education" (Schiller), deployed by Rancière and later Spivak, has consequences for disciplinarity within the academy too. The politics of an artwork is linked to its derangement of literal communication by figurative language. This displacement within an artwork demands an adisciplinary approach toward it that respects the disrespectful borrowings between art forms. The following (last) section will explore precisely how the internal displacement within artworks, and their borrowings from other art forms repartitions the boundaries of disciplines.

Aesthetic Displacement and Disciplinarity

> The object can no longer be contemplated peacefully and with composure. As in emancipated film, thought uses a handheld camera.
> —Theodor Adorno

> A discipline is always the anticipated implementation of a decision about the relation of thought and life, about the way thought is shared.
> —Jacques Rancière

Why is a discipline "the anticipated implementation of a decision" of the relationship between thought and life?[38] In "Thinking between Disciplines" Rancière offers one type of answer to this question by conjoining two forms of knowledge: knowledge (*connaissance*) as "know-how [*savoir*] and knowledge as the distribution of roles."[39] In this specific take on Kant's *Critique of Judgment*, knowing how to do something and knowing one's place are both a conjunction and a displacement. Rancière terms this displacement "aesthetic experience." He argues, "For Kant, aesthetic experience implies a certain disconnection from the habitual forms of sensible experience."[40] The customary expectations of the subject's capacity for sensible experience, knowledge, and its social position are displaced. An "aesthetics" of knowledge names the displacement between a place in the social order and the potential to know how to do something. An aesthetics of knowledge, furthermore, has consequences for how a discipline is understood as the codified and habitual practice of specialized knowledge. To be able to practice within a discipline is accompanied by the potential of somebody outside the discipline knowing how to engage in this practice. This is why a discipline is always an anticipation and not a given, produced by the displacement in the relation between the practice of knowledge as *savoir* and those who wield this knowledge as a tool. "Aesthetic experience" as the anticipatory destabilization of disciplinarity parallels the anticipatory experience Rancière describes in the movement of forms in art. Bresson's strategy of deploying images by thwarting anticipations and rendering indeterminate what "happens to meet them" is not specific to cinema but borrows this displacing potential from literature (Flaubert). Given that the power of art as an aesthetic experience borrows from the other arts, the specific domain of its intelligibility codified within disciplinary practice is displaced. Cultural critique of a specific art form requires borrowing from the knowledge accumulated by the analyses of other art forms. This accumulation is thus also a displacement across disciplinary boundaries—the power of Bresson's cinema manifests itself through a reading of Flaubert's literature. The term "aesthetic experience" describes both the displacing logic between knowledge and social roles, and the displacement of medium-specificity by thinking between art forms. The consequences for unthinking disciplinary divisions will be developed in this last section by exploring the precise conjunction of "discipline as anticipation" and the aesthetic experience of displacement in specific artworks.

"Cinema," Rancière writes, "is not the art of the movie camera—it is the art of forms in movement, the art of movement written [*écrit*] in black-and-white forms on a surface."[41] This script of broken meaning (Adorno) projected on the screen, transforms the meaning of the medium of cinema: "A medium is neither a basis, nor an instrument, nor a specific material. It is the perceptible milieu [*milieu sensible*] of their coexistence."[42] By understanding cinema as the art of forms in movement, Rancière argues that this specific movement of forms on a surface is part of a common history of the movement of forms preceding it (his example here is Chaplin's reception in the 1920s): "A new art [cinema] seeks to define itself through the discoveries of poets, choreographers, painters and theatre directors."[43] The disciplinary study of cinema is interrupted and extended by the recognition of this common history of forms of movement. The undisciplined trajectories of a medium's wanderings through the terrain of other arts, like "Charlot's 'life'[,] is thus nothing other than the very life of a new art, an art that crosses the borders separating different arts, as it crosses the ones that separate art from prosaic life and live performance from mechanical movement."[44] The provocation of the "new art" of cinema for disciplinarity resides in a demand. Like Charlot's crossing across the arts, and between the arts and prosaic life, the study of cinema must factor into its protocols first, cinema's borrowing of the potentials of other art forms, and the conjunction between cinema's inscription of forms of movement and the powers of movement in the world.

The cinema of Dziga Vertov exemplifies this double meaning of "movement" as the power to connect every element of life to any other, and of the image to connect to any other image.[45] Rancière argues in his reading of Vertov's *Man with a Movie Camera*, "Cinema offers itself as the immediate achievement of a communism existing solely in the relationship between all movements and all intensities. The self-dismissal of the eye, always in control or being controlled, to the profit of movement, gives us the formula not only for a new art, but for the immediate realization of a new world."[46] Chaplin's and Vertov's cinema perform the newness of the "new art" in specific ways. For Chaplin, cinema establishes a continuum between the already existing forms of movement in life and the forms on the screen. For Vertov, the communism of all forms of the movement of images subtracted from the eye's organizing mastery registers directly on screen the political movement of communism in the construction of a new world. Cinematic communism and the new world of communism coincide. The loss of medium specificity and the recognition of the coincidence between the arts "as forms of movement" and the movement of the world through a political movement generally equates the study of cinema with the study of the world. Political struggle and cinematic movement coincide in a specific knotting of their powers.

This cinematic provocation replays in a different form the disturbance that photography caused between those enraged artists who saw it as a mere instrument for recording and those proponents of the technology who saw it as an art form. Refusing that distinction, Walter Benjamin had argued, remaining faithful to an expansive understanding of aesthetics as sense-perception, that photography's (technically enabled) alteration of the senses was integral to the artistic manipulation of the senses.[47] The registration of reality and its manipulation were one and the same, this coincidence marking both art's potential to alter perception and its intervention and response to a changing, moving world. Sense perception as both a conditioned response to and effect of modernity, Benjamin argued was being registered in the debates between what counts as art and what does not with the advent of photography.[48] What mattered were the choices made in using a tool, whether the paintbrush and easel or the camera, toward a particular end. And this "end" or goal was one always susceptible to displacement by the choices made in (de) constructing the movement of forms through inscription.

In Adorno's filmic metaphor of knowledge production in the epigraph, approaching an object from a disciplinary position implies wielding a handheld camera to register the object in its movement. This potential is explored in Rancière's reading of the body in movement in art. In the chapter "The Dance of Light" in *Aesthesis*, Rancière frames Loïe Fuller's performance not as the imitation of something else (the Serpentine Dance) but as the bodily inscription of the transformation of forms through the use of light and fabric. Paraphrasing Mallarmé's review of Fuller, Rancière argues, "The figure is the potential that isolates a site and builds this site as the proper place for supporting apparitions, their metamorphoses, and their evaporation."[49] The body is an operator much in the same way as the image is in Bresson. Here it constructs a site (rather than performs on a site) on which forms appear, transform, and disappear. This staging of inscription interrupts the temptation to see dance as the performance of mimesis: the snakelike undulations of Fuller are not "serpentine"; they are the dance of light. This inscription is repeated again, Rancière asserts, when her dance is written into the field of legal patents submitted to the U.S. copyright office in Washington.

This displacement of one form of inscription into another brought into relief what was at stake in Fuller's performance of dance, for when the patent application was rejected, it made clear the split between a regime of art understood (by the New York court) as mimetic, and Fuller's inscription through dance of its displacement. Rancière argues, "Loïe Fuller's dance . . . is not dance anymore [mimesis], but the performance of an unknown art, or rather a new idea of art: a writing of forms determining the very space of its manifestation."[50] Electricity, fabric, the body are the materials of inscription through which dance as mimetic performance is displaced. This "new art is first an art of the indistinction of the arts . . . it negates the supposed specificities of material and processes anterior to these specifications. Before dance, there is movement; before painting, gesture and light; before the poem, the tracing of signs and forms: world-gestures, world-patterns. The new art, symbolized by Loïe Fuller's dance, captures the common potential of these patterns through its artifices."[51] The inscription of forms through movement exploit the "common potential" of all anterior arts, rather than the specificity of their material.

Understanding the significance of Fuller's "dance of light" as inscription requires reading other inscriptions in other forms (patents, poems, paintings). If one borrows the common potential of the arts however, rather than their particularity and specificity as separate arts, every new art is built on a specific disturbance in what "the common" means. It is Hegel who, in the 1820s, announces this rupture or delinking between "the arts" that at the same time makes them construct something in common (their potential). Rancière argues (paraphrasing Hegel), "The separation between spheres of rationality entailed not the glorious autonomy of Art and the arts but the loss of their power of thinking in common, of thinking, producing or expressing something in common; and from the sublime gap invoked there possibly resulted nothing but the 'entertainer's' indefinitely repeated abrupt switch of subject, capable of combining everything with anything."[52] Fuller's dance embodied this combination. He goes on, "The loss of any common term of measurement between the means of art does not signify that henceforth each remains in its own sphere [literary specificity, filmic materiality, the dance performance, etc.]. Instead it means that any common measurement is now a singular production."[53] Fuller's dance is a singular production enabled by the borrowing of the common *potential* of the other arts. The singularity of a specific aesthetic encounter is this construction through "artifice" of a common measurement between the means of art. Disciplinarity is displaced precisely by this letting go of separate rules for measuring different arts, by attending to how a common measurement is the effect of a specific production (film, dance, poem).

Rancière's cross-medial rendition of cinema's paradoxical specificity, and his reading of dance as part of a larger nexus of evolving arts of movement are paralleled in Adorno's close readings of works of literature. Immersing himself in small passages of Proust, Adorno identifies how the specificity of Proust's writing practice dissolves the "unity and wholeness of the person."[54] This specificity resides in the production of *images* and their passage through time. Adorno describes the transformations in Proust's characters as "the process of dissolution," which produces "a fugitive series of images."[55] Adorno goes on, "What changes in people . . . are the images into which we transpose them . . . Proust knows that there are no human beings in themselves beyond this world of images."[56] Eschewing the rhetoric of psychological depth and the wholeness of individuality, Adorno's reading of Proust displaces the power of words from communicating "mere psychological or sociological data."[57] Instead, "the process by which the novel unfolds is the description of the path travelled by these images."[58] The literary text becomes a cinematic trajectory of appearance, transformation, and dissolution in Adorno's hands, in a manner not unrelated to Rancière's Flaubertian reading of Bresson's sequencing of fragmented images. Kafka too appears in Adorno's *Notes on Kafka* through the language of musical composition ("notes") and photographic practice. Employing the language of the photographic camera, Adorno asserts, "Eternalized gestures in Kafka are the momentous brought to a standstill. The shock is like a surrealistic arrangement of that which old photographs convey to the viewer."[59] He goes on, echoing Eadweard Muybridge's photographic studies of motion, "Anything that balances on the pinnacle of the moment like a horse on its hindlegs is snapped." His dialectical rendition of opposites ("eternalized gestures are the *moment*ous") invokes the freezing of eternity into a moment. This rendition in the critic's words of the writer's words as images frozen in time converts reading Kafka into the leafing of a photo album. Yet Adorno does not succumb to a simplistic displacement. Words operate as a camera shutter to freeze an image, but words also produce "long and fatiguing imageless sections."[60] The text is a surface of conversion where words both function as images and produce imageless passages. The dynamic of displacement in Kafka's writing produces a specific knot between knowledge in all its direct momentousness and its mediated monotonous passing. This knotting produces a dissonant aesthetic experience through the excision of the moment from *durée*. What endures is both the duration and the interruption. For Adorno, these two processes in Kafka's writing are graspable only through the metaphor of photographic capture.

The movement of forms and the forms of movement across specific arts can be glimpsed by moving from the nineteenth and early twentieth centuries to a slightly more contemporary example. The dialectic of duration and interruption is given a further twist in the play between presence and absence here. The writer, essayist, and photographer Hervé Guibert thought through the specificity of each medium precisely through its other.[61] Absorbing this method of displacement in his own work, his collection of essays on photography, *L'image fantôme* is completely absent of images, precisely because the visual is not limited to the image. The written word in these essays does not substitute for the visual, they operate visually. In the essay "L'écriture photographique," Guibert describes Goethe's *Voyage en Italie* as a postcard, while his description of the Palladio convent is viewed by Guibert as "a sort of architectural photo, then he isolates a detail, a nuance of matter."[62] Midway through the collection, the essay functions as an instruction on how to read each of them as absent photographs. The collection, then, far from being absent of images, like Goethe's diaries, is a collection of impressions, a contact sheet (*planche-contact*) that requires a form of reading that is not strictly literary. Or rather, it is literary in the precise sense of exploiting the power of relation between writing (*écriture*) and photography. The diary is "like a contact sheet, an alignment of shots."[63] The absence of photographs does not prevent seeing Guibert's own diarylike collection of essays as any less a collection of perspectives from which photographs are snapped. Duration and interruption, presence and absence are two strategies by which the word transforms into an image or registers the latter's absent presence.

This constructive disruption of the word-image separation is exemplified in the many photographs which Guibert took but which never *illustrated* any text between the covers of a book. The photographs circulate separately, their presences appearing by reference in a written text but never accompanying the text. The literary critic Ralph Sarkonak is thus obliged to move between text and photograph, though both function as visual inscriptions. Sarkonak argues,

> The photo of absence generates a fiction in the same way that the absence of a photograph can—and often does—lead to the writing of a Guibert text. This helps explain the problematic relationship between photos and texts, for to provide the story of a photo directly, immediately—in the same space, as in a photo text—would have the effect of cancelling the absence, filling the void, and curtailing our imagination. It is no doubt for this reason that when there is an intertext to a particular photo, it is usually fragmented, dispersed, and disseminated among the written works, rather than directly juxtaposed to the image that it "explains." The figures of past, present, and future absences that haunt Guibert's writing are thus reified in a photo . . . by the play of light and shadow that

> emphasizes the link between photography and an absent referent . . . the eerie concomitance of presence and absence.[64]

The disciplinary displacement provoked by the object of analysis is registered as a play of absences and presences. AIDS and death are registered both photographically and literally/literarily by displacing one form of inscription (*écriture*) into another (photography). But the photographs figure only absence, or rather through the copresence of elements which comprise its perceptible milieu, they figure forth no literal meaning, no substantive presence but the material trace of an absence. It is for this reason that Benjamin too compares a photograph to a "crime scene."[65]

Providing the "story of a photo" with a written text produces in Adorno's words "a picturebook without pictures." In Rancière's words, it would close the gap between an anticipation and whatever happens to meet it. Explanation would fill the gap between word and text (both as images) reducing the dissonant and dissensual productivity of aesthetic experience. Playing in the interval between presence and absence rather than closing the gap, the artist exercises a choice among possible options of inscription. Guibert's different forms of *écriture* (diaries, essays, novels, photographs, films) demand different vantage points from which they can be viewed through a process of continual alignment and dislocation. Their continual reference to each other across different forms of inscription puts forms into movement through the play of absence and presence. Just as Chaplin's films exploit the cinematic medium's borrowings from theater, painting, and poetry by setting shadows into movement, Guibert's photographs traverse the boundaries between writing as text and writing as the play of light and shadow. Forms of movement across art forms and within them produce a momentary constellation of aligned perspectives which disrupt disciplinary protocols. Releasing the imagination to wander between art forms is not a function of subjective will, however. It is the effect of an encounter between artworks and the sensory experiences they produce.

If Sarkonak reads Guibert's photographs as the displaced presence of absent words, Adorno's reading of philosophical texts often detects the presence of what Rancière calls "the prosaic world" in conceptual thought. In his reading of "the construction of the aesthetic" in Kierkegaard, Adorno locates in language the knot tied between the philosophical and the poetic, between existence in all its prosaicness and the demands of philosophical rigor. The linkage between these two disciplinary boundaries is identifiable for Adorno in those moments where the "poetic" invades the philosophical text.[66] This poetic element is not the result of Kierkegaard's failing as a philosopher, but the registering of philosophy's failure to capture everyday existence conceptually. At issue then is not reading Kierkegaard the philosopher poetically but recognizing the coexistence of different uses of language in the same text. The conceptual rigor of philosophy fails and this failure productively interrogates the limits of restricting a particular discipline to a specific use of language. The aesthetic in "the construction of the aesthetic" is not a branch of philosophy, it is the experience within philosophical thought of a failure which the poeticity of Kierkegaard's text registers. Adorno reads this retraction of meaning through the presence of the poetic in the philosophical text, and as a cipher of precisely that in experience which cannot be conceptually explained. This is why Adorno argues that "everything in philosophy that could not be integrated into the ideal of science was dragged along behind as a stunted appendage under the title of poetry."[67] In Rancière's terms in the epigraph, thought comes up against what resists it.

Similarly, in his literary criticism, just as he had undone the separation between the word and the image in Kafka, Adorno establishes the link between science and literature by displacing their separate fields of operation. Adorno plays off Proust the writer against Bergson the scientist. Proust's writing is marked by an "allergic reaction to ready-made thought, to the pre-given and established cliché."[68] Proust's "objectivity," Adorno argues, is "not the verification of assertions through repeated testing but rather individual human experience, maintained through hope and disillusionment."[69] The word "objectivity" points both to notions of neutral scientific language and to the resistance the object offers to conceptual capture. The novelist's writing is adjacent to, if not overlapping with, science and philosophy, yet its deployment of language, in its labyrinthine weaving of miniaturized descriptions of reality as theater, expresses thought's yearning for a future reconciliation between subject and object. Reading Proust as a sensory and cognitive *experience* (*Erfahrung*) constructs a different path to the scientific critique of reified experience (*Erlebnis*) of temporality in Bergson. This proximity of art and science not only undoes the claims of exclusivity which structure much scientific thinking; the reading of Proust also disturbs the vantage point from which he can be read as a writer. Adorno argues that "although art and science became separate in the course of history, the opposition between them should not be hypostatized. Aversion to an anachronistic conflation of the two does not render a compartmentalized culture sacrosanct."[70] The practice of inscription, by writer and scientist, is both acknowledged in their distinctive uses and undermined.

Circling back to the opening quote of Rancière in the first section of this essay, inscription as both aesthetic displacement and disciplinary displacement coincide. This coincidence can be found in the concept of "literariness" and its elaboration in Rancière's history of nineteenth-century workers. Looking back at this historiographical intervention, Rancière observes, "While proletarians appropriated for themselves the leftovers of the outmoded high poetics and rhetoric, it [the aesthetic way of writing *as reading*] framed a new poetics giving flesh to a 'voice from below,' an eloquent voice of the mute. It framed what would afterwards be endorsed by social science and criticism: a hermeneutic of social truth."[71] The sociologist stabilizes the aesthetic displacement produced by proletarian appropriation of "high culture" by reading it as the *failure* of worker-being. This failure attributed to the worker however, is predicated on positing a pure worker as the starting point of the hermeneutics of social truth. Artistic practice by the laboring body can only be seen as a mistake by the traditional sociologist because a discipline already delineates the proper object of study. For this kind of sociologist, "a discipline, in effect, is not first of all the definition of a set of methods appropriate to a certain domain or a certain type of object. It is first the very constitution of this object as an object of thought, the demonstration of a certain idea of knowledge—in other words, a certain idea of the rapport between knowledge and a distribution of positions."[72] Rancière and Adorno's reconstitution of the artwork as the site for the exploitation of the common potential of different art forms, undoes the rapport between art objects as objects of habitual sensible experience and the demonstration of specific forms of knowledge and expertise constituted by disciplines.

Conclusion

Adorno's critique of the real segregation of the life-world precipitated by the dialectic of the Enlightenment is well-known. The aesthetic harbors the potential for destabilizing this segregation by, in Rancièrian terms, undoing the separation between the arts, and between the arts and life. The visual reading of words and the "scientific" reading of the novel register the singular transformations of such intermedial exchange. These exchanges also trouble the borders between disciplines encouraging an adisciplinary perspective on the study of aesthetics. The reading of the Adornian aesthetic as the figuration of art's withdrawal from life, of its nonutility to a world in which everything has been subordinated to exchange, must be supplemented by understanding how such a withdrawal is simultaneously an expansion of an understanding of the aesthetic. If "life does not live," aesthetic experience registers the weak hope of life's continuation amid this death of life in life that the social order announces as reality.[73]

The pessimistic reading of Adorno is thus both invited and negated in his readings of artworks. Aesthetic experience's registration of the evisceration of life in the "aesthetic shudder" is also the starting point for rethinking thought's own relation to life. Art registers thought's incapacity to grasp sensible experience and everyday life as concept. Hence the undisciplined eruption of the poetic in the philosophical. As both registration in the form of witness to, and deixis in the sense of pointing to, art, thought, and unthinking itself are related. Art, thought, and life enter into a constellation brought to a standstill in moments of aesthetic displacement.

Rancière's reading of worker's aestheticization conjoins art, thought, and life subjunctively. By viewing the palace as an object of aesthetic contemplation rather than the site of his labor, the "as if" by which the worker transforms his tools from their destined purpose of work displaces his place in the social order. "Aesthetics means, in effect, a 'finality without end' [*finalité sans fin*], a pleasure disconnected from every science of ends. It is a change in the status of the as if. The aesthetic gaze which sees the form of the palace is without relation with its functional perfection, and with its inscription in an order of society," argues Rancière.[74] The "without end" (*sans fin*) of the worker's aestheticizing gaze and the nonutilitarian *political* utility of the aesthetic in Adorno are tied together in a specific way. The Adornian "no" that art says to society's ordering of life is a refusal. However, this refusal is not a deluded attempt to escape the real functioning of the world. When framed through Rancière's understanding of the displacing potential of the "aesthetic gaze," this refusal resists the philosophical emplacement of the reign of thought by linking thought to its own volatility and fragility manifested in the dis-ordering of social space.

That is why, in words similar to Adorno's, Rancière states, "the worst calamity for a theory is when nothing resists it."[75] The subjunctive character of aesthetic contemplation in Rancière's reading of aesthetics (the worker's "aesthetic gaze") distances aesthetic appreciation from the gaze's "inscription in an order of society." Both the making of art by anybody of that which is not capable of being appreciated aesthetically, and the dissonant experience through the subjective "shudder" of art's bearing witness to the violence of social ordering, figure aesthetic experience as an experience of displacement. Rancière's notion of the aesthetic can frame Adorno's understanding of experience's displacement by doubling the meaning of "witness" (*témoin*). Witnessing (*témoignage*) implies both the right kind of body speaking truth as it does the capacity of any body to incorporate truth. The latter form of incorporation displaces the stability of the former. This latter form of witnessing "attests to an unconditioned of truth, to its irreducible factuality, indifferent to the diverse authorities linked to power, knowledge or prestige."[76] The double incarnation of the witness, as obedient to social power, and as attester to the unconditioned nonprescribed understanding of truth, disrupts the stabilization of aesthetic experience understood broadly. The spatial redistribution of capacities and the aesthetics of disinterestedness are joined. "In relation to Kant," Rancière argues, "it's definitely a question of a priori forms of experience but, of course, the space we're dealing with in these a priori forms of distribution of bodies in society and capacities attributed to those bodies is, from the outset, its own metaphor."[77]

Through Rancière, Adorno's embodiment of Kant's reading of aesthetic distance becomes perceptible not just as an elaboration, but also as an expansion of art's specific potential for displacement. The field of art is a space in which aesthetic distance and disinterestedness produce the destabilizing potential of sensory experience. Through terms such as the "phrase-image," Rancière introduces into aesthetic experience the displacement of thought's end-driven stabilization of meaning by asserting pure materiality's registration by the senses. Conjoining and separating thought and the sensorial (Kant's "a priori sensorium") he constructs shifting alignments of thought, art, and life. The effects of these singular arrangements can be sensed in the experience of artworks and their provocation to disciplinary thought. Anticipation rather than habituation, interruption rather than continuity, mark the trajectory of aesthetic experience within the landscape constructed through the writings of both thinkers. Aesthetic experience as an aesthetics of displacement reorients aesthetics by moving into artworks to go beyond the narrowly artistic into the sensorial experience of the "prosaic world." Aesthetic experience turns thought, art, and life into moving dissensual elements which resonate in singular constellations as dissonances in the sensible fabric of life.

Notes

The first epigraph for this chapter is from Jacques Rancière, *Aisthesis*, trans. Zakir Paul (New York: Verso, 2013), x–xi. The second epigraph is from Rancière, *La méthode de l'égalité: Entretiens avec Laurent Jeanpierre et Dork Zabunyan* (Paris: Bayard, 2012), 100; see note 75 in this chapter for the original French. The third epigraph is from Theodor Adorno, *Aesthetic Theory*, trans. Robert Hullot-Kentor (Minneapolis: University of Minnesota Press, 1997), 79.

1. T. W. Adorno, "Cultural Criticism and Society," in *Prisms*, trans. Shierry Weber Nicholson and Samuel Weber (Cambridge, MA: MIT Press), 22, my italics.

2. Adorno, "Cultural Criticism and Society," 20.

3. Jacques Rancière, "Re-visions—Remarks on the Love of Cinema: An Interview with Oliver Davis," *Journal of Visual Culture* 10, no. 3 (2011): 298.

4. This accompaniment is constructed in the argument that follows. However, the presence of Adorno's thought can be found scattered across Rancière's work. My argument is not a reconstruction of this presence but the construction through the term "aesthetics of displacement" of their relation to each other.

5. Jacques Rancière, "From Politics to Aesthetics?," *Paragraph* 28 (2005): 13.

6. Jacques Rancière, "The Aesthetic Revolution and Its Outcomes: Emplotments of Autonomy and Heteronomy," *New Left Review* 14 (2002): 136.

7. Jacques Rancière, "Aesthetics against Incarnation: An Interview with Anne Marie Oliver," *Critical Inquiry* 35 (2008): 173.

8. Jacques Rancière, *Dissensus: On Politics and Aesthetics*, ed. and trans. Steven Corcoran (London: Continuum, 2010), 176.

9. Rancière, *Dissensus*, 173, italics in the original.

10. Rancière, *Dissensus*, 173.

11. T. W. Adorno, *Minima Moralia: Reflections from Damaged Life*, trans. E. F. N. Jephcott (London: Verso, 2002), 127.

12. Adorno, *Minima Moralia*, 127.

13. Adorno, *Aesthetic Theory*, 123, italics in the original.

14. Adorno, *Aesthetic Theory*, 124.

15. Adorno, *Aesthetic Theory*, 125.

16. Adorno, *Aesthetic Theory*, 292.

17. Adorno, *Aesthetic Theory*, 292.

18. Adorno, *Aesthetic Theory*, 292.

19. Adorno, *Aesthetic Theory*, 75.

20. Adorno, *Aesthetic Theory*, 269.

21. Adorno, *Minima Moralia*, 141.

22. Adorno, *Minima Moralia*, 124.

23. Max Horkheimer and T. W. Adorno, *Dialectic of Enlightenment: Philosophical Fragments*, trans. Edmund Jephcott (Stanford, Calif.: Stanford University Press, 2002), 155.

24. Adorno, *Aesthetic Theory*, 78.

25. Adorno, *Aesthetic Theory*, 79.

26. Theodor Adorno, "On Epic Naiveté," in *Notes to Literature*, vol. 1, trans. Rolf Tiedemann (New York: Columbia University Press, 1991), 25. The term is Karl Theodor Preuss's.

27. Adorno, "On Epic Naiveté," 27.

28. Jacques Rancière, "Future of the Image," in *Future of the Image*, trans. Gregory Elliot (London: Verso, 2007), 7.

29. Rancière, "Future of the Image," 3.

30. Rancière, "Future of the Image," 5.

31. Rancière, "Future of the Image," 5, my italics.

32. Rancière, "Future of the Image," 7.

33. Rancière, "Re-visions," 298.

34. Rancière, "Re-visions," 298.

35. Jacques Rancière, "The Politics of Literature," *SubStance* 103, vol. 33, no. 1 (2004): 11.

36. Jacques Rancière, *The Politics of Literature*, trans. Julie Rose (Cambridge: Polity, 2011), 6.

37. Gayatri Chakravorty Spivak, *An Aesthetic Education in the Era of Globalization* (Cambridge, Mass.: Harvard University Press, 2012), 38.

38. Epigraphs for this section: Theodor Adorno, "The Handle, the Pot, and Early Experience," in *Notes to Literature*, vol. 2, trans. Rolf Tiedemann (New York: Columbia University Press, 1992), 216; Jacques Rancière, "Democracy, Dissensus and the Aesthetics of Democracy: Interview with Max Blechman, Anita Chari and Rafeeq Hasan," *Historical Materialism* 13, no. 4 (2013): 300.

39. Jacques Rancière, "Thinking between Disciplines: An Aesthetics of Knowledge," *Parrhesia* 1, no. 1 (2006): 4.

40. Rancière, "Thinking between Disciplines," 1.

41. Rancière, *Aisthesis*, 193.

42. Rancière, *Aisthesis*, 193.

43. Rancière, *Aisthesis*, 193.

44. Rancière, *Aisthesis*, 194. "Charlot" is the name for both Chaplin's "Tramp" and Chaplin himself in French.

45. Jacques Rancière, "Après la littérature," in *Les écarts du cinéma* (Paris: La Fabrique, 2011), especially the section "Hitchcock-Vertov et retour."

46. Rancière, *The Intervals of Cinema*, trans. John Howe (London and New York: Verso, 2014), 34.

47. Walter Benjamin, "Little History of Photography," in *Selected Writings*, vol. 2 (Cambridge, Mass.: Harvard University Press, 1999).

48. For an incisive account of the centrality of sense perception in the relationship between cinema and modernity, see Miriam Bratu Hansen, *Cinema and Experience: Siegfried Kracauer, Walter Benjamin, and Theodor Adorno* (Berkeley: University of California Press, 2012).

49. Rancière, *Aisthesis*, 94.

50. Rancière, *Aisthesis*, 103.

51. Rancière, *Aisthesis*, 106.

52. Jacques Rancière, "Sentence, Image, History," in *Future of the Image*, 43.

53. Rancière, "Sentence, Image, History," 42.

54. Adorno, "Short Commentaries on Proust," *Notes to Literature*, vol. 2, trans. Rolf Tiedemann (New York: Columbia University Press, 1992), 177.

55. Adorno, "Short Commentaries on Proust," 177.

56. Adorno, "Short Commentaries on Proust," 177.

57. Adorno, "Short Commentaries on Proust," 177.

58. Adorno, "Short Commentaries on Proust," 178.

59. Theodor Adorno, "Notes on Kafka," in *Prisms*, 252–53.

60. Adorno, "Notes on Kafka," 255

61. My thanks to Romain Caudron for discussions of Guibert's work.

62. "une sorte de photo d'architecture, puis il isole un détail, une nuance de matière"; Hervé Guibert, *L'image fantôme* (Paris: Les éditions de Minuit, 1981), 73–74. English translation by Scott Durham.

63. "comme une planche-contact, un alignement de prises de vues"; Guibert, *L'image fantôme*, 75. English translation by Scott Durham.

64. Ralph Sarkonak, "Traces and Shadows: Fragments of Hervé Guibert," *Yale French Studies* 90 (1996): 196–97.

65. Benjamin, "Little History of Photography," 527.

66. Theodor Adorno, *Kierkegaard: The Construction of the Aesthetic*, trans. Robert Hullot-Kentor (Minneapolis: University of Minnesota Press, 1996), 5.

67. Adorno, *Kierkegaard*, 3.

68. Adorno, "Short Commentaries on Proust," 175–76. Adorno calls attention to Bergson's critique of the classificatory concepts employed in "causal-mechanistic science" and aligns Proust to this critique. Adorno argues that "Proust was equally capable [as Bergson] of expressing a scientific or metaphysical relationship" so that the "powers" of intuition "are counterbalanced by those of French rationality" ("Short Commentaries on Proust," 175).

69. Adorno, "Essay as Form," *Notes to Literature*, vol. 2, trans. Rolf Tiedeman (New York: Columbia University Press), 8.

70. Adorno, "Essay as Form," 7.

71. Rancière, "From Politics to Aesthetics?," 17–18.

72. Rancière, "Thinking between Disciplines," 6.

73. "Life does not live" is borrowed from Ferdinand Kürnberger as the epigraph to part 1 of Adorno's *Minima Moralia*.

74. Rancière, "Thinking between Disciplines," 5.

75. Rancière, *The Method of Equality: Interviews with Laurent Jeanpierre and Dork Zabunyan*, trans. Julie Rose (Cambridge: Polity, 2016), 54: "Le plus grand malheur d'une pensée, c'est quand rien ne lui résiste." Rancière, *La méthode de l'égalité*, 100.

76. "atteste d'un inconditionné de la verité, de sa factualité irréductible, indifférente aux autorités diverses liées au pouvoir, au savoir ou au prestige"; Rancière, "Figures du témoignage et démocratie: Entretien avec Maria Benedita Basto," in *Et tant pis pour les gens fatigués: Entretiens* (Paris: Éditions Amsterdam, 2009), 531. English translation by Scott Durham.

77. Rancière, *The Method of Equality*, 58. "Par rapport à Kant, . . . il est bien question de formes *a priori* de l'expérience mais, bien sûr, l'espace dont il est question dans ces formes *a priori* de la distribution des corps en société et des capacités attribuées à ces corps est d'emblée sa propre métaphore." Rancière, *La méthode de l'égalité*, 107.

The Politics of the Aesthetics of Theory

Nico Baumbach

I will start, as Jacques Rancière often does, by offering a preliminary explanation of my title. Much of Rancière's work from the last two decades has been focused on the interrelation of aesthetics and politics through a critique of a wide range of discourses that have attempted to define what makes art art or what makes politics politics. The uptake of, and debates about, this recent work has correspondingly been largely around the status of these objects: either art in terms of the concepts Rancière has used to reframe it—the aesthetic regime of art, the distribution of the sensible, and so on—as compared to more familiar concepts he rejects, such as critical or committed art, modernism, postmodernism, and so on. Or Rancière's conception of politics as axiomatic equality or his definition of democracy in terms of dissensus have been debated in relation to the theories of politics he is in opposition to, such as those grounded in strategies of power or conceptions of community and organization.

Implicit, but rarely foregrounded, in this growing literature on Rancière's work are questions about the place or function of the very discourse within which these debates about art and politics take place. It is this discourse that I will focus on in this essay. This is the third term in my title, which goes here by the name of "theory."

Readers familiar with Rancière's work might already know the answer to the question of what place his discourse seeks to occupy—it is no place at all or at least no fixed place, a place in between discourses that effects a displacement. If it is a place at all, it is a heterotopic space. Rancière has repeatedly made clear that he seeks to mix discourses that are not meant to be mixed and do so without creating a hierarchy between them. His method is meant to work against the idea of disciplines. He has pitted this way of working against discourses that pursue the opposite course, that seek to define and establish the specificity of their practices and determine the conditions that make these practices efficacious.[1]

Significantly, these discourses that Rancière has challenged are not only those that are invested in the autonomy of disciplines and preserving realms of expertise; they also include those framed as political interventions or as subverting regimes of common sense. For example, Rancière has shown how political theorists or philosophers often create a theater in which the concept of politics is threatened by forces that corrupt its meaning and dilute its radical emancipatory potential. To preserve that potential, the theorist must wrest the proper concept from its corruptions and return it to its specificity. But, as Rancière has argued, this discourse of the proper is strictly antipolitical because it fixes the definition of the concept whose value is dependent on the possibility that its meaning can be contested.[2]

But doesn't this criticism of political philosophy also rely on a distinction between politics proper and its opposite? Indeed, Rancière has insisted on the rarity of politics defined against what he calls "the police," which is a name for any count without supplement or lack, a partition of the sensible. To make the case that politics always opposes the police logic that says what politics is and politics is not, he too must define politics and differentiate it from what it is not, from the uses of the concept that define politics in ways that erase its very possibility. Similarly, he must differentiate his conception of the aesthetic regime of art from the stultifying conceptions of modernism and postmodernism that dominate theories of art and aesthetics. Thus, the charge can be, and has been, raised that Rancière does not escape the logic he criticizes, as he must define the terms that he claims have no fixed definitions.

Rancière has responded to this criticism in an essay called "The Use of Distinctions." Distinctions, he explains, are necessary for undoing distinctions. As he states, "I put forward these distinctions as replacements for other distinctions, and against them. They effectuate less another type of classification than a declassification. Which is to say . . . they put into question the received distribution of the relations between the distinct and the indistinct, the pure and the mixed, ordinary and exceptional, the same and the other."[3]

This same process of drawing distinctions between terms to demonstrate their interdependency can be seen in the relation between aesthetics and politics in Rancière's work. According to Rancière, art has its own politics and politics has its own aesthetics, which is to say that questions of aesthetics and politics are always intertwined, since both are ways of reframing the partition of the sensible. He thereby undermines the reductive assumptions that, for example, aestheticizing politics leads directly to fascism or universal commodification; or, on the other hand, that art might be secured as a domain that should be analyzed separate from politics. But to preserve the entwinement of art and politics he must also separate them; he must also say that art is not politics and politics is not art.

What is the discourse of Rancière's own writing through which this double operation can be understood? Or, rather, to return to our central question: If, as Rancière has put it, art has its own politics and politics has its own aesthetics then how can we think of the aesthetics and politics of the discourse that asserts these claims?

We can start by giving it a name, and in my title I called it "theory"—with some hesitation, admittedly, but I have decided to embrace it and see where it takes me. "Theory" is the word used most frequently in North America as a shorthand for what it is that Rancière, and the various names he is most closely associated with, do. To say, for example, that I am writing a chapter on Jacques Rancière is to suggest to someone that I work on "theory." I take it that readers of this essay will have an idea of what I mean and the kind of baggage that accompanies this signifier in its singular generic form.[4]

Theory here means something both specific and vague—specific in the sense that it is associated with specific proper names and a specific history within the academy, and vague in the sense that there is no unified concept of theory that encompasses the practice of those specific names or the ways they have been used. If I sound vague myself, I intend to leave it that way. I realize that it is customary at this point to give you a more precise history of how the concept of theory has morphed into the one I am referring to however indirectly. Better yet, I might give you the various meanings in the *Oxford English Dictionary* or take the time to rehearse the etymology of the word.

I do not want to repeat here the familiar and often tiresome debates about "theory" in the American humanities, or to insist that Rancière be understood as a theorist and not, as he has claimed, a philosopher. Nonetheless, for the sake of argument I would like to take seriously, for the moment at least, this idea of "theory" in what may seem to be its most debased or discredited form—that is, as a way of writing or speaking about things such as science, art, politics, or philosophy about which one knows nothing. This characterization may be familiar from some newspaper think piece or magazine article, in which a public intellectual—nonacademic and happily so, but grounding his claims in the authority of good modest disciplinary academics working as native informants—reveals his or her own skills in the arts of critical unveiling or the hermeneutics of suspicion to tell us that this fancy academic-speak, this jargon we may be intimidated by, in fact means nothing at all. Theory, it is well-known, is stupidity masquerading as intelligence, resentment and elitism masquerading as radical politics.

The broad dismissal of this reductive concept of theory contains two charges that I take to be central: On the one hand, theory is considered a discourse of mastery. Certain proper names and accepted jargon signal an in-the-know discourse with no ramifications outside its own hermetic language games. On the other, theory is criticized for not knowing its place, for mixing disciplines, for being without a proper object, for not being empirically verifiable, and so on. It is criticized for being too academic and not academic enough, being too reliant on a foundation and having no foundation.

In the first charge, that theory is a discourse of mastery, we might recognize a critique Rancière might be sympathetic to in that it resonates with his own critique of his former intellectual master, Louis Althusser. Rancière's critique of Althusser is worth dwelling on because Althusser has been enormously influential in defining a certain conception of theory that has shaped the analysis of the politics of art and literature in Anglo-American academia.

For Rancière, Althusser's "lesson," the real message behind the pedagogy he practiced, was hierarchical and antiegalitarian. The problem, as Rancière saw it, was the positing of a subjectless science not reducible to ideology. According to Althusser, the production of the Marxist theorist is not outside ideology; rather, it is the only standpoint from which to properly say, "I am in ideology." But in Rancière's reading, Althusser, by drawing a distinction between good and bad forms of knowing, in effect repeats the discourse on alienation that he had previously dismissed as irredeemably humanist. The good Marxist no longer says, "I am outside ideology but the masses are not." Rather, he says, "We are all in ideology. The difference is I know it, but the masses (and the bad Marxists) do not." Knowledge as production is valorized and placed in opposition to understanding as sight.[5]

Significantly, this opposition of knowledge of the system versus sight is seen again in Althusser's conception of art. In Althusser's text published as "A Letter on Art," he states that "the real difference between art and science lies *in the specific form* in which they give us the same object in quite different ways: art in the form of 'seeing' and 'perceiving' or 'feeling', science in the form of *knowledge* (in the strict sense, by concepts)."[6] He continues, "Art makes us 'see' 'conclusions without premises,' whereas knowledge makes us penetrate into the mechanism which produces the 'conclusions' out of the 'premises.' "[7] Art, in other words, is not capable of theory.

For Rancière, the importance of the aesthetic regime of art is that it undoes this distinction between sight and knowledge. Literature, according to Rancière, is a letter without an addressee; its egalitarian basis means that there is no ground that can guarantee its transmissibility—a ground which is necessary for the teachings of Marxist science. At stake, then, is the relation between politics, science, and art—a relation that, we might say, remained unthought in Althusser's own theory of reading.

Rancière's disagreement with Althusser about science was necessarily a disagreement about aesthetics. By separating his own practice from aesthetics and reserving it for science, Althusser helped define a conception of theory as mastery that, as we shall see, led to an impoverished conception of art and politics. Theory, in the sense that Rancière has developed it, is "a discourse that declassifies discourses," and the discourse that declassifies discourses goes by another name in Rancière: literature or aesthetics. Rancière's work has followed the consequences of recognizing the necessity of thinking theory as a matter of aesthetics. As he states explicitly, "I think that a theoretical discourse is always simultaneously an aesthetic form, a sensible reconfiguration of the facts it is arguing about. Claiming that any theoretical statement has a poetic nature is equivalent to breaking down the borders and hierarchies between levels of discourses."[8]

Yet he will also say, "Literature works, as politics does, in order to undo the consensual forms of gathering and counting. But it does it in a different way."[9] The hierarchies may not return, but the borders do, even if they have shifted. Having exposed the police logic of Althusserian symptomatic reading, which allowed one to determine the hidden cause from the surface effect, Rancière has nonetheless developed his own kind of symptomatic reading that seeks to think constitutive absences or, in his terms, the "part of those who have no part."[10] But now it identifies this practice not with production of knowledge or science but with a fiction, theater, montage, or mise-en-scène which allows him to claim that he seeks no longer primary causes but ways of reframing by unhinging the very logic of cause and effect.[11]

Rancière argues that symptomatic reading was possible only through a poetic revolution in which literature and art of the nineteenth century overthrew the hierarchies of the representational norms that had defined the legibility of artistic practices in favor of discovering a world of mute speech, either incorporeal, or in the form of hieroglyphs, written on the body of material things. According to Rancière, the Marxist theory of fetishism and Freudian theory of the symptom inherited this revolutionary aesthetic logic. Here we can see how a rethinking of the relation between aesthetics, politics, and theory are central to this concept of theory.[12]

This brings us to the second charge against theory: that it does not know its place, that it has no object. Rancière's work might be used to suggest that we turn this charge around and see it as a feature rather than a bug. This caricature of theory that sees it as the enemy of academic respectability might recast theory as a useful site of contestation in which we would then separate theory from the antitheoretical discourse of mastery and consensus. Theory's foundationless foundation can be understood as the site of its potential. Theory is necessarily political because, like art or literature, it is a way of framing a polemical common world. As Rancière explains about his own work, writing about himself in the third person, "The works of Rancière are not 'theories of,' they are 'interventions on.' They are polemical interventions."[13]

In the remainder of this essay, I will show how Rancière's conception of theory helps us rethink how we analyze the politics of art. In challenging Althusser's conception of theory, he was also challenging one of the dominant practices of theoretical inquiry within literature, film, and cultural studies. Because it came out of an Althusserian conception of ideology critique, theory has always knotted together aesthetics and politics in a particular fashion. We could put it this way: theory shows how aesthetics are political.

I will take my example from the discipline I know best: film theory. In their influential statement of purpose "Cinema/Ideology/Criticism," first published in *Cahiers du cinéma* in 1969, Jean-Louis Comolli and Jean Narboni claim, "Every film is political."[14] No film is outside politics because each film necessarily positions itself in relation to dominant ideology, which it can either conform to or disrupt. Correspondingly, theory can show how aesthetics is political in one of two ways: If a film is political because it is ideological (which is to say, in some sense, not political at all), then theory reveals its ideological subservience. If a film is political because it disrupts ideology, then it does what theory also does, which would seem to make theory's role unnecessary.

Among the eight possible relations that films can have to ideology, the authors of "Cinema/Criticism/Ideology" regard two of the categories as the "essential" ones—political films that disrupt the dominant mode either through both signifier and signified or just at the level of the signifier. Comolli and Narboni write, "For *Cahiers* these films (b and c) constitute the essential in the cinema, and should be the chief subject of the magazine."[15] These are the films that the journal says it will focus on, but among the eight categories, the explanations of the essential ones are, with category (g) the one documentary category they endorse, the briefest in the taxonomy. In other words, there is not much to say about the films they have agreed to focus on, because those films already do what theory does. Or, rather, if there is a role for theory in relation to the essential films, it was never clear what it would be. The division of labor between the work that film did when it showed up its own work—which involved a knowledge effect, and what theory did to show you how it did it—remained ambiguous. It is no wonder that so few films were discussed in the pages of *Cahiers* over the following decade.

What scientific criticism adds to this disruption that the films already show is necessarily ambiguous when the idea of a Brechtian cinema filtered through Althusserian-Lacanian language was thought to provide a conceptual model for film to pass from recognition to knowledge or the Imaginary to the Symbolic. Tellingly, this formula for political modernism contradicted Althusser's distinction between science and art, which could be ignored, since Althusser wrote so little about art.

The difficulty of thinking the interrelation and separation of politics, art, and theory is perhaps most transparently illustrated in an unfinished piece, "On Brecht and Marx," that Althusser wrote in 1968. In this piece, he begins by drawing an analogy between Brecht and Marx. This analogy is based on the claim that they both generate within their respective domains, theater and philosophy, a new kind of practice based on a knowledge of the repression of politics that founds both their practices.[16] Politics is the ground of both practices, but it speaks only when its silence is revealed. To demystify theater does not mean that theater can become politics. It can only reveal how politics is its absent cause through its own means.[17] Althusser reaches the conclusion that the specificity of theater, its difference from philosophy, politics, science, and life is that it shows and entertains but showing and entertaining are the very things that disguise theater's difference from philosophy, politics, science, and life. To show what theater is, we have to betray what it is, but it must remain theater and only theater in the process without generating a new mystification. Althusser concludes by asking rhetorically, how is it that theater can still provide entertainment through mere showing while also thwarting this logic at the same time? No answer was forthcoming and the piece remained unfinished.

This paradoxical logic can be found smoothed over using Althusser's Lacan-inspired definition of ideology throughout 1970s film theory. Christian Metz provides us with the formula: The role of film theory, according to Metz, is "to disengage the cinema-object from the imaginary and win it for the symbolic."[18] Peter Wollen linked this logic explicitly back to Brecht to advocate for a materialist cinema that countered ideology. According to Wollen, "Brecht wanted to find a concept of 'representation' which would account for a passage from perception/recognition to knowledge/understanding, from the imaginary to the symbolic."[19] Whether conceived of as an immanent break within the artwork itself or through the intervention of theory, the goal is a passage or break out of appearance or sensory experience and into knowledge. In film, like theater, distance is perceived as immediacy, but once we become aware of the distance through distancing we are restored to real immediacy in the form of knowledge.

But if the artwork effectively accomplished the knowledge-effect, why did we need theory to point it out? One solution for "theory" that proved agreeable to many American academics was to rely on "bad objects," because then theory could perform its criticism and provide the politics.

Some may claim that this era of film theory is over because it has been discredited, but it is instructive to briefly compare one example of the logic that has sought to discredit it. David Bordwell has been one of the most influential advocates in American film studies of saving film theory from itself by advancing piecemeal theories that serve to address specific answerable questions. According to Bordwell, theories underdetermine politics.[20] On the other hand, he implies that politics overdetermine certain forms of film interpretations that get called film theories but really are no theories at all.[21] The idea that theory underdetermines politics presupposes a certain conception of theory and a certain conception of politics and a relation between the two. Since Bordwell means by "politics" such matters as his position on gun control or abortion, and means by "theories" generalizations about the principles by which films achieve specifiable effects, he is no doubt correct. But this is an extremely narrow conception of what makes theory political. Meanwhile, to qualify as genuine theory in Bordwell's terms, and not mere interpretation, means never to introduce supplement or lack into the distribution of the sensible. It corresponds precisely to Rancière's conception of "the police," according to which both aesthetics and politics should be eliminated from theory.

Whereas Althusserian/Brechtian film theory wishes to show up the film work, Bordwell wishes just to show how films work. And whereas the former takes politics as the motor for theory, its absent cause, and the latter sees it as noise, they both share the desire to purge theories of their aesthetic dimension in Rancière's sense—the "as if" that makes theory a contingent operation that frames a polemical world.

Theory, understood not as having an object but rather as the operation of intervening in a constellation of meanings under contestation, may then be a useful concept after all. To undo definitions, Rancière must continually reassert them and risk repeating the same operation he is critiquing. He has not solved the problem of untying the knot of aesthetics, politics, and theory, but he has not tried to, because the knot is not of his own devising. His efforts at clarification do not end the confusion but attempt to make use of the potential it affords—to frame both art and politics not as objects of theoretical knowledge, but as war zones in which the stakes are resources for emancipation.

Notes

1. See, for example, Jacques Rancière, "Afterword: The Method of Equality. An Answer to Some Questions," in *Jacques Rancière: History, Politics, Aesthetics*, ed. Gabriel Rockhill and Philip Watts (Durham, N.C.: Duke University Press, 2009), 281. In this essay, Rancière aligns his own "method of equality" with "philosophy." As he puts it, "History, sociology, political science, literary theory, art history, and so on contend that they have their objects and the methods of fitting them. Philosophy instead would say: your objects belong to everybody; your methods belong to anybody."

2. See his critique of political philosophy in *Disagreement*: Jacques Rancière, *Disagreement: Politics and Philosophy*, trans. Julie Rose (Minneapolis: University of Minnesota Press, 1998).

3. Jacques Rancière, *Dissensus: On Politics and Aesthetics*, ed. and trans. Steven Corcoran (London: Continuum, 2010), 205.

4. In case examples are needed, I am referring to the use of the word "theory" in the title of books such as *Theory's Empire: An Anthology of Dissent*, ed. Daphne Patai and Wilfrido Corral (New York: Columbia University Press, 2005); Terry Eagleton, *After Theory* (New York: Basic Books, 2004); and Francois Cusset, *French Theory*, trans. Jeff Fort (Minneapolis: University of Minnesota Press, 2008).

5. See Jacques Rancière, "On the Theory of Ideology—Althusser's Politics," in *Radical Philosophy Reader*, ed. Richard Osborne and Roy Edgley (London: Verso, 1985), 101–92.

6. Louis Althusser, "A Letter on Art," in *Lenin and Philosophy and Other Essays*, trans. Ben Brewster (London: Monthly Review Press, 1971), 223.

7. Althusser, "A Letter on Art," 224.

8. Jacques Rancière, *The Politics of Aesthetics* (London: Bloomsbury, 2005), 61.

9. Rancière, "Afterword: The Method of Equality," 284.

10. Rancière, *Disagreement*, 123.

11. Peter Hallward has written with some skepticism about we he sees as the centrality of the metaphor of theater in Rancière's conception of politics We should note first that it is a mistake to think that Rancière accords a privileged place to theater in particular: the metaphor of "staging" is only one of the metaphors from various artistic realms that Rancière uses to think the aesthetics of politics. Second, these metaphors are equally central to Rancière's aesthetics of theory or poetics of knowledge. See Peter Hallward, "Staging Equality: On Rancière's Theatrocracy," *New Left Review* 37 (January/February 2006): 109–29.

12. Rancière, *The Politics of Aesthetics*, 30.

13. Jacques Rancière, "A Few Remarks on the Method of Jacques Rancière," *Parallax* 15, no. 3 (2009): 115.

14. Jean-Louis Comolli and Jean Narboni, "Cinema/Ideology/Criticism," trans. Susan Bennett in *Film Theory and Criticism*, 7th ed., ed. Leo Braudy and Marshall Cohen (New York: Oxford University Press, 2009), 688.

15. Comolli and Narboni, "Cinema/Ideology/Criticism," 691.

16. Louis Althusser, "On Brecht and Marx," in *Louis Althusser*, ed. Warren Montag (New York: Palgrave, 2003), 141.

17. Althusser, "On Brecht and Marx," 142.

18. Christian Metz, *The Imaginary Signifier: Psychoanalysis and the Cinema*, trans. Celia Britton, Annwyl Williams, Ben Brewster, and Alfred Guzzetti (Bloomington: Indiana University Press, 1982), 3.

19. Peter Wollen, "'Ontology' and 'Materialism' in Film," *Screen* 17, no. 1 (1976): 18–19.

20. David Bordwell, "Slavoj Žižek: Say Anything," accessed April 16, 2018, http://www.davidbordwell.net/essays/zizek.php.

21. See David Bordwell, "Film Interpretation Revisited," *Film Criticism* 17, nos. 2 and 3 (Winter/Spring 1993): 19.

Who's the Subject of Politics? Language in Jacques Rancière

Giuseppina Mecchia

Jacques Rancière's most enduring contribution to the contemporary debate about the nature and possibility of political action is certainly his unwavering affirmation that the conditions for it are always necessarily in place. There is no postmodern irony or cynicism in Rancière: as long as language as human faculty exists and governmental powers keep wronging those they claim to represent, the people will always have both the linguistic ability and the historical pretext to rise up and demonstrate their fundamental equality with their rulers, forcing them to acknowledge their political agency and give in to their demands. At the beginning of the 1990s, after the wholesale liquidation of communist models of sociopolitical organization, this message was a refreshing and much needed reminder of the extant viability of oppositional politics on an apparently sedated global scene. The triumph of the Western capitalist model of social organization, with the attached "policing" systems of government that enable its smooth functioning, was still insufficient to declare that the age of political struggle had ended, precisely because of the inevitability of *wrong*-doing on the part of any bureaucratic state apparatus. Rancière's arguments still appear, in this respect, unassailable; however, in the pages that follow, I will try to underscore how much is left unsaid—or, rather, willingly excluded—in Rancière's version of political struggle, as a consequence of both his dependency on a recurring historical archive and his mainly polemical, "contrarian" mode of argumentation.

In Rancière's works, what is omitted has to be read against the grain of what is included: I will argue that the most compelling aspects of Rancière's political philosophy need to be contrasted with a number of notions present in the thought of his contemporaries, which act as a more or less explicit foil for the building of his own conceptual toolbox. Such a contrast might redirect our allegiance to Rancière's theses in a more critical, but also more finely tuned understanding. Toward this end, in the final section of this essay I enlist the theoretical help of other contemporary thinkers, such as the Italian philosopher and media-activist Franco "Bifo" Berardi and the Swiss economist Christian Marazzi, who also refer us to earlier thinkers, from Marx to Deleuze and Guattari.

As an illustration of my thesis I start with one of Rancière's readings of Deleuze as an example of his combative philosophical style and of the necessity to bridge the distance that separates Rancière's understanding of politics—and of the political character of aesthetic activity—and the views expressed by other critics of contemporary capitalist democracies interested in exploring the space that might still be available for egalitarian, freeing political interventions. While Rancière's polemical style can impose significant torsions to the theses of "rival" thinkers, thereby risking alienating some readers, it is by juxtaposing them with his own discourse that we can understand what is at stake, today, when a vision of politics makes its way into the public, although apparently elitist, debate surrounding the practice of political philosophy.

Misreading as a Polemical Tactic

Gilles Deleuze famously said in an uncharacteristically raunchy comment that if he had written so many monographs on previous philosophers, some of whom seemed quite distant from his own theoretical orientation—most notably Kant, of course, but also Leibniz—he had done so in the spirit of "buggery":[1] he hoped that this sort of intercourse, penetrating these venerable fellows "from behind," would generate an unpredictable, even monstrous conceptual offspring. It might thus appear rather incongruous that we should spend some time in trying to expose the distortions created by Rancière's reading of Deleuze. Shouldn't Rancière have the right to treat Deleuze as he treated others in order to collect a similar conceptual prize? But things are not so simple.

On the one hand, we notice that Rancière's attack on his own contemporary's philosophical positions goes much deeper than any Deleuzian readings of philosophical classics. As Gabriel Rockhill, one of Rancière's translators and earliest commentators, wrote in a rather understated manner, Rancière "is not known for his lack of controversial spirit."[2] On the other hand, there is a specific meaning in focusing on Deleuze, and more precisely on Deleuzian aesthetics in the context of an argument underscoring the difference between Rancière's own and other approaches to building a progressive theory of politics. To make my own strategy clear, I will mostly address two tactical misreadings of the Deleuzian corpus and conceptual apparatus.

The first—and the most obviously symptomatic—is that Rancière never acknowledges the double signature of some of the texts that he comments on: for instance, in "The Monument and Its Confidences; or Deleuze and Art's Capacity of 'Resistance,' "[3] when critiquing the political-aesthetic theses in *What Is Philosophy?* and *Kafka: Toward a Minor Literature,* Rancière makes no mention of Félix Guattari as the coauthor of these texts. What might seem a simple oversight is in fact the sign of a much deeper unavailability, on the part of Rancière, to engage with these texts in a way that would surpass the will to undermine the political credentials of their presumed single author. This is a befuddling move that nonetheless Rancière shares with other thinkers and critics, all equally intent at dismissing "Deleuze's" relevance for political philosophy—most notably Alain Badiou and his followers—although their approach and philosophical presuppositions are otherwise quite different.[4] Dismissing the importance of the encounter with Guattari automatically removes the most "militant" guarantor of the duo's political credentials: as it has been pinpointed several times, "Deleuze's statement that between the two of them 'there is a politics, micro-politics,' " is taken to apply above all to Guattari. As a longtime "political activist and a practicing analyst,"[5] the younger coauthor could not be dismissed as a good example of political engagement as easily as Deleuze, who was rarely involved in militant forms of collective organization. Often gravely ill, Deleuze mostly used his seminars as a public forum, refusing to be blackmailed into more organized forms of militancy even in the late 1960s and early 1970s at Vincennes, where he coexisted for a certain time not only with Badiou but with Rancière himself.[6] The refusal to recognize the philosophical authorship of the duo Deleuze and Guattari even before engaging with the content of the texts studied is then far more symptomatic than it might appear, since it excludes precisely the texts where the political dimension of their philosophy is more openly developed.

Second, and perhaps more interestingly from a conceptual point of view, Rancière critiques Deleuze's (and Guattari's) understanding of the political subject because, according to him, it remains indistinguishable from the category of the "living" being, missing the specificity of the political act in itself. But why is it that one of Rancière's most pointed attacks on Deleuze's politics comes obliquely, in an essay dealing mostly with issues of aesthetics? Rancière reminds us that for Deleuze, the work of art expresses a "resistance" of sorts, because while revolutions are subject to history's travails and defeats, the sensorial vibrations emitted by the physical "blocks" of aesthetic creations find a durable life in the public that they create for themselves not only in the present, but also in the future of artistic reception. Rancière finds this position highly questionable, because for him, the word "resistance" is irrevocably tied to a completely different form of subjectivation, which has nothing to do with physical bodies and blocks of sounds, paint, or images. For him, the very use of the word "resistance" in the domain of art implies that Deleuze thinks that art is political *by itself*, thereby making an implicit leap "from the artistic torsion of sensations to the struggle of men."[7]

Rancière's critique, at this point, continues on two separate levels: on the one hand, Deleuze seems to attribute to art in general the main aspects of what Rancière considers to be specific only to "the modern regime of art, which [he has] proposed to call the 'aesthetic regime of art.'"[8] Deleuze is then said to repeat and generalize what Rancière considers to be a time-specific, post-Kantian, Romantic gesture toward an aesthetic of the sublime. On the other hand, even if we might want to admit that art can give shape and establish a living testimony of the confrontation with the chaotic forces of nature, it would be wrong, according to Rancière, to attribute a political value—and therefore use the word "resistance" to describe it—to this kind of experience. There is no true revolution to be achieved by the works or the philosophers tied to the "aesthetic" regime of art, since their public, the "people" that they create is not actualized in a specifically political, dissensual gesture. As Rancière understands it, for Deleuze "art . . . is the transcription of an experience of the heteronomy of Life with respect to the human," which per se is rather ill-suited to create or rein in "the power of a human collective in struggle."[9]

If Deleuze had ever said or written that the resistance of art to the forces of the universe was a political practice, Rancière's critique might be justified. And it is true that for Deleuze, the function of art is much closer to the ethical dimension of philosophical inquiry, that is, to the post-Nietzschean question of *how to live* in a chaotic world. But Deleuze never said that the ethical coincides with the political, nor that the artist and her public are the equivalent of the political militant. So if Rancière willingly misses the mark in his critique of Deleuze, since he has to twist Deleuze's use of words and displace their context of appearance in order to express his theoretical distance with his positions, then we are left with the question of *why* that needs to happen, and why he starts from the aesthetic when presenting a language-based notion of political agency. I believe that the single meaning that Rancière wants to attribute to the word "resistance" is in fact somehow related to the larger issue of how words function in his understanding of both politics and language.

The Aesthetic Detour

To start addressing this question, we need to consider very closely the negative connotations that Rancière attributes to both the concept of "life," of living being, and consequently to the domain of the ethical in establishing his vision not only of politics, but *also* of the *aesthetic* experience. For Rancière, the subject is not "the living," it is not a body, but a linguistic subject, according to a definition of language very close to Plato's concept of logos, that is, as intellectual faculty and process. In this respect, he is part of a certain reception of Saussure, Mallarmé, and Lacan that he shares with other post-Althusserian thinkers, and most notably, once again, Alain Badiou. In fact, several of Rancière's readers have recently noticed how difficult it is for Rancière to create an aesthetics with such a restricted understanding of the subject, since all that is related to the physicality of such a subject is willingly excluded from his definitions of both the political and the artistic act.

It could even be argued that in Rancière's thought, art and aesthetics end up falling mainly in the domain of *signification,* and in more than one way: according to a neohistoricist recognition of different "artistic regimes," the work of art makes visible and becomes the sign of a larger sociohistorical "partition of the sensible" that is equally intelligible in a certain political partitioning of public life. In Rancière's chronology, the French Revolution causes a deep break in such arrangements and coincides with the advent of a new aesthetic regime in continental Europe—while in England the beginning of a similar phenomenon had already occurred, to a certain extent, after Cromwell's regicide in 1649 and its aftermath. This happens because the democratic principles of the Revolution are signified in a breakdown of the hierarchy of artistic subjects, in such a way that now "there are no longer appropriate subjects for art . . . but a general availability of all subjects for any artistic form whatsoever."[10] Such a change from the Classical modes of representation ushers in not only the realistic forms, such as the novel or bourgeois drama, but also the modernist turn toward abstraction, since now, in both cases, there is the belief in the "absolute power of making on the part of the artwork, pertaining to its own law of production and self-demonstration."[11] In other words, we now have a "democratic" art, ready to be seized on by the workers-poets of the mid-nineteenth century in a political affirmation of their subjective worth.

Art, therefore, first and foremost signifies its politics, both in the sense of the context in which it can appear, and in what is expressed by the new subjects that come to life thanks to their artistic involvement. What these subjects really say is not only—or even mainly—what appears in their canvas or in their verses, but an intellectual message of equality. Far from being a purely aesthetic phenomenon, or even an ethical issue—how to be happier, how to keep sane—this highly intellectual version of the artistic experience allows Rancière to formulate a critique of a vast array of postmodern aesthetic and political positions.

In this regard, Rancière's negative pantheon houses not only Deleuze's ethical stoicism, and implicitly Guattari's therapeutic political aesthetics, but also, for instance, Baudrillard's apocalyptic assessment of the circulation of both images and words as simulacra in today's mediatic world, precluding all intellectual and political exchange based on intellectual contents. If the image—cinematic, pictorial, literary—is apprehended for the most part through language as inalienable faculty, such a tragic assessment of today's political landscape becomes senseless. The nexus between perception and signification is absolute in Rancière. In a delayed, implicit torsion of Deleuze's cinematic categories, for instance, Rancière talks about "image-sentences" and "image-metaphors,"[12] which are attached to "operations: relations between whole and parts; between a visibility and a power of signification."[13] Even Rancière's later critique of Badiou's Platonism, which affirms the supremacy of the Idea in modernist art, is predicated on the fact that "the specificity of the arts resides in their respective languages."[14] What other critics would have called conventions or techniques, are called "languages" by Rancière, precisely because he finds in the aesthetic domain first and foremost a place where a certain kind of intellectual process and political signification can occur.

This is the basis for a critique of Rancière's understanding of art that has been recently proposed by Joseph Tanke, who affirms that the flattening of the aesthetic impulse on the plane of public affirmation is not without its dangers. When considering the character of Julien Sorel, the hardworking, normally quite self-possessed protagonist of Stendhal's *The Red and the Black*, whose ability for aesthetic feeling allows him—among other things—to find lovers much above his own station, Rancière only sees him as the perfect example of the new, "aesthetic" regime of art, which allows anyone to participate in the aesthetic experience. But Tanke reminds us that Sorel accomplishes this feat only by risking—and eventually losing—his own life, since the experience of the sublime can in fact be a heterogeneous, irrational moment of self-annihilation: "In these scenes that outstrip the logic of the narrative, we experience the violence that defines the aesthetic in its heterogeneity . . . which has been forcefully withdrawn from the cognitive and the moral."[15] Rancière's quite explicit Kantian heritage therefore appears strangely truncated, a point that Tanke makes elsewhere with regard to the imaginative faculty.[16]

And in fact, we can see quite clearly that in his eagerness to escape what he considers a trend toward a postmodern nihilistic quietism in the face of oppression and inequality, Rancière constructs what is still conceived as an experiential subject, though inexplicably deprived not only of the faculty of imagination but also, and perhaps most importantly, of perceptions, sensations, and emotions. The advantages of such a radical reduction of the notion of subjectivity are evident: if we, as aesthetic and political subjects, can always be conceived as relatively unaffected by external and internal forces that we might not be immediately able to name and "think through" in linguistic terms, then there is no obstacle to what we can do, and both politics and aesthetics are always available to us. But is this really the case? And how can this availability make itself present?

On the Present/ce of Democratic Politics

If we want to transition from the theoretical availability to the practical appearance of both politics and aesthetics, we need to address how *time* functions in Rancière's philosophy. It is evident that his philosophical positions are so appealing to us today because there is an expectant, joyful side to his understanding of the recurrent, insuppressible temporality of political intervention. Since the foundation of democratic politics, that is, the political admission of the equality among linguistic subjects, is always in place, politics itself will keep occurring, whether we expect it or not. Faced with the inevitable "wrongs" that various policing powers inflict on them, the people are sure to rise in a truly political act of contestation. This is perhaps the most persuasive and certainly the most heartening of Rancière's arguments: from the ruins of twentieth-century political projectuality and historical teleology, Rancière has extracted the conviction that the time for politics cannot be predicted, and even less announced. Against the Marxist necessity of subordinating revolutionary projects to the calculation of the socioeconomical forces involved in a certain state of affairs, Rancière affirms that equality is always an operative principle for a people constituting itself in its absolute affirmation.

In all of Rancière's political discourse, from *The Ignorant Schoolmaster* to *Disagreement* and *Hatred of Democracy*—first published, respectively, in 1981, 1995, and 2005—we find the rejection of the future as hypostasized time of realization, as the category guiding political action. If we start thinking about the "good" time for action, we become the slaves of a merciless tyrant, the servants of a revolutionary imperative just as binding as the industrialist's clock: "Time is not the leader of a liberal company, it is an old-fashioned monarch. It wants to be obeyed and loved before all else. It does not only want for us to follow its march. It wants us to go ahead of it, to give it in advance the gifts of our persons and our thoughts . . . The future, to be built cautiously, step by step, becomes the Future which calls us and does not wait."[17] If the revolutionary, or simply the insurgent, were to wait for the right time to act, there simply would be no politics, because the time is never right. Caught in the inevitable discrepancy between what is right in principle and what is "wrong" in terms of governmentality,[18] the time for politics is always now, in the supreme inactuality of the unexpected. In the nineteenth century, when the rise of Marxist socialism gave a "futurist" horizon even to immediate demands, the workers still wanted something right there and then, for instance "to separate clearly between leisure time and work time, and strictly limit the latter to the advantage of the former."[19] In other words, emancipation—and even communism—is always affirmed not on the basis of, but actually *against* the simple analysis of a certain "conjuncture" that necessarily subordinates the people's immediate struggles to its own historicist logics. This is why Rancière is radically committed to disenfranchise the political principle—the emancipatory affirmation of equality in the face of governmental "wrongs"—from its various usurpers: Marxist economicism, sociological necessity, historicist determinism, capitalist command, and so on.

This is, however, one of the main reasons why Rancière can and does fall prey to the double accusation of abstraction and arbitrariness: first of all, if the subject of politics is still now who it was for the Greeks, that is, the linguistic subject of equality, couldn't we say that such an abstract subject risks being voided of all substance in the quasi-tautological affirmation of its existence? In Rancière's understanding of the history of political philosophy, the Greek polis and the Roman republic described in *Disagreement* already contain the germs of all future appearances of political discord. It is governmentality—or "policing"—itself, as the ordering of bodies and feelings proper to a certain structure of power and rationality, that endlessly *re*-presents both its own appearance and the sporadic emergence of egalitarian movements. But such a steadfast adherence to one and only one political principle, ends up functioning as a reduction that never takes into consideration the changes in the bodies engaged in such egalitarian movements, intended as flesh-and-blood living beings, whose brains and organs are caught in the different technological dynamics of their time.

In fact, we can readily understand that language is not a simple, undisputed faculty that can be retrieved and used by anyone at any moment in any way. For instance, Rancière never truly addresses the fact that in Antiquity itself—where so many of his political "fables" take place—women and slaves were not part of the democratic polis, although they certainly possessed language, and therefore were not qualified to protest against the "wrongs" imposed on them by the so-called "democratic" ordering. Things, of course, only get more complicated when we deal with the technological and economic changes modifying the way we live in our body and use our brain—the latter being the indispensable physical support for the linguistic faculty, something that Rancière chooses to ignore in order to keep the space for politics open against all determinist odds.

In the way he avoids discussing these issues, it is clear that Rancière wants to reject both Althusser's Marxist scientism and the post-Heideggerian emphasis on the "enframing"[20] power of technology on our physical and mental existence, which is given a quasi-ontological status in later critiques of postmodernity, from Baudrillard to Lyotard to Agamben. Rancière addresses both tendencies in his works, throughout the thirty or so years going from *Althusser's Lesson*, originally published in 1974, to *Hatred of Democracy*, which appeared in 2005. In the former, Rancière denounces Althusser's misunderstanding of the student movement, rooted in what is considered a dogmatic adherence to Marx's economic and historicist understanding of class struggle. In the latter, Rancière denounces the apocalyptic posturing of some of his contemporaries who, coming from different perspectives, all seem to concur in an equally nihilistic move threatening to suppress the very possibility of political action on the part of a "people" that they reduce to the stupor of passive suffering. Here Rancière is taking issue with an unspecified—in this case, but elsewhere he makes it quite clear who they are—group of intellectuals, who "learnt their first lessons in Marxism" but now "find it harder to cope with the fact that Marxism disappointed their expectations," to the degree that "their enthusiasm has transformed into *ressentiment*."[21] From this disappointment and melancholic bitterness, the new "imprecators" formulate a critique not only of capitalist consumerism, or of the democratic State, but of the "democratic individual that is dragging humanity to its ruin."[22]

The targets of this critique are recognizable in the shortened references to some of their works: Giorgio Agamben, for instance, is probably first alluded to in the denunciation of "one" who says that "he is a communitarian and without community," for whom the consumerist citizen of Western democracies has lost "the sense of family values and the sense of their transgression, the sense of the sacred and that of sacrilege."[23] Without going into the detail of Rancière's further critique of Agamben—which for certain aspects might even be justified—one should stop at the repetition of a word that is otherwise quite absent from Rancière's own theoretical apparatus, and appears here only as part of a polemical rebuke. It is the word "sense," appearing twice in Rancière's parody of Agamben's discourse: the "*sense* of family values" and the "*sense* of the sacred" both belong to an understanding of the subject of the polis that Rancière constantly denounces as inherently conservative: possessing or not possessing the "sense," the feeling for something, is clearly something that occurs in the margins of linguistic elaboration.

Such "gut feelings" bring the subject of modern democracies—which for Rancière are not institutions, but political potentialities to be enacted by a "people" that constitutes itself in each political action—into the domain of affectivity and therefore illusion. This kind of reasoning is the mark of intellectuals who end up denouncing not only the current, oligarchic institutional democracies typical of Western capitalist societies, but the concept of democracy itself, which Rancière has revitalized by thrusting it out of historical realizations and redefining it as the appearance of any new political manifestation. Those who think the Nazi state is the logical *aboutissement* both of Enlightenment rationalism and of technological development—in a post-Heideggerian move that Rancière parodies in a quite scandalized tone—denounce the subject of contemporary democracies "as if" we were still living in camps, while for Rancière the word "democracy" cannot be rejected, because when it is inscribed in a society's self-definition, it inevitably reappears as a demand aimed at wresting "the monopoly of public life from oligarchic governments, and the omnipotence over lives from the power of wealth."[24]

I have already said that Rancière's contrarian affirmation, in the face of his contemporaries, of the continued possibility for political intervention and democratic subjective constitution remains his most welcome contribution to the contemporary debate in political philosophy. However, as Gabriel Rockhill pointed out some years ago, Rancière's very use of the term "democracy" is unusual enough to appear strategic in the context of the 1990s, when the historical collapse of the Eastern socialist states caused a wholesale disparaging of all forms of Marxist critique of contemporary capitalist societies. It is at this point in history that "this suspicious rhetorical strategy" can be construed as being tied to a general strategy of "conceptual transcendentalism consisting in detaching certain concepts from their concrete use and from specific political situations." Once again, we can compare Rancière's position with that of Alain Badiou, who also posits "formal ideas that overdetermine the social and political world." In fact, Rockhill goes as far as accusing Rancière of "exploiting the positive resonance of the name democracy in order to crown his own political reflection with a sacred halo."[25]

Although the suspicion of bad faith implicit in Rockhill's remark is completely out of place, it is still a fact that Rancière's political concepts seem to be particularly *timely*, since both Marxist critique and postmodern theories were taking quite a beating in the years that saw Rancière's philosophical stock rise both internationally and on the French scene. In that respect, a thought founded on the reconceptualization of quite unassailable principles in modern, republican Western societies, such as "equality," "democracy," and "the people" is not particularly bothersome to the powers in place, who also use the same terms in their everyday discourse, although admittedly with different meanings attached to them.

Rockhill also addresses the impossibility, in Rancière's thought, to assign with any certainty the place that real politics—that is, a movement of contestation that creates a new people—or simple policing or even postmodern eschatology play in any specific occurrence, since the assignation in the actual world of transcendental concepts "rests, in the last instance, with the master's whims."[26] As an example of the unchecked position occupied by Rancière, one episode that Rockhill finds particularly baffling is the negation of political status to the young rioters who took to the streets in France's major cities in 2005, protesting against the racist and ruthless treatment on the part of the French police of the French youth of Arab and African descent. For Rancière, politics is predicated as speech, and until a coherent speech, or program declaration, is heard from these groups, they cannot be given "true" political status.[27] It goes without saying that the French republican officials would have readily agreed with Rancière, since they were intent on labeling the young protesters "scum" (*racaille*)—in the words of Nicolas Sarkozy, who at that time was Minister of the Interior—that is, several degrees below what could be recognized as a legitimate political interlocutor. As I have said elsewhere, Rancière can spuriously attribute "speech" to certain political actors when he wants to take them as "real" examples of political—or democratic—subjectivation,[28] but here we see the opposite move, as he withdraws political subjectivity from protesters who presented themselves not primarily as rational subjects of speech, but as embodied racial and economic minorities reacting violently to their being "wronged" by the police—this time in both the literal and the extended sense of the word.

We see that Rockhill puts his finger on something that reminds us very closely of the critique articulated by Tanke of Rancière's philosophy of aesthetics: we have seen how, instead of presenting to us an actual, embodied account of the aesthetic experience that would talk to us about the sensorial and affective qualities of its works as well as of their creators and audiences, Rancière offers us a quite traditional version of the history of art in its relation to forms of social organization. Now it is also clear that this excessive reliance on linguistic rationality creates a strange political paradox, since the present of both art and politics, is a physical, temporal, sensorial, emotional, and perceptual embodiment, as some of the contemporaries that Rancière attacks in his writings have shown quite compellingly. How can we accept Rancière's reduction of the subject of politics—and therefore of history—as the subject of a language formally described as a function apparently completely independent from the physical supports that sustain it? And how does an acknowledgment of the material supports for the linguistic act modify the approach taken by Rancière in his account of the aesthetic-political experience?

Toward a Politics for the Living

We have already seen that like Badiou, Rancière has always manifested a strong opposition to philosophies of life, such as Deleuze's, since for him the simple fact of being alive is a passive datum, completely unrelated to the possibility of constituting oneself as a political actor. Linguistic equality is affirmed as an a priori, according to a descriptive, Saussurian approach both to language as human faculty and to individual languages in their differences. For Saussure, however, this was a practical limitation that left to psychology and sociology the essential task of studying the wider material context of "linguistics proper."[29] As I have said at the beginning of this reflection, one of the most surprising features of Rancière's philosophy, in fact, might be that, although it makes the linguistic function the primary guarantor of both politics and aesthetics, it presents *no theory of language itself*, be it from a philosophical, social, or physiological point of view.[30] Clearly, doing so would imply an involvement with many other disciplines—linguistics included—which Rancière considers not only superfluous, but actually damaging to the possibility of philosophically defining a truly political subjectivity. As a support for his arguments, Rancière sticks to a recurring archive of historic, literary, and cinematic documents, limiting his discussion of other disciplines to attacking those of his contemporaries who use them for shaping their philosophical outlook on politics and aesthetics.

In the last few pages of this essay, I would like to outline how, on the contrary, some of Rancière's contemporaries present a different view both of language and on political subjectivation, which I consider indispensable if we want to go beyond the reductions operated by Rancière with the aim of preserving the possibility for political action. While the goal is laudable in itself, Rancière's procedure might be not only unnecessary, but potentially counterproductive, because it does not allow for an analysis of any "present" of politics besides the presupposed availability of rational faculties. But if we think that the present of politics is the contemporary, we need to take a further step on the path of reflection.

It is true that *Homo sapiens*, as Paolo Virno said at the beginning of the 2000s, is characterized by "certain empirical, historically determined facts" that are "*icons* of an invariable human nature,"[31] but he was quick to add that founding a metahistory on such "facts"—and first and foremost language—risks becoming a "materialist version, rigorously atheistic, of the theological Revelation."[32] And in fact, the very principle of the equality of all human beings, and the privileging of the "wronged" as the downtrodden or "the salt of the earth," are transhistorical Christian values that are always valid in any and all historical circumstances. While I would not go as far as to consider Rancière's philosophy a secular version of Christian ethics, I think that one can extend to his aesthetic-political vision the criticism that Virno directs at Chomsky's attempt to found his critique of contemporary capitalism on the "inalterable biological patrimony of *Homo sapiens*."[33] As the Italian philosopher explains, this kind of position completely ignores the transformations in the capitalist mode of production in the last few decades, which have made language an essential factor in the creation of new commodities and structures of command: "Today, rather than being the springboard and the inspiration for a possible emancipation, our innate linguistic creativity manifests itself as a component of the despotic organization of work. In fact, it appears as a profitable economic resource. In so far as it achieves an immediate empirical consistency, the biological invariant is part of the problem, not the solution."[34]

Of course, for Rancière, language per se is not always an emancipatory instrument: it only becomes such in certain speech acts, when a new "people" stages its linguistic ability in the theater of a specific request for the redressing of a historical "wrong." However, Rancière's approach can give us absolutely no indication of *how, when*, or thanks to *whom* this scene will be played out. In fact, his historical archive functions mostly as a collection of vignettes, described simply in terms of visibility—they *ex-ist* as monumental reminders—and not of empirical conditions. In an age when language has been theorized quite compellingly as the ultimate resource for contemporary capitalist control, invoking it as the necessary and sufficient condition for the unpredictable emergence of the people can hardly be sufficient.

In fact, what we need most of all might very well be an analysis of *the order that denies equality* today. This is why we need to turn to the thinkers who have theorized the functioning of what has been called "cognitive capitalism." I am referring to sociologists such as Maurizio Lazzarato and economists such as Christian Marazzi, who add a very strong political dimension to their theoretical investigations.

In a seminal book originally published in 1994, but that has only recently been translated into English, Marazzi explains how information and communication techniques already began to pervade contemporary production since the 1950s, when Toyota started to implement "lean production" methods. This is when we stopped creating a certain amount of goods for a consumer who was going to be willed into existence by the commodity itself—according to the Fordist model that dominated industrial production in the first half of the twentieth century—starting instead to respond "in real time" to data collected among the public and transmitted through new, faster, language-based technologies. In this way, the people's language was transferred to the impersonal plane of productive imperatives, whose goal is "to organize the firm as a 'data bank' able to self-determine its actions by virtue of a smooth, fluid, 'interfaced' linguistic communication process."[35] This was, of course, only the very beginning of the capture of linguistic processes by the capitalist push for value creation, which has quickly spread from the reproduction of human language for mechanized processes of data collection and retrieval, to the production of copyrighted instruments of economic valorization of speech itself, such as Facebook, Instagram, or Twitter.

The social bonds created by language, the potentiality for the creation of a politicized "people" capable of bursting onto the scene of history, are often reduced to the actualization of the aims of the commodity itself, the social media which are at least equally apt at creating street protests and "flash mobs" enacting the tritest of cultural refrains. The principle of linguistic equality, in itself, cannot differentiate between inane instances of human materialization and other, truly political events, such as the 2011 commotions known as the Arab Spring and the international Occupy movements.

As a quick, and certainly insufficient example, we can take the event that ignited the first of these two political upheavals, Mohamed Bouazizi's self-immolation on the streets of Tunis on December 17, 2010. He said nothing, left no note, had no manifesto, and created no aesthetic monument for his action, just like the French youth in 2005 who set cars and buildings on fire in what Rancière could not bring himself to recognize as a "political" gesture. In the case of the Occupy movements, one of the most common reproaches directed at the activists from more conservative forces, even on the Left, was the fact of not being able to come up with a clear, common plan, articulated in plain language, that all could understand and agree on. In this respect, the physical act of occupying either a former public space now administered by a corporate entity—such as Zuccotti Park in New York City—and of intimidating, even if only for a few weeks, the traders of the nearby Stock Exchange—is indeed a moment of aesthetic, that is, sensorial and affective, "redistribution of the sensible." However, its legacy is inherent to the current articulations of capitalist command, and to a financial crisis unleashed by the hyper-symbolic processes of value creation typical of "bundling" packets that reduced physical properties and their supposed owners to tradable data.

In a way, of course, we can certainly say that "the people" of Zuccotti Park did replicate in many ways the third-century B.C.E. secession of the Roman plebs on the Aventine Hill, by removing their bodies from the production sites and battlefields of the republican oligarchy. We can also rejoice in the fact that, contrary to some dire predictions, politics is indeed always possible, just as Rancière maintains. On the other hand, such an analogy leaves us completely unable to assess and plan for the new, for the ways in which technological, economic, and social change continuously reassign the circulation of language among its subjects, human and not. As Franco "Bifo" Berardi has said, we are living in an age when "the question of sensibility becomes one with politics,"[36] reaffirming the vital bond between the aesthetic and the political.

It is now clear, I hope, why I believe that neither the aesthetic nor the political coming into being of a new subject can be reduced to the level of a more or less historicized linguistic actor. Today, not only language but also its conceptual function as well has been rethought and diverted according to the most recent productive imperatives: as Deleuze and Guattari said in *What Is Philosophy?*, our ability to think is never a datum, but a field of struggle that extends from the places of education to those of political organization. Against the risk of reducing the task of the critic to the reiteration of an archival patrimony of past struggles, we need to practice a continuous involvement with the present of our own contemporary and sensible condition. Only in this way can we hope to extract new thoughts and affects from the stronghold of capitalist production, and a quote from Deleuze and Guattari's last book will be a good way to conclude my argument: "If the concept's three ages are the encyclopedia, pedagogy and commercial professional training, only the second can safeguard us from falling from the heights of the first into the disaster of the third—an absolute disaster for thought, whatever its benefits may be, of course, from the viewpoint of universal capitalism."[37]

Notes

1. Gilles Deleuze and Claire Parnet, *Dialogues II* (New York: Columbia University Press, 2007), 26.

2. Gabriel Rockhill, "La démocratie dans l'histoire des cultures politiques," in Jerôme Game and Aliocha Wald Lasowski, *Jacques Rancière: Politique de l'esthétique,* 52–71 (Paris: Editions des Archives Contemporains, 2009), 55, my translation.

3. Jacques Rancière, *Dissensus: On Politics and Aesthetics,* ed. and trans. Steven Corcoran, 169–83 (London: Continuum, 2010).

4. In *Deleuze: The Clamor of Being* (Minneapolis: University of Minnesota Press, 1999) Badiou was mostly intent on demonstrating that Deleuze is an "aristocratic" thinker of *life* who nonetheless equates the event with a *death* of the subject. Politically, Deleuze's reliance on a Spinozian concept of the One as existing only in the world of multiplicities cannot oppose a solid enough response to "the powers of decomposition that our grandiose and decaying capitalism liberates on a large scale" (*Deleuze,* 98). Not a word is said of the works coauthored with Guattari, where capitalism is discussed at great length. For reasons of brevity, I cannot engage here with other contemporary thinkers who explicitly adopt a similar approach—such as Slavoj Žižek, who, like Rancière, does not mention Guattari at all as the author of their coauthored books, or Peter Hallward, who, like Badiou, tries to argue explicitly that the coauthored works don't belong to Deleuze's thought.

5. Eleanor Kaufman and Kevin Jon Heller, *Deleuze and Guattari: New Mappings in Politics, Philosophy and Culture* (Minneapolis: University of Minnesota Press, 1998), 7.

6. For details about the founding of the Department of Philosophy at Vincennes under the direction of Michel Foucault, and the split during the years 1969–71 between the Lacano-Maoists (Badiou, Miller, Milner) and the Hegelo-Spinozists (Deleuze, Châtelet), see chapter 19 of the excellent double biography by François Dosse, *GillesDeleuzeFélixGuattari, biographie croisée* (Paris: La Découverte, 2007).

7. Rancière, *Dissensus,* 171.

8. Rancière, *Dissensus,* 173.

9. Rancière, *Dissensus,* 181.

10. Jacques Rancière, *The Politics of Aesthetics* (London: Continuum, 2007), 118.

11. Rancière, *The Politics of Aesthetics,* 119.

12. In *Cinema 1* and *Cinema 2,* Deleuze had distinguished between the image-movement of early cinema, and the image-time of postwar movies. Gilles Deleuze, *Cinema 1: The Movement-Image,* trans. Hugh Tomlinson and Barbara Habberjam (Minneapolis: University of Minnesota Press, 1986; original French edition, 1983), and *Cinema 2: The Time-Image,* trans. Hugh Tomlinson and Robert Galeta (Minneapolis: University of Minnesota Press, 1989; original French edition, 1985).

13. Jacques Rancière, *The Future of the Image* (London: Verso, 2007), 3.

14. Jacques Rancière, *Aesthetics and Its Discontents* (Cambridge: Polity, 2009), 70.

15. Joseph J. Tanke, "Why Julien Sorel Had to Be Killed," in *Rancière Now: Current Perspectives on Jacques Rancière,* ed. Oliver Davis, 123–42 (Cambridge: Polity, 2013), 140.

16. See Joseph J. Tanke, *Jacques Rancière: An Introduction. Philosophy, Politics, Aesthetics* (London: Continuum, 2011), 152–62.

17. Jacques Rancière, *Chronicles of Consensual Times* (London: Continuum, 2011), 9–10.

18. I use this Foucauldian term as a somewhat tendentious translation of what Rancière calls *la police*, that is, the way a certain political power organizes the spaces of public life, such as education, religion, and the distribution of professional and social status.

19. Rancière, *Chronicles*, 10.

20. This is the accepted English translation for Heidegger's notion of *Gestell*, that is, the mode of presentation of Being to man through modern technology. Heidegger specifically addresses the issue of rationality and language, saying that language might lose its potential and become a simple instrument of information. See Martin Heidegger, *The Question concerning Technology and Other Essays* (New York: Fordham University Press, 1982), 26–28.

21. Jacques Rancière, *Hatred of Democracy* (London: Verso, 2007), 87.

22. Rancière, *Hatred of Democracy*, 89.

23. Rancière, *Hatred of Democracy*, 90.

24. Rancière, *Hatred of Democracy*, 96.

25. Rockhill, "La démocratie," 61

26. Rockhill, "La démocratie," 61.

27. Rockhill, "La démocratie," 62.

28. See Giuseppina Mecchia, "The Classics and Critical Theory in Contemporary France: The Case of Jacques Rancière", in *Jacques Rancière: History, Politics, Aesthetics*, ed. Gabriel Rockhill and Philip Watts (Durham, N.C.: Duke University Press, 2009), 67–81.

29. While its approach has been dismantled from many angles, from deconstruction to gender studies, it is still useful to go back to Saussure's *Course in General Linguistics* (New York: Columbia University Press, 1994), where the proper object of linguistics is painfully extracted in the introduction and the first five chapters. After having recognized at different junctures that there are many things in the fact of language that need to be considered from other disciplinary angles, we read that "the actual object we are concerned to study, then, is the social product stored in the brain, the language itself" (24).

30. One might want to think, for instance, about the thought of somebody who also thinks that language is the main guarantor of the political: Paolo Virno, who nonetheless roots his theories in a strong engagement with philosophers of language such as Wittgenstein or Peirce, as well as linguists like Austin or Frege. See Paolo Virno, *When the Word Becomes Flesh: Language and Human Nature* (Los Angeles: Semiotext[e], 2015).

31. Virno, *When the Word*, 210.

32. Virno, *When the Word*, 212.

33. Virno, *When the Word*, 219.

34. Virno, *When the Word*, 219–20.

35. Christian Marazzi, *Capital and Affects* (Los Angeles: Semiotext[e], 2011), 35.

36. Berardi "Bifo," Franco, *The Soul at Work: From Alienation to Autonomy* (Los Angeles: Semiotext[e], 2009), 132.

37. Gilles Deleuze and Félix Guattari, *What Is Philosophy?* (New York: Columbia University Press, 1994), 13.

Emergence: Dissensus in a Global Field of Instrumentality

Pheng Cheah

This essay concerns the pertinence of Jacques Rancière's account of aesthetic politics for understanding the quandary of the emergence of new subjects on the nonhegemonic postcolonial side of the international division of labor in contemporary globalization. The process of decolonization is often characterized as the emergence of a new collective subject—a people—from a prior condition of subjugation in which its members inhabited a world, that of colonialism, where they did not count. They were doomed to wretched obscurity because they did not have access to the light of the political public sphere. In Frantz Fanon's Hegelian-Marxist vocabulary, emergence is a process of self-actualization that necessarily entails the destruction of a prior world through a process of dialectical negation when that world is confronted by a new world in which a new subject becomes visible to its constituent members, who then recognize themselves as part of it. Commenting on the importance of oral narrative to the continuing process of the creation of this new world and the interpellation of a decolonizing people, Fanon notes that "every time the storyteller narrates a new episode, the public is treated to a real invocation. The existence of a new type of man is revealed to the public. The present is no longer turned inward but channeled in every direction. The storyteller once again gives free rein to his imagination, innovates, and turns creator."[1] In this primal scene of revolutionary national culture, the awakening national consciousness is the animating force and the highest end of cultural innovations. But at the same time, energies in the cultural sphere also anticipate and stimulate political struggle, because they express and give sensuous objective shape to the new national consciousness, thereby stimulating, strengthening, and cultivating it. Such cultural processes are literally the media through which the national consciousness recognizes itself as something new and changes its perception of the world, thereby enabling it to change the world. As Fanon puts it,

> Well before political or armed struggle, a careful observer could sense and feel in these arts the pulse of a fresh stimulus and the coming combat. Unusual forms of expression, original themes no longer invested with the power of invocation but the power to rally and mobilize with the approaching conflict in mind. Everything conspires to stimulate the colonized's sensibility, and to rule out and reject attitudes of inertia or defeat. By imparting new meaning and dynamism to artisanship, dance, music, literature, and the oral epic, the colonized subject restructures his own perception. The world no longer seems doomed. Conditions are ripe for the inevitable confrontation.[2]

We see here in embryonic form the theological figure of absolute sovereignty: this emergent subject is not only self-legislating. It is a self-causing being who creates itself in a self-recursive feedback loop of culture and organized struggle.

Fanon had cautioned against the blockage of this ongoing, potentially open-ended teleological process of a people's emergence by neocolonial forces. But it is more accurate to say that the figure of sovereignty underlying any quasi-Hegelian conceptualization of emergence is no longer viable in contemporary globalization. It is not only that postcolonial nations cannot be free because they exist in a neocolonial global political economic system hierarchically organized in terms of center and periphery. The primacy of the economic dimension of life, its thorough penetration of all other spheres through biopolitical technologies, and the accompanying spread of formal mathematical models based on calculative reason for the organization of every aspect of life has led to the formation of a field of means and ends that now extends throughout the mathematical totality we call the globe. All human populations now live according to such calculations. This global field, which I have elsewhere called a field of instrumentality, is more thoroughly pervasive than what the Frankfurt School diagnosed as instrumental reason because all the capacities of human beings, including the powers we take to be constitutive of humanity such as dignity, freedom, and even critical reason, are generated within it.[3] This is best illustrated by the concepts of social and human development. How then are we to reconceptualize emergence in postcolonial space, where the discourse of social and human development is especially prevalent?

Jacques Rancière's thought is a productive opening onto this question because it offers an account of emergence as the process of a becoming-visible of a contentless political subject—what he calls subjectification—generated by specific situations of inequality and exclusion. This essay is divided into three sections. In the first section, I reconstruct what I take to be Rancière's socio-anthropologistic account of emergence, focusing on its link to the aesthetic. The second section considers more carefully Rancière's reinscription of Kant's formulation of the "as if" in order to draw a contrast between his socio-anthropologistic account and a quasi-transcendental, deconstructive account of emergence. For Rancière, any distribution of the sensible takes as its fundamental premise a division of labor, which is thereby the general material condition of a social world of appearance. What are the consequences of emergence when a division of labor is transposed onto a global scale as an international division of labor? The final section of the paper looks at the problem of emergence in subalternity, a space that lies outside the international division of labor and argues for the need to supplement a socio-anthropologistic account of emergence with a deconstructive account and vice versa.

Emergence and the Dream of Another World

The tenor of emergence as a metaphor for the genesis of new political subjects is most likely the surprising transcending leaps by which life arises spontaneously from inanimate matter and rational consciousness from brute biological life. In a mechanistic world, the coming-into-being of something, when it is not determined in advance by laws of nature or programmed by human calculative manipulation of these laws, is the advent of the new, the unexpected that interrupts the natural order and routine of the world that existed before. Although Rancière does not often explicitly use the term, emergence is a motif that runs through his entire corpus in a set of images depicting the interruption or suspension of a hierarchical world that puts it in confrontation with another world. This confrontation becomes the backdrop for the coming-into-being of a new subject who can be the bearer or recipient of the experiences afforded by this new envisioned world and also the agent who will bring this new world into existence. In his poignant study of the lives and dreams of nineteenth-century French worker-writers, *Nights of the Proletariat,* Rancière uses the term in relation to workers who have managed to elude the darkness and obscurity of an anonymous existence by undoing in their thoughts, action, and writing the hierarchy of manual and intellectual labor.

> *Most of them, however, will spend their lives in anonymity, out of which will emerge an occasional name*: a worker-poet or a strike leader, the organizer

> of an ephemeral association or the editor of a journal that quickly disappeared . . . What are they by comparison with the anonymous masses of the mills or the innumerable militants of the workers' movement? What weight can be attributed to the verses of their poems or even the prose of their "workers' journals'" by comparison with the multiple array of daily practices, oppressions, resistances, murmurings, and clashes of workshop and city?[4]

This emergence is variously figured as theft, interruption, and suspension in relation to the grinding routine of work and rest. It is "snatched from the normal round of work and repose." It is "an interruption of the normal round . . . in which our characters prepare and dream and already live the impossible." It is "the suspension of the ancestral hierarchy subordinating those dedicated to manual labor to those who have been given the privilege of thinking" (*NL*, viii).

The energy of this emergence, this leap from obscurity, comes from the anger and resentment that arises in response to the experience of inequality and exclusion that constitutes the visible world, the world of appearance. The visibility in question is that of a social world, for we are concerned with the social status and significance accorded to certain occupations by a hierarchical division of labor in which the manual labor that is the material basis of the social world is invisible, excluded from visibility in two senses. In the more obvious sense, manual labor has no visibility because of its devalued social status. But, more importantly, those engaged in occupations involving manual labor are barred from having access to and sharing the visible world because they are fixed in their occupations by the calculations of the division of labor. They are denied not merely visibility but also, more significantly, the *capacity for* and *right to* visibility, namely the capacity and right to engage in intellectual, signifying, and image-producing activities. The latter activities do not only afford visibility. Precisely because they also determine the *conditions* of visibility, the denial of the capacity for and right to these activities amounts to an eternal banishment of workers from the visible world. Rancière emphasizes that what is alienated from workers is not only the objects produced by their work but also their very image, "the lost glory of pictures that they themselves have not made, that they are doomed never to make" (*NL*, 5). The worker is denied "another place in the world of images" (*NL*, 5), a place in which workers have the right to make images of themselves, where image production is precisely what enables one to come into presence, to emerge in the phenomenal world. The poverty that results from this alienation of the image is not only the material poverty of bodily needs but that of the soul. It is the poverty of the inability to choose what one can do for a living, the inability to "dream of another kind of work" (*NL*, 8). Indeed, these worker-artists and worker-writers are doubly excluded: they are excluded from the respectful gaze because they lived as workers, and they are excluded also because they engaged in intellectual activity like the bourgeoisie. They are "ghostly doubles" and "shadow images" that are incomprehensible to bourgeois intellectual discourse and to the scholarly discourse that attempts to excavate and retrieve the truth of proletarian labor in all its pure simplicity.

There are at least three moments in the process where the worker emerges as a new subject. First, one must imagine another world in which the worker is liberated from the strictures of a hierarchical division of labor and its organization of time. Second, such a liberation enables the worker to participate as an equal in determining the conditions of visibility in the world. Third, this participation will lead to the creation of a new world of free workers. But in the current world, the first moment is a matter of the eruption of a new time, or more precisely, a new division of time, within the endless cycle of work and rest. Speaking of Gauny, the floor-layer who has left the workshop to become a free worker, Rancière notes that the rest that comes with uncertain employment is reinscribed not as the negation of enslaving work but as the positive opening of a space for activity:

> How can one establish, in the intervals of servitude, the new time of liberation: not the insurrection of slaves but the advent of a new sociability between individuals who have already, each on his own, thrown off the servile passions that are indefinitely reproduced by the rhythm of work hours, the cycles of activity and rest, and the alternations of employment and unemployment? A society of free workers. (*NL*, 67)

> [A] positive presence of nonbeing—absence, illusion, future—in being, where it is no longer death *but rebirth that is anticipated.* And so the dead time of unemployment is no longer the slow erosion of life, dispossession of the environment, flight pursued by fate. On the contrary, it is the march of a conqueror through the streets of the city, intoxicated with his liberty and receiving from the multitude of slaves the respects due to a superior type of humanity. (*NL*, 83)

In *Disagreement,* Rancière generalizes the three moments of emergence into the structure of politics by way of a reading of Plato's and Aristotle's political writings. First, the structure of disagreement is that of an argument over incommensurable meanings attributed to the same object by different parties because of the situations from which they speak and the meaning-making and signifying capacities that follow from these situations.[5] This dispute concerning "the tangible presentation of [a] common object, the very capacity of the interlocutors to present it" (*D*, xii) corresponds precisely to the confrontation between two worlds in which the occupation of the worker has different meanings. Rancière characterizes this confrontation of two worlds as a process of subjectification that involves a transformative reinscription of a prior naturalized identity whereby the distance between the part attributed to the naturalized identity in the social order (that identity's function in society) and its lack of access to or inability to share in the social order is measured and expressed as a dispute. Accordingly, the proletariat is "the subject that measures the gap between the part of work as social function and the having no part of those who carry it out within the definition of the common of the community. All political subjectification is the manifestation of a gap of this kind . . . Any subjectification is a disidentification, removal from the naturalness of a place, the opening up of a subject space where anyone can be counted since it is the space where those of no account are counted, where a connection is made between having a part and having no part" (*D*, 36). Subjectification involves the transformative denaturalization of social space and its divisions. As Rancière puts it, "A mode of subjectification does not create subjects ex nihilo; it creates them by transforming identities defined in the natural order of the allocation of functions and places into instances of experience of a dispute" (*D*, 36). Second, disagreement nevertheless presupposes a common world of argument where the parties interact as equal interlocutors. This corresponds to the demand of workers to equality in defining the conditions that determine what counts as work and, therefore, the manner in which they can work for a living.

Third, the process of subjectification points to the creation of a new world in which the reinscribed identity and its meanings will have a continuing viability, for the gap between an emergent political subject's function in the existing social order and its lack of access and recognition in the social order (the gap manifested in the process of subjectification), when thematically expressed as a demand by the subject, unfolds as a gap between the existing social order and a new social order where the first gap is overcome. The third moment of emergence indicates that there are two related orders or levels of emergence: the leap that creates a new political subject and the leap from an old world to a new world. The difference between *The Nights of the Proletariat* and Rancière's theory of politics is merely that the three moments of emergence are no longer chronologically successive stages of a discursive expression of a dream and its actualization. The discursive expression is now a force of making-real because as a capacity for presentation, it also brings the disputed object (the disputed meanings of the object) into the light of phenomenality, thereby making it real. In Rancière's words, "The *demonstration* proper to politics is always both argument and opening up the world where argument can be received and have an impact—argument about the very existence of such a world" (*D*, 56). For argument to have an impact on or to convince its addressee, it must open up a shared world in which the addressee can hear the argument. The world that is opened up is thus a virtual world that automatically heralds and paves the way for its factual existence. This is why subjectification is "a reconfiguration of the field of experience" and even "the production of a new field of experience" through a series of corporeal actions and enunciations (*D*, 35). It gives us the capacity to see a different world, and in so doing it also gives us a different world to see. This reinscription does not obey the logic of dialectical negation but is instead a positive neither/nor.

The fundamental connection Rancière postulates between politics and aesthetics must be understood within this framework. First, insofar as the realm of visibility is opened up by and anchored in the socioeconomic fact of a hierarchical division of occupations where some occupations do not have a share in the community and are excluded from the visible world, or, more generally, when groups that are part of a community are excluded from sharing in it/having a part of it, when such groups are not counted because they are seen as uncountable, that is, as what does not count, the contestation of such exclusions and the demand for equal participation in decisions concerning the apportioning of parts and shares—what Rancière calls "politics"—necessitates a dispute about the realm of visibility and the current criteria that determine visibility. Rancière calls this the revelation of a given "distribution of the sensible."[6] This distribution concerns the aesthetic in the Kantian sense of transcendental aesthetic, an investigation into the a priori conditions of visibility and appearance, the conditions that open up the field of experience in general. For Rancière, however, these conditions are socially and historically constructed. In his reading of Plato, he detranscendentalizes the conditions of appearance by connecting visibility in the philosophical sense of appearance to the social recognition of occupation.[7] The distribution of the visible by means of an ordering of spaces according to occupations, he argues, is most clearly seen in Plato's proscription of mimeticism for destabilizing the proper ordering of space that determines what is visible. Since in Rancière's view "politics revolves around what is seen and what can be said about it, around who has the ability to see and the talent to speak, around the properties of spaces and the possibilities of time" ("DS," 13), politics is based on an aesthetics and, which is the same thing, there is necessarily an aesthetics at the core of politics.

Second, and more importantly, if the making-explicit of a given distribution is to lead to a redistribution, reconfiguration, or transformation of the sensible, then the dispute itself must not be exhausted after its action or utterance. It must have an aesthetic dimension in the sense that it must leave behind sensuous forms (which can be art objects in the narrow sense of aesthetics) that either crystallize and embody a new field of the sensible or function as doorways that open onto this new field. As Rancière puts it, "The aesthetic configuration in which what the speaking being says leaves its mark has always been the very stakes of the dispute that politics enlists in the police order" (*D*, 57).

Modalities of the *"als ob"*: Rancière's Detranscendentalization of the Aesthetic in the Kantian Sense

Because he detranscendentalizes the conditions of appearance by rooting them in the exclusion of groups of a community, the typecase of which is the hierarchical division of labor, Rancière gives a meaning to the aesthetic that radically transforms the two main senses of the term as Kant bequeathed it to German idealism. In that tradition, the aesthetic is grounded in and irreducibly marked by the passivity of the human sensibility, which being merely receptive, requires that the matter of its intuitions be given to it. In contradistinction, Rancière regards the aesthetic as a mode of articulation of the activities of doing (*praxis*) and making (*poeisis*) and the forms of visibility they produce. The visible world is no longer merely given and passively received but actively made by human production such that doing/making and seeing are indissociably connected. The aesthetic thus refers to "the formation of a shared sensible world, a common habitat, by the weaving together of a plurality of human activities," where the shared world of the visible is a dynamic space constituted by polemical struggle ("DS," 42). The aesthetic in the narrower sense of the human relation to beautiful forms plays an important role in this formation of the visible world.

In a manner of speaking, Rancière's weaving together of action and sensibility revives the key motifs of an intellectual intuition and an absolute infinite self-positing subject that can also posit the objects of its senses and consciousness found in German idealism. German idealism saw in the aesthetic project the desired reconciliation of the sensible material and rational-intellectual aspects of being. But because Rancière has detranscendentalized the conditions of experience, the aesthetic is no longer governed by the vocation of absolute idealism. Its autonomy is not achieved at the cost of being divorced from daily work activities. This detranscendentalization of the aesthetic, Rancière suggests, is fully accomplished in the early Marx's understanding of work as human species-being. Work, elaborated in terms of production, is anticipated by German idealism's understanding of art as the external objectification of thought in the realm of sensible matter and the medium for a community's recognition of its inner spiritual principle.[8]

Rancière's account of emergence is resolutely socio-anthropologistic because for him the dynamic plasticity of sensibility arises from human activity of configuring the sensible. We can better appreciate the key features of such an account by focusing on his interesting interpretation of Kant's *als ob.* In several places, Rancière suggests that the distribution of the sensible operates in terms of an "as if" mode of seeing that he takes to be the defining feature of Kant's understanding of aesthetic judgment. In *Disagreement,* he notes that an aesthetic judgment is an evaluation of a perceived object that does not consider that object's utility. As such, it defines "a world of virtual community," as opposed to the instrumental world of existing community, a hierarchical world of means and ends in which everything and everyone has its place and use.

> That a palace may be the object of an evaluation that has no bearing on the convenience of a residence, the privileges of a role, or the emblems of a majesty, is what, for Kant, particularizes the aesthetic community and the requirement of universality proper to it. So the autonomization of aesthetics means . . . constituting a kind of community of sense experience that works on the world of assumption, of the *as if* that includes those who are not included by revealing a mode of existence of sense experience that has eluded the allocation of parties and lots. (*D*, 58)

The passage from §2 of Kant's Third Critique to which Rancière refers is of central importance to his understanding of the distribution of the sensible. In a subsequent article, he returns to it again, this time elaborating on Kant's doctrine of the faculties and glossing the "as if" through an analogy with Gauny, the joiner from *Nights of the Proletariat,* who views the room in which he is working with pleasure and enjoyment by ignoring that it is the possession of someone else.

> The joiner agrees with Kant on a decisive point: the singularity of the aesthetic experience is the singularity of an as if. The aesthetic judgment acts as if the palace were not an object of possession and domination. The joiner acts as if he possessed the perspective. This as if is no illusion.

> It is a redistribution of the sensible, a redistribution of the parts supposedly played by the higher and lower faculties, the higher and the lower classes . . . The ethical ordering of social occupations ultimately occurs in the mode of an as if. The aesthetic rupture breaks this order by constructing another as if.[9]

Put simply, Rancière makes two main points about the disinterestedness that Kant attributes to aesthetic judgment. First, the "as if" acknowledges the governing distribution of the sensible, the configuration of the visible realm, at the same time that it willfully turns away and ignores this governing distribution. The disinterestedness of aesthetic judgment expresses a willed ignorance and suspension of knowledge ("AD," 15–16). However, this ignorant pleasure is not an ideological illusion that hides the reality of possession. Instead, it reconfigures and redistributes the sensible by opening up a new belief and new way of looking. "It is the means for building a new sensible world, which is a world of equality within the world of possession and inequality . . . This dismantling of a worker's body of experience is the condition for a worker's political voice" ("AD," 8). Second, aesthetic judgment foregrounds the fact that the sensible is always necessarily configured on the basis of hierarchy—that of the cognitive faculties and the ethos of the different social groups who correspond to these faculties as their proper bearers by virtue of their occupations. But the aesthetic gaze that willfully turns away from a given distribution of the sensible by looking differently is thereby also an act of force that neutralizes and dismantles this twofold hierarchy ("AD," 2). The aesthetic disinterestedness characterizing Gauny's gaze is "the dismantling of a certain body of experience that was deemed appropriate to a specific ethos, the ethos of the artisan who knows that work does not wait and whose senses are geared to this lack of time" ("AD," 7–8).

What is decisive here is the correlation between social hierarchy and the relation of subordination between the various cognitive faculties or even the superimposition of the former onto the latter. This superimposition is the defining feature of Rancière's socio-anthropologistic understanding of emergence. Since the sensible is always a social given and not merely a phenomenological given, it can be actively reconfigured by human endeavor. Two important consequences follow from Rancière's emphasis on the active character of the distribution of the sensible. First, where Kant had subordinated sensibility to reason and the understanding on the basis of sensibility's inherently receptive and passive nature, this subordination is now overturned. A dynamically plastic sensible that can be redistributed is nothing other than freedom as the human capacity to transform the given and, indeed, to re-give, to give in a nonhierarchical way. Second, this means that for Rancière the finitude of our powers is merely a social limitation, the limitation imposed by social hierarchy in its organization of the sensible. The aesthetic viewpoint is therefore a means of overcoming or, dare one say, transcending these limitations. The "as if" is a persistent force that resists social exclusion. One instance of this is the perpetual disruption of all essential identities since the definition of essential identities is the fundamental means of social exclusion. This is why Rancière insists that the political subject views itself not as the demos through a determinative judgment but always through an "as if" judgment.

But does not Rancière's socio-anthropologistic interpretation of the "as if" of Kantian aesthetic judgment involve a willful turn away from its irreducible transcendental structure? First, the "as if" is not unique to aesthetic judgment and therefore may not be its defining feature. It is a formulation that Kant first used in his moral philosophy to describe the application of the supersensible moral law to the sensible world and the test to which practical reason subjects our maxims to see if they have a universal rational form. In the well-known formulation of the categorical imperative from the *Groundwork of the Metaphysics of Morals*, we are enjoined to "act as if the maxim of your action were to become by your will a universal law of nature."[10] Or in another formulation from the Second Critique, Kant suggests that "we are conscious through reason of a law to which all our maxims are subject, as if a natural order must at the same time arise from our will."[11] Far from neutralizing hierarchy, the "as if" is an analogy that facilitates the imposition of the command of the supersensible moral law onto nature by having us see it as something similar to a law of nature. It functions as a bridge between the sensible and supersensible. The representational principle of the faculty of judgment that embodies this analogical perspective is the type. The type performs the work of subordination and rule through which the sensible world can be given the form of the supersensible world.

The formulation is used with much greater frequency and variability in the Third Critique, where it refers variously to the potentially misleading similarity between a reflective judgment of taste and a determinative judgment when we speak of beauty as though it were a property or predicate of the object; the paradoxical conjunction between the singularity of an aesthetic judgment, which makes it incapable of proof and similar to a subjective judgment based on sensation, and its claim to universality, as if it was uttered by a universal voice; the regarding of fine art as if it were a product of nature; the presentation of nature as if it were based on an understanding and was made possible through techne (the technic of nature); and, finally, the figuring of the apparent purposiveness of nature for our cognitive faculties because of their harmony with nature as a system of contingent particular empirical laws as if it were a favor of nature. For reasons of economy, I only quote the last instance of the "as if."

> This transcendental concept of a purposiveness of nature is neither a concept of nature nor of freedom, since it attributes nothing at all to the object (of nature), but rather only represents the unique way in which we must proceed in reflection on the objects of nature with the aim of a thoroughly interconnected experience; hence, we are also delighted (strictly speaking, relieved of a need) when we encounter such a systematic unity among merely empirical laws, just as if it were a happy accident which happened to favor our aim, even though we necessarily had to assume that there is such a unity, yet without having been able to gain insight into it and to prove it.[12]

Two points are important here. First, the disinterested pleasure that Rancière focuses on is a response to what we take as nature's purposiveness for us, the pleasure aroused by the thought that it is "as if" nature favors us. Hence, although the free accord between the understanding and the imagination is a relation among the faculties where there is no hierarchy or subordination, this free accord itself is grounded in a relation of obligation to or dependency on nature judged as if it were intelligent, generous, and giving. Second, the importance of aesthetic judgment in Kant's thought lies in the fact that it was needed to bridge the gulf between the realm of the given and the transcendent realm of freedom because of the fundamental incapacity of our finite human cognitive powers. This means that instead of indicating our active power to reconfigure the realm of visibility, the "as if" of aesthetic judgment points to a fundamental passivity and constitutive deficiency of the human faculties. The magnificent resourcefulness and inventiveness of the aesthetic attempts to cover over our finitude. Or, better yet, the distribution of the sensible is a response to our transcendental stupidity. In both cases, freedom or autonomy is grounded on a prior heteronomy.[13]

The Quasi-transcendental Account of Emergence and Postcoloniality

I have suggested that Rancière's account of emergence as the resistant force that necessarily haunts the force of exclusion in the social constitution of the sensible involves a willful turning away or refusal to see the aesthetic as a response to the finitude of the sensible. In this latter view, the source of emergence lies beyond the realm of the anthropos. Of course, unlike Fanon's national subject, the demos, Rancière's political figure for emergence, is not a form of sovereignty but a power without a self-identical subject or underlying concept because it acts in the mode of the "as if," where those who are excluded and invisible act as if they were identical with the community.[14] I am also aware that in suggesting that the source of emergence lies outside the plasticity of anthropologistic form, I am perilously close to the position that Rancière critically rejects as the figure of the outsider celebrated by what he calls the ethical approach exemplified by Lyotard's figure of the inhuman. We can flesh out the difference between Rancière's approach to the "as if" and the transcendental approach from which he turns away in his reading of Kant by briefly comparing his position to that of Hannah Arendt. There are many similarities between Rancière's and Arendt's understandings of emergence, not least their rejection of the argument that action should be grounded in the fulfillment of bodily needs and utilitarian interest.[15] But although Arendt also views emergence in terms of the action of a human subject, in her concept of natality, she conceded that the source of action lies beyond the human, in the sheer force of the human being's coming into the presence of an existing visible order *before* that force is transposed into and appropriated by that human figure of action that she calls the newcomer.

> The crucial difference between the infinite probabilities on which earthly human life is based and miraculous events in the arena of human affairs lies, of course, in the fact that in the latter case there is a miracle worker—that is, that man himself evidently has a most amazing and mysterious talent for working miracles . . . The miracle of freedom is inherent in this ability to make a beginning, which itself is inherent in the fact that every human being, simply by being born into the world that was there before him and will be there after him, is himself a new beginning.[16]

Although Arendt distinguishes this coming into phenomenality from merely earthly biological life because it requires the permanent order of a world, this coming is also not reducible to human action, since it involves the sheer force of being born that erupts into and disrupts the world made by human action. Instead, it is human action that inheres in natality. The propulsion of natality occupies the same place as the favor of nature that is inseparable from the "as if" of aesthetic judgment. In my view, Derrida, whom Rancière places in the camp of the ethical approach, radicalizes this force of coming by referring it to the absolute otherness of the giving of time as the nonanticipatable coming of the event:[17] "Birth itself, which is similar to what I am trying to describe, is perhaps unequal to this absolute 'arrivance.' Families prepare for a birth; it is scheduled, forenamed, caught up in a symbolic space that dulls the arrivance. Nevertheless, in spite of these anticipations and prenominations, the uncertainty will not let itself be reduced: the child that arrives remains unpredictable; it speaks of itself as from the origin of another world, or from an-other origin of this world."[18]

But why is it important that emergence and the opening of the visible world also be approached in this quasi-transcendental manner? Because the organization of human existence into a field of instrumentality is so thorough and pervasive that it is difficult to envision emergence solely in terms of a force of heterogeneity that is purely internal to the dynamic of the formation of communities through exclusion. The problem becomes more acute in postcolonial space. For Rancière, the inaugural example of the distribution of the sensible is the socioeconomic fact of a hierarchical division of labor that fixes occupations involving manual labor and excludes them in the determination of the realm of social visibility. If we transpose the division of labor onto an international stage where it becomes an international division of labor, a redistribution of the sensible is obstructed for two reasons. First, in the current neoliberal dispensation of global capitalist accumulation, manual work no longer lacks visibility. Although there is a hierarchy among different kinds of agricultural, industrial, and postindustrial production, these types of production are part of a developmental scale along which a given country can progress in the manner of upward class mobility. Global capital is fundamentally inclusionary rather than exclusionary, and it includes all kinds of labor that are indispensable to its functioning. Second, as part of this inclusionary dynamic, the oppressive consequences of work are now alleviated by a regime of global governmentality that produces needs, capacities, and interests and then codifies them in the juridical form of rights that will be respected. With second-generation human rights—namely economic, social, and cultural rights, including the right to work, the right to health, and so on—manual work has achieved the greatest possible recognition. In other words, work in all its forms is no longer stigmatized or excluded from but now included within a global community.[19] The acquiescence of postcolonial states to developmental discourse and the alleviation of the negative consequences of developmentalism by human rights make it hard to envision a genuine emergence that will reconfigure the international division of labor.

But in the event that a redistribution of the sensible occurs, we must also ask what the realm of the sensible as such can show in its greatest inclusivity. Here it is important to note that despite the inclusiveness of global capitalism, significant sections of the population in postcolonial countries remain excluded from the international division of labor. These sections have no access to its benefits, its international civil society, or the transnational public realm. For example, in the South Asian subcontinent this excluded part is the shifting space of subalternity. As Ranajit Guha puts it, "The terms 'people' and 'subaltern classes' have been used as synonyms . . . The social groups and elements included in this category represent the demographic difference between the total Indian population and all those whom we have described as the 'elite' . . . Some of these classes and groups . . . who 'naturally' ranked among the 'people' and the 'subaltern,' could under circumstances act for the 'elite' . . . and therefore be classified as such in some local or regional circumstances."[20] Rancière's notion of the distribution of the sensible and the "as if" character of the demos is potentially of great analytical probity in helping us understand the fundamentally ambiguous, mobile space of subaltern resistance.

However, notwithstanding the multiplication of subjectification processes in modern politics, "the opening up of common . . . worlds where the subject who argues is counted as an arguer" is fraught with difficulty when we are confronted with the extreme variegation and ambiguity of subaltern space (*D*, 58). The problem here is that just as the exclusion that constitutes any sensible realm is always an exclusion of or by a specific community, the heterogeneity that suspends and disrupts this exclusion is likewise a heterogeneity of a specific community, a force internal to that world. The common world that Rancière presupposes is tacitly a modern secular world. The examples of the politics of virtual communities he discusses are primarily Western and claim the lineage of Greek antiquity. The three regimes of art he outlines as cobelonging with politics belong to the Western tradition. The problem here is that this kind of common world where a disagreement can be heard and a redistribution of the sensible can take place may already be a world that obscures cultural traditions that do not count as having modern political cultures.

Exclusion can take place within a territorially bounded community or a global community. Hence, a common world can be opened up that permits dispute between peoples throughout the world and within non-Western nations. But insofar as this common world is irreducibly "modern" as a result of the global dissemination of modern Western political and legal culture and institutions, non-Western cultural elements can be automatically disabled from emerging in the common world of disagreement and argumentation. This is emphatically not a matter of a dispute among the various peoples of the Book or "a clash of great civilizations," such as the West versus Islam or Confucianism. The cultural elements I am referring to are unconnected to modern state institutions or socioeconomic class divisions, where "supernatural" forces are part of everyday life and action. How can they emerge in relation to the modern culture of the postcolonial state? Can such forces appear in the light of dissensual redistribution of the visible, given that they are conventionally "dark" or "invisible" precisely because they are not demonstrable by rational argumentation? Here, where the distribution of the sensible is based not just on the hierarchical division of socioeconomic class but also on caste and religion, including the animism of tribal groups, the notion of the human-social configuration of the sensible itself may be put into question.

This is why it is important to insist that we must go beyond thinking of visibility only as the visibility of the social world of the anthropos and thinking of that which cannot be fixed in its proper place as the heterogeneity at work in the constitution of human community. We must think of the incalculable that disrupts calculation as that nonhuman force which opens up the realm of visibility in general. For the human being in general may already be a culturally limited invention. The world or community that is opened up, however much it is based on the antagonistic principle of human equality, however universal it is in its vocation, will never be able to admit what is not human without giving it a human face. Hence, it will always have obscured elements in postcolonial space that can never be capable of making or receiving a dissenting human argument. On the one hand, to insist on the inhuman character of emergence is to make room for emergence in a world thoroughly saturated by human instrumentality. But on the other hand, it is also to allow to come into phenomenality inhuman forces that speak through human beings, the human belief in the actuality of nonhuman forces.

Let me end with a literary example that stages the unsettling enablement of a progressive distribution of the sensible by an inhuman force. Amitav Ghosh's *The Hungry Tide* portrays the Morichjhapi massacre of the 1970s, when thousands of refugees who had fled persecution in East Bengal and settled in the Sundarban region were killed, injured, and forcibly evicted by the West Bengal government on the grounds that they had violated the Forest Acts by illegally occupying a government reserve forest area that is the habitat of endangered tigers. The massacre is recorded by Nirmal, one of the novel's main characters and narrative voices, a retired Marxist schoolteacher and a failed writer. He was initially invited to the refugee settlement in order to promote their cause by publicizing it to the wider world. As a refugee leader tells Nirmal, "We need to let people know what we are doing and why we're here. We have to tell the world about all we've done and all we've achieved. Can you help us with this? Do you have contacts with the press in Calcutta?"[21] We can understand Nirmal as attempting to help bring about a redistribution of the sensible so that these refugees from the subaltern sections of the population can be made visible, or can make themselves visible, by suspending the calculations in which they are so devalued and made uncountable as parts of the community that they have a status that is even lower than the tigers who need to be saved from them.

Two things about the novel's climax are significant for present purposes. First, although Nirmal decides to stay on the island to be a witness during the siege, his notebook does not actually document the atrocious violence, since he has entrusted it to someone else to be delivered to his nephew for circulation before the massacre takes place. Indeed, by the end of the novel, his nephew, who has read the notebook, loses it in a cyclone storm and can only circulate its contents by writing a story about the origins of the notebook. Subalternity still cannot be heard despite a redistribution of the sensible in which the plight of the subalterns is made visible. But, second, although the subaltern cannot be heard, the force for the subsequent redistribution of the sensible is actually subaltern religious animism. The main female protagonist, Piya, is saved during the cyclone by Fokir, a subaltern fisherman, who sacrifices himself and uses his body to shield her from the storm because he lived his life according to the animistic beliefs of the region that promise protection by the forest goddess, Bon Bibi. "For this boy those words were much more than a part of a legend: it was the story that gave this land its life. That was the song you heard on Fokir's lips yesterday. It lives in him and in some way, perhaps, it still plays a part in making him the person he is."[22] Fokir dies without any last words, but the legend pulsing through his actions, what cannot be understood as rational argumentation and dissensus, causes the woman he saves to make him and others like him count and to give him and them visibility by starting an environmentalist foundation in his name.

Notes

1. Franz Fanon, *The Wretched of the Earth*, trans. Richard Philcox (New York: Grove, 2004), 174.

2. Fanon, *The Wretched of the Earth*, 176.

3. See Pheng Cheah, *Inhuman Conditions: On Cosmopolitanism and Human Rights* (Cambridge, Mass.: Harvard University Press, 2006), 4–13, 259–66.

4. Jacques Rancière, *The Nights of Labor: The Workers' Dream in Nineteenth-Century France*, trans. John Drury (Philadelphia: Temple University Press, 1989), viii, my italics. Hereafter cited parenthetically in the text as *NL*.

5. Jacques Rancière, *Disagreement: Politics and Philosophy*, trans. Julie Rose (Minneapolis: University of Minnesota Press, 2004), xii. Hereafter cited parenthetically in the text as *D*.

6. Rancière, "The Distribution of the Sensible," in *The Politics of Aesthetics*, trans. Gabriel Rockhill, 7–45 (London: Continuum, 2004), 12–13: "The distribution of the sensible reveals who can have a share in what is common to the community based on what they do and on the time and space in which this activity is performed. Having a particular 'occupation' thereby determines the ability or inability to take charge of what is common to the community; it defines what is visible or not in a common space, endowed with a common language." Hereafter cited parenthetically in the text as "DS."

7. See also Rancière's comments on the transcendental in "The Distribution of the Sensible," 50: "I would say that my approach is a bit similar to Foucault's. It retains the principle from the Kantian transcendental that replaces the dogmatism of truth with the search for conditions of possibility. At the same time, these conditions are not conditions of thought in general, but rather conditions immanent in a particular system of thought, a particular system of expression . . . The visibility of a form of expression as an artistic form depends on a historically constituted regime of perception and intelligibility . . . I thus try at one and the same time to historicize the transcendental and to de-historicize these systems of conditions of possibility."

8. "Romanticism declared that the becoming-sensible of all thought and the becoming-thought of all sensible materiality was the very goal of the activity of thought in general. In this way, art once again became a symbol of work. It anticipates the end—the elimination of oppositions—that work is not yet in a position to attain by and for itself. However, it does this insofar as it is a production, the identification of a process of material execution with a community's self-presentation of its meaning. Production asserts itself as the principle behind a new distribution of the sensible insofar as it unites, in one and the same concept, terms that are traditionally opposed: the activity of manufacturing and visibility. Manufacturing meant inhabiting the private and lowly space-time of labour for sustenance. Producing unites the act of manufacturing with the act of bringing into light, the act of defining a new relationship between *making* and *seeing*. Art anticipates work because it carries out its principle: the transformation of sensible matter into the community's self-presentation. The texts written by the young Marx that confer on work the status of the generic essence of mankind were only possible on the basis of German Idealism's aesthetic programme, i.e. art as the transformation of thought into the sensory experience of the community" (Rancière, "The Distribution of the Sensible," 44).

9. Jacques Rancière, "The Aesthetic Dimension: Aesthetics, Politics, Knowledge," *Critical Inquiry* 36 (2009): 1–19, quotation on 8. Hereafter cited parenthetically in the text as "AD."

10. Immanuel Kant, *Groundwork of the Metaphysics of Morals*, in *Practical Philosophy*, trans. and ed. Mary J. Gregor, 43–108 (Cambridge: Cambridge University Press, 1996), 73; *Grundlegung zur Metaphysik der Sitten*, in *Werkausgabe*, ed. Wilhelm

Weischedel, 7:10–102 (Frankfurt am Main: Suhrkamp, 1996), 51; Ak. 4:421. See also 87; 72; Ak. 4:438: "Every rational being must act as if he were by his maxims at all times a lawgiving member of the universal kingdom of ends. The formal principle of these maxims is, act as if your maxims were to serve at the same time as a universal law (for all rational beings)."

11. Immanuel Kant, *Critique of Practical Reason*, in *Practical Philosophy*, trans. and ed. Mary J. Gregor, 137–271 (Cambridge: Cambridge University Press, 1996), 175; *Kritik der praktischen Vernunft*, 158; Ak. 5:44.

12. Immanuel Kant, *Critique of the Power of Judgment*, 71; *Kritik der Urteilskraft*, in *Werkausgabe*, vol. 10, ed. Wilhelm Weischedel (Frankfurt am Main: Suhrkamp, 1996), 93; Ak. 5:184.

13. I have discussed this grounding of freedom in the prior heteronomy of a gift or favor (*Gunst*) from nature in Pheng Cheah, *Spectral Nationality: Passages of Freedom from Kant to Postcolonial Literatures of Liberation* (New York: Columbia University Press, 2003), 99–113.

14. "The demos is the subject of politics inasmuch as it is heterogeneous to the count of the parts of a society" (Rancière, "The Aesthetic Dimension," 10). It is the power of the whoever or anyone. A dissensus puts two worlds or heterogeneous logics on the same stage in the same world and is the commensurability of incommensurables. Accordingly, for Rancière, "the political subject acts in the mode of the as if; it acts as if it were the demos, that is, as the whole made by those who are not countable as qualified parts of the community. This is the aesthetic dimension of politics: the staging of a dissensus—of a conflict of sensory worlds—by subjects who act as if they were the people, which is made of the uncountable count of anyone" (ibid., 11).

15. For a succinct statement of Rancière's critique of Arendt, which focuses on Arendt's insistence on a specifically political sphere and political way of life that is defined through the policing exclusion of bare or nonpolitical life determined in terms of the social or the economic, see Jacques Rancière, "Ten Theses on Politics," in *Dissensus: On Politics and Aesthetics*, ed. and trans. Steven Corcoran (London: Continuum, 2010), and "The Thinking of Dissensus: Politics and Aesthetics," in *Reading Rancière*, ed. Paul Bowman and Richard Stamp (London: Continuum, 2011).

16. Hannah Arendt, *The Promise of Politics*, ed. Jerome Kohn (New York: Schocken, 2005), 113.

17. See Jacques Rancière, "Should Democracy Come? Ethics and Politics in Derrida," in *Derrida and the Time of the Political*, ed. Pheng Cheah and Suzanne Guerlac (Durham, N.C.: Duke University Press, 2009), 274–88.

18. Jacques Derrida, "The Deconstruction of Actuality," in *Negotiations: Interventions and Interviews, 1971–2001*, trans. and ed. Elizabeth Rottenberg, 85–116 (Palo Alto, Calif.: Stanford University Press, 2002), 95. I can only remark here on the radical distance between Arendt's newcomer and Derrida's *arrivant* and the to-come (*à-venir*).

19. Rancière would most likely characterize this recognition of work in terms of the fetishization of work into the identity of the laboring class and a

worker's culture (see Rancière, *The Nights of Labor*, 11–14) and insist on distinguishing proletarian political subjectification from giving voice to a collective worker's ethos (see Rancière, *Disagreement*, 36, 59).

20. Ranajit Guha, "On Some Aspects of the Historiography of Colonial India," in *Selected Subaltern Studies*, ed. Ranajit Guha and Gayatri Spivak, 35–44 (Oxford: Oxford University Press, 1988), 44.

21. Amitav Ghosh, *The Hungry Tide* (New York: Mariner Books, 2006), 143.

22. Ghosh, *The Hungry Tide*, 292.

"Plunge into Terrible Readings": Rancière, Badiou, and the Thought of Libidinal Economy

Eleanor Kaufman

This essay attempts to situate the work of Jacques Rancière, particularly the early work, within what I argue is a shift from the terrain of the economic to that of the political in late twentieth-century French thought. The claim is that Rancière's work, though squarely in line with the turn to the political, also harkens back to questions of the economic and in particular unbalanced or unequal economies. It is important to note at the outset that the terms "economic" and "political" will be employed not in the fashion that an economist or a political theorist would be likely to use them, but more nearly as they are marshaled by a lineage of French thinkers that includes Jacques Derrida, Alain Badiou, and Rancière, among others. To be sure, in this particular milieu these terms are not always entirely separate, yet they are *separable* in the context of their philosophical if not structural valences in twentieth-century French thought, and that thought's strong link to Marx and Freud.

Some of the greatest insights of twentieth-century French philosophy might be grouped under a rubric or logic of the economic, and this in distinction from the political. This is not to suggest that contemporary French philosophers have not had a pronounced impact in real politics, nor is it to suggest that there is an absence of engaged writing about political situations. We might look back to Sartre, Beauvoir, and even Maurice Blanchot, and their engagements with the Algerian cause, or to May '68, or to the French Maoist moment and its ongoing legacy, such as Badiou's activism in the Organisation Politique. Yet Badiou will locate politics as *one* of *four* generic procedures (alongside art, love, and science) that *might* lead to an "event," a revolutionary rearrangement of a situation through a fidelity to making universal what is uncounted in that situation. Notably, though, Badiou will pose it as a question in his book by that name, *Can Politics Be Thought?*.[1] It seems he would answer this question with a careful affirmative—yes, it can, while warning against a suturing of philosophy to politics (or to any of the other generic procedures).[2] Rancière, by contrast, is more decisively affirmative with respect to the possibility of the political, or more nearly, *politics*, being thought, but it is not clear that it is really philosophy that is doing that thinking, whereas the preeminence of philosophy is more explicit for Badiou—although at many points he calls it antiphilosophy. In *Metapolitics*, Badiou goes so far as to accuse Rancière's notion of politics of not being properly philosophical: "Admittedly, no one is obliged, in order to do politics, to deploy an underlying ontology. It may even be advisable to do without one. But Rancière doesn't do politics. If, on the other hand, one does philosophy, there is an obligation to make use of explicit ontological categories and to argue their cohesion. However, all things considered, Rancière doesn't do philosophy either."[3] It is not exactly clear if, in Badiou's estimation, it would be viable to do *both* politics and philosophy, but according to this pronouncement Rancière is doing neither. In the French tradition in which both thinkers are grounded, it seems that a joining of the economic and the philosophical is in fact more tenable.

Fredric Jameson makes a strong claim for "the priority, within Marxism, of economics as some ultimately determining instance."[4] Though he cautions that it is a very specific use of the economic that he is upholding and that "to be sure, the term *economics* is no more satisfactory to characterize Marxism than sexuality is to characterize Freudian psychoanalysis," he still regards the shift from the economic to the political as a "mistake." He writes that "the substitution of the political for the economic was of course the standard move of all the bourgeois attacks on Marxism" and moreover that "the very force and originality of Marxism was always that it did not have a [structural] political dimension . . . , and that it was a completely different thought system of unity-of theory-and-practice altogether. The rhetoric of power, then, in whatever form, is always to be considered a fundamental form of revisionism."[5] Among other things, this is a not-so-veiled attack on Foucault's middle period in the 1970s during which he placed particular emphasis on relations of power, though this by no means subsumes Foucault's work in its entirety. Jameson even cites those points where Freud defends the priority of the sexual against disciples such as Adler, Jung, and Rank who sought to diffuse it or water it down, and he in turn defends these as "the most admirable and heroic moments in Freud."[6] So, too, I would locate a thought of the economic, if not at all points strictly Marxist—indeed, a more Ricardian variant appears in the early Foucault[7]—as similarly marking the most "admirable and heroic" moments of twentieth-century French philosophy.

Following a similar logic of bifurcation, I would claim that in the realm of mid-twentieth-century French thought until the late 1970s there is a premium placed on the economic above and beyond—and at many points in contradistinction to—the political, even in writings that deal directly with political topics.[8] Jameson refers to the "*structural* priority of economics over politics" for Marxism, and this reflects the strong link between the economic and the structural that reaches its height in the late 1960s and early 1970s.[9] With this framework in mind, I wish to outline four essentially structural if not numerical logics that dominate mid-twentieth-century French thought, logics that I would consider to be fundamentally economic. The first two are clearly traceable to Marx and Freud; the third is part and parcel of the synthesis of Marx, Freud, and gift theory that I would characterize by the term "libidinal economy" and that will be the primary focus here; and the fourth is the category of the serial, which links such seemingly disparate thinkers as Sartre and Deleuze.

1. The first economic model is the dynamic of two forces that may appear as one. According to Marx in *Theories of Surplus Value*,[10] this difficulty of distinguishing between the two and the one is none other than the mark of crisis. The crisis is the recognition that two forces (here purchase and sale, M-C and C-M) that generally come together so seamlessly so as to seem like one, are in fact completely delinked. In this fashion, by being torn asunder and forcibly dissociated, the truth of their always tenuous duality emerges.

Freud describes a similar structure with respect to two drives that may appear as one: not only the pleasure principle and the reality principle but more fundamentally the pleasure principle and the death drive, which coexist and exert force on each other. Even before this, distinctive economic models emerge in the writings from the mid-1910s, in particular the essay "Repression."[11] Repression, for Freud, is not just a force holding something back; it is the interplay between that force and the counterforce of what is trying to emerge. Unless the repression is entirely successful, there is an imbalance of forces and some of what is trying to get out does so, symptomatically, thereby unbalancing the economy—for the symptom appears precisely when the forces do not stay balanced. I will return to this example in a literary context in what follows. In short, so much of twentieth-century French thought might be charted through the lens of a pulsional economy of forces, whether they are active and reactive forces, or good and bad forces in a Nietzschean sense, or joyous and sad passions, in a Spinozist one (and Deleuze's early single authored works achieve a synthesis of the two).

Even in Badiou's more overtly political discussions, we still see the same economic logic of the two being the truth of the one. This is the explicit motif of *The Century*, where Badiou will claim of the twentieth century that "the century is a figure of non-dialectical juxtaposition of the Two and the One."[12] Badiou follows Mao in opposing the bad model of the fusion of the two into one with the superior model of the one dividing into two. At issue is a structural logic whereby the challenge of recognizing the structure (and its model) is intrinsic to the structure itself, the recognition consisting on the one hand in realizing that there are two forces at work in what might appear as a unique one.

2. Related to this is a second economic or structural model, which is the belated recognition that an event is being repeated. For Freud, this is epitomized by the workings of trauma, whereby the trauma only becomes recognizable in the belatedness of its repetition. In both *Beyond the Pleasure Principle* and then later in *Moses and Monotheism,* Freud gives the example of walking away from a train accident seemingly unscathed, where symptoms emerge only belatedly when some element from the environment of the accident is repeated or brought to mind.[13] This is a strong model of unconscious repetition, in which the trauma is bound up with the recognition of repeating something that has taken place and that went unrecognized at the initial moment.

To be sure, this structure occurs in the political domain, but it follows a structural-economic logic, which is that of the repetition and true or false recognition of sequences and patterns. Taking one of Marx's most overtly political writings, *The Eighteenth Brumaire of Louis Bonaparte,* we might still follow Jameson in maintaining that even here it is an essentially economic logic at issue, one of repetition. *The Eighteenth Brumaire* is the recounting of the second Napoleon's repetition, between 1848 and 1851, of the tragedy of his uncle, but this time as farce and in a fashion eminently more banal, passive, and bourgeois.[14] As with Freud, the crisis becomes apparent with its repetition, the key being the ability *to recognize* the repetition for what it is, which is above all a structural apprehension.

We might again turn to some of Badiou's most overtly political writings, in particular his analyses of the sequences of the Paris Commune, the 1917 Revolution, and the Chinese Cultural Revolution. In these discussions, one recurrent theme is the difficulty of discerning which of the aforementioned events marks the decisive appearance of the party: does 1871 mark the first appearance of something like a thought of the party? or does the party appear in the disjunction between the Commune and October 1917? or is it in Mao's reworking of the Lenin from *What Is to Be Done* up until October 1917? or might we say that it is only with the Cultural Revolution that we get a true instantiation of the thought of the party, a moment which might also be said to represent the definitive failure of the party?[15] Notably, Badiou's own thought will shift from a more party-oriented one in the 1970s and 1980s to one that attempts to think political organization without the framework of a party structure. In short, questions that are fully political are nonetheless presented in an eminently structural logic of repetition and event recognition.

Marxian and psychoanalytic thought, if not Marx and Freud themselves, provide the lens through which each of the above economic logics becomes perceptible, where two or more replicable patterns—whether on a historical or individual level—are discerned from what might appear to be one. In both models what is striking is that the economic dimension may easily go unrecognized. Rather than something akin to a permanent state of exception, here it is a question of perceiving something that has been there all along, but the occurrence of repetition or of forcible disjoining makes the structure more apparent.

3. The third model represents a synthesis of the Marxian and Freudian elements as they are also filtered through anthropological work on gift dynamics. Crucial to mid-twentieth-century French discussions of the gift is the question of whether or not there remains an effective balanced or imbalanced economy. One of Marcel Mauss's signal observations in his book *The Gift* is the idea that there is no pure gift as such, but that the gift is entirely bound up with an elaborate system of exchange and reciprocity.[16] Studying cultures of Polynesia, Melanesia, and the North American Indians, he proposes that even if the return of the gift is displaced by as much as a generation, there is nonetheless an expectation of such exchange and return for any gift given. Mauss's analysis extends to an act of destruction or a throwing away of wealth, as in the potlatch ritual. If the gift must exist outside a system of reciprocation for it to be a true gift, then to follow Mauss to the letter of his analysis, we would have to say that the gift as such does not really exist but is entirely bound up in an economy of exchange. This is the challenge Derrida poses in *The Gift of Death*, before querying what a gift would look like if it were somehow possible to extricate it from this exchange economy.[17]

Mauss's gift economy rests, then, on a standard of balance and reciprocity, where, much like Freud's model of a perfectly functioning repression, the forces at issue are effectively balanced (though we might inquire, in the counterspirit of Derrida, if repressions ever function perfectly). Directly counterposed to this is an emphasis on imbalance, excess, indeed the dimension of potlatch, that Georges Bataille as early as the 1930s and 1940s will designate as a *general economy* of imbalance and asymmetry as opposed to the *reserved economy* of balance and reciprocity.[18]

The sum of the varied writings on libidinal economy theory that reach a short-lived crescendo in France between 1969 and 1974 might be grouped under this third category of the explicitly imbalanced economy. Examples include Deleuze and Guattari's *Anti-Oedipus*, Lyotard's *Libidinal*

Economy, as well as a range of other works synthesizing Marx and Freud, such as Baudrillard's *For a Critique of the Political Economy of the Sign*, and Pierre Klossowski's *Living Currency*.[19] All emphasize the pulsional dimension of use value, so that, translating backward into Marx's formulas from *Capital*, at issue is an endless desiring economy of use as well as exchange (C-M-C as well as M-C-M). It is this libidinal economic model that will be a crucial framing point for Rancière's discussion of the laborer in his early writings.

The fourth and final economic logic that emerges from this constellation of mid-twentieth-century French philosophy might be categorized as that of the serial. The serial is different from the imbalanced economy model that tends to favor a dynamic of excess, although it still entails a play of forces. Here, however, as opposed to repetition, the one dividing into two, or balanced or imbalanced economies, there is a movement from multiplicity to singularity and back to multiplicity. Deleuze, following something of a Spinozist procedure, describes human affect in terms of this waxing and waning of focus. In *Proust and Signs*, Deleuze notes the way the Proustian narrator at first cannot distinguish Albertine from the group of girls she is part of, in which she is effectively one element of a series.[20] For Deleuze, as for Sartre in *The Critique of Dialectical Reason* with the opposition between seriality and praxis, the issue is not so much to understand how the serial is singularized—how the narrator falls in love with Albertine—but more significantly how the love relation, or the political organization for Sartre, recedes from the focalized realm back into the series from which it emerged.[21] Whereas Deleuze emphasizes the genuine joy in apprehending the structure of one's amorous patterns, as opposed to the negativity of the waning of affect, Sartre regards the descent from the organized group back into inert seriality as something of a step backward.

In Badiou's work there is also a negative valence to an event's losing its properly "evental" quality, and indeed he critiques Proust precisely for this, for the way that love is depicted as receding, or as waxing and waning. By contrast, in *Logics of Worlds*, he will intersperse his discussion of the Paris Commune with a reading of Rousseau's *Julie, ou la nouvelle Héloïse*, seeing the latter as a model of fidelity to an impossible love that does not recede from the group to the serial in the fashion of Proust's narrator's love for Albertine, but remains at the apex of its trajectory.[22]

In short, we see at least four models of the economic that pervade even the most "political" of examples in a range of thinkers from Sartre to Badiou: the two in one, the belated repetition, the logic of general economy and excess, and the serial structure. Although these models may be distributed in different fashions, their fundamentally economic structures of cognitive mapping dominate a substantial trajectory of twentieth-century French thought.[23]

Yet in the last two decades of the twentieth century and into our current moment, we see a turn away from the synthesis of Marx and Freud, one carried out in a fundamentally structural-economic register, to a more univocal focus on the political. It is not that the political has ever been absent, but in the more recent theoretical terrain it takes on a more overarching dimension, and one severed from the economic. This thought of the political takes at least two forms. The first, which will be left aside for the most part here, is the domain of political theology, which is certainly not a new phenomenon but has nevertheless reached a peak of critical attention in the last three decades.[24] Addressing this fully would entail a return to Carl Schmitt, but notable here is the important turn inaugurated by Derrida's *Specters of Marx* from 1993, in its revival for the more secular fields of the humanities and social sciences of the term of the messianic, or a "messianicity without messianism."[25] This is a companion volume to *The Politics of Friendship* from the following year, with its even more direct engagement with Schmitt and the question of the political.[26] It could be argued, above all for Derrida but also to no small degree for Badiou, that these thinkers' early work is dominated by economic models, specifically the four outlined above. Such models never quite disappear, but there is a pronounced turn in Derrida's work after about 1989 to a focus on questions of ethics, justice, hospitality, and the democracy to come,[27] all topics which move Derrida's thought into a more political register.[28] Leaving Derrida aside in what follows—though his is by far the most important and complex case history to consider for this analysis—I wish to chart the emergence of economic logics at the heart of what is otherwise a more political focus in the late twentieth-century spectrum of French thought. It is at this juncture that Rancière's work will finally make an appearance.

Rancière's work is to be most squarely situated under the second political rubric, distinct from political theology, of a late twentieth-century French turn to the question of the political, specifically the question of the *practice* of politics and an affirmation of the terms democracy and equality. These questions are in no way new in fields such as political theory, but they represent a strikingly different turn within the literary-philosophical domain of French philosophy at issue here. Once again, Derrida's work is the bellwether for this shift in its open embrace of democracy, a term usually treated with great philosophical suspicion, in late works such as *Rogues*. While acknowledging there has never been a democratic philosopher, Derrida instead gestures toward a democracy to come (*à venir*).[29]

In this setting, then, Rancière's work is exemplary if not extraordinary for its affirmation of terms and formulations that his French philosophical cohort will treat with far more reticence. Not only does he embrace politics in its proximity to philosophy (Rancière will suggest that a suppression of politics can be equated to a suppression of philosophy);[30] he will also provide a rubric for how politics takes place. For Rancière, here not unlike Badiou, politics does not just happen every day. It is precarious, it occurs in the midst of a dominant police model, and it must arise from a radical insistence on equality.[31] The following passage, from the section "The Uses of Democracy" in *On the Shores of Politics*, illustrates this rare twentieth-century French philosophical position that readily affirms, along with equality, the idea of democracy:

> The democratic experience is thus one of a particular aesthetic of politics. The democratic man is a being who speaks, which is also to say a poetic being, a being capable of embracing a distance between words and things which is not deception, not trickery, but humanity; a being capable of embracing the unreality of representation. A poetic virtue, then, and a virtue grounded in trust. This means starting from the point of view of equality, asserting equality, assuming equality as a given, working out from equality, trying to see how productive it can be and thus maximizing all possible liberty and equality. By contrast, anyone who starts out from distrust, who assumes inequality and proposes to reduce it, can only succeed in setting up a hierarchy of inequalities, a hierarchy of priorities, a hierarchy of intelligences—and will reproduce inequality ad infinitum.[32]

It bears emphasizing the striking difference between Rancière's foundational and quasi-humanist assumption of equality and the economic models outlined above, with their insistence on a driving imbalance of forces—particularly in the third, or libidinal economy, model. This libidinal economy model is anything but an assertion of a basic underlying equality (which would fall into Bataille's debased restrictive economy). Furthermore, there is virtually no sustained discussion or even mention of democracy in these previous economic models. By contrast, the synthesis of Marx and Freud emerges from a fundamental asymmetry and imbalance, which is none other than the logic of the symptom, of the crisis; it is the marker by which we come to recognize repetition, serial formation, the two terms that appear as one. These imbalances and asymmetries, which are the distinctive mark of general economy, are considered fundamental and generative for a strain of thought that dominates the middle part of the French twentieth century.

It is useful in situating Rancière to draw once again on Badiou, insofar as Badiou is a mediating figure of sorts between Derrida and Rancière on the economic/political spectrum under consideration. He retains a certain proximity to Rancière, for Badiou takes up some of the same problematics with respect to the question of politics and, like Rancière, would see the political event emerging from something that is not counted or included in the situation. Another point of proximity is that a true evental occurrence for Badiou opens onto a space of universal access (Badiou does not use the word "equality," but arguably equality is at least on some level implicit when he takes up the question of universalism). This comes out most distinctly in Badiou's book on the apostle Paul, *Saint Paul: The Foundation of Universalism*, and the way Paul's fidelity to Christ's resurrection introduces a militant insistence on the universalizability of the Christian message—something not restricted to the Greek or the Jew but available to all Gentiles. Notably, for Badiou this is a political and not a theological event. This, however, is about as far as the similarities between Badiou and Rancière extend, for in fact Badiou criticizes Rancière in stringent terms for trying to reverse Platonism (almost all of twentieth-century French thought for Badiou is subject to this critique), for not having a concept of the militant, and for basically espousing a parliamentary logic.[33] Badiou, who will privilege, in his *Logics of Worlds*, the materialist dialectic over democratic materialism, is certainly not about to embrace the category of democracy, or even equality. He writes in *Metapolitics* that "Rancière's doctrine can be identified as a democratic anti-philosophy that identifies [or revolves around] the axiom of equality."[34] This, to be sure, is not a favorable assessment.

Badiou is notably at odds with the libidinal economy movement, and in fact he attacks it quite forcefully in his *Théorie de la contradiction* (1975), where he parodies Marx's ridicule of Stirner in *The German Ideology* but here substitutes the names Saint Gilles, Saint Félix, and Saint Jean-François for Marx's Saint Max.[35] In this regard, despite Badiou's distance from Rancière's model of democracy, he shares Rancière's distance from the exuberant tones of the libidinal economy theorists. Indeed, we might say that both Badiou and Rancière, and in a different fashion Derrida, react to this frenetic synthesis of Marx and Freud by proposing a more sober turn to the question of the political. However, in the time that remains, I wish to link Rancière's work back to one of the least sober moments in the libidinal economy movement, perhaps the least sober moment of all. Beyond anything even in *Anti-Oedipus*, the most extreme articulation of a radical rethinking of use value is voiced in Lyotard's *Libidinal Economy* (though Baudrillard's *For a Critique of the Political Economy of the Sign* likewise uses an in-your-face shock effect to illustrate that all use value is inextricably bound to desire, indeed even the physical fact of exploitation).[36] This is Lyotard's extreme claim that the English proletariat in fact experience a form of *jouissance* in the destruction of their laboring bodies, something that would otherwise appear to be a straightforward instance of bodily exploitation rather than a scene of masochism.[37]

Rancière gives a much more sustained and nuanced attention to the figure of the worker. His early works engage in detailed archival analysis of writings by workers, such as the joiner Gabriel Gauny, whose letters and fictional writings Rancière reproduces in his book on Gauny, as well as in the slightly earlier *The Nights of Labor*. Rancière's excerpts and analyses show the full range of workers' writings, and what comes out repeatedly is that there is a very pronounced aesthetic sensibility—a realm of the sensible—in these writings, one that doesn't at all correspond to Plato's hierarchy (in *The Republic*) of gold, silver, and bronze races, where workers occupy the lowest rung. He documents with detail and precision the way in which the life of the worker, as shown through the writings and the archives of those rare workers who took up writing and whose writings were preserved, is entirely in excess of the worker's position as a cog or token of labor or use value. This reorientation of use value constitutes a certain affinity between Rancière's work on nineteenth-century laborers and the libidinal economy movement in the wake of May '68, epitomized by Lyotard's *Libidinal Economy*.

Rancière's presentation of the full complexity of the worker's perspective, including the embracing of activities such as writing that are not always related to bodily subsistence—to the point even of being destructive of that working body's subsistence—puts him strangely in line with the very antiequality libidinal economy theorists he would seem to be at odds with. This comes out particularly in his evocation of the destructive side of the worker. If we might equate the worker's extraproductive side, his surplus literary production in excess of his physical labor, with a proletarian republic of letters that gets its impetus from a fundamental assumption of equality, that anyone (as Rancière emphasizes) can take part in literary production, then what do we make of the worker's extradestructive side, something like a death drive, which is what Lyotard figures as the worker's enjoyment of his body's destruction? Rancière gestures to this at significant moments, such as his commentary at the beginning of *The Nights of Labor* on the "hieroglyphs of the anticommodity, products of a worker know-how that retains the creative and *destructive* dream of those proletarian children who seek to exorcise their inexorable future as useful workers."[38] It is this mixture of the creative and the destructive as a *resistance* to an inexorable future, one in excess of that future, but in no way *equal* to it, that comes out in both Rancière's and Lyotard's discussions of the worker. In this regard, Rancière's analyses of the body and mind of the worker have considerable resonance with some of the fundamentally economic logics of the synthesis of Marx and Freud that reached its heyday in France in the early 1970s. Clearly, Rancière's work is much more restrained and careful in tone than Lyotard's rant—perhaps that is the mark of it coming a decade later in the early 1980s—but it shares with Lyotard the willingness to engage with the destructive.

One might ask if this emphasis on destruction is simply the mark of the early part of a thinker's oeuvre, a sort of youthful exuberance, for such claims might be made of Derrida, Deleuze, Foucault, and Badiou, among others. Rancière himself makes something of this connection in an afterward to the collection *History, Politics, Aesthetics: Jacques Rancière,* but instead insists on connecting his later work on the relation of politics to aesthetics, in particular the concept of the "distribution of the sensible," to the early work on the joiner Gauny. In what follows, Rancière describes the worker's creative remapping of his exploitation as something beyond mere awareness and instead at the level of the body's celebratory drives, or to impose Lyotard's term from *Libidinal Economy*, beyond awareness toward *jouissance.* Rancière writes:

> In the construction and the writing of his sensory experience, the joiner implements a different *as if* that overturns the whole logic which allotted him his place. But this overturning is far from the canonical idea of the freeing power of awareness. The jobber frees himself by becoming *less aware* of exploitation and pushing aside, thereby, its sensory grip. He frees himself by nurturing a power of self-delusion. That power makes him work still more for the benefit of his enemy, against his own employment and the conservation of his health. But this counter effect, which results from his way of reframing the space and time of exercise of his force of labor, is the source of a new pleasure, the pleasure of a new freedom.[39]

This destructive drive in which the worker indulges at the expense of his own health is acutely reminiscent not only of Lyotard's *Libidinal Economy* but also of Klossowski's monumental study of Nietzsche from 1969, where the force and joy of weakness and sickness are read as the key to Nietzsche's entire oeuvre.[40] And, significantly, Klossowski's brilliantly unorthodox economic treatise *Living Currency* (1970), a text that Lyotard glosses at length and with extreme lucidity in *Libidinal Economy*, makes many of these same points in a different framework. In brief, Klossowski suggests that all values, both exchange *and* use, are bound by a desiring structure which is tantamount to prostitution, and according to Klossowski there is a "voluptuous" exuberance in this position.[41]

This is certainly not to imply that Rancière takes up the libidinal economy rhetoric as fully or in the explicit fashion of Lyotard and Klossowski, yet there is an undeniable resonance. Indeed, as soon as one moves past the ready equivalent of the worker as a useful laboring proletarian body and considers what the worker is actually thinking and feeling, it is hard to avoid an engagement with some dimension of extremity and contradiction. In *The Philosopher and His Poor*, Rancière remarks in a discussion of Plato's *Republic* that "if the city began with the clearcut distribution of useful workers, politics begins with the motley crowd of the *unuseful* who, coming together into a mass of 'workers,' cater to a new range of needs."[42] It would seem that, intimately connected to the spirit of the worker, is something of a disorientation from an easy or straightforward equivalence of use and usefulness. While for Rancière this complicating of use inaugurates the sphere of the political, for the libidinal economists, whose work is in explicit dialogue with Bataille's *Accursed Share* and its emphasis on the generative force of imbalanced or "general" economy, this bringing together of labor and desire, of use value and surplus value, of Marx and Freud, is an *economic* above and beyond a *political* logic. We are left, then, with something of a conundrum: while the interrogation of use would seem to align Rancière with the libidinal economy theorists, his even more stringent emphasis on politics and on equality as foundational could not be more opposed to their line of thinking.

In conclusion, I will note a striking instance where these seemingly diametrically opposite discourses converge, and converge around the exuberantly active body of the worker. For Rancière, "The emancipated worker's new 'awareness' of his situation means the 'ignorance' of the logic of inequality. The balance of knowledge and ignorance is what our joiner calls a passion."[43] Rather than regarding, with Rancière, the new awareness as an ignorance of inequality, it might be considered by contrast an *awareness* of inequality that counterintuitively pushes that inequality to its limit. Supporting this reading is a passage from Gauny that Rancière himself cites in his afterword, just after the statement on ignorance and inequality. He continues à propos of Gauny, citing a letter Gauny writes to one of his fellows: "This is how [Gauny] demonstrates to one of his fellow companions the necessity of new passions: 'Plunge into terrible readings. That will awaken passions in your wretched existence, and the labourer needs them to stand tall in the face of that which is ready to devour him. So, from the *Imitation* to *Lélia*, explore the enigma of the mysterious and formidable chagrin at work in those with sublime conceptions.' "[44] Gauny here extols an economy of excess, though he also authors a tract on "cenobitic economy" that promotes an economic imbalance in the other direction, toward that of restriction.[45] In either case, the worker's body is the site of a calculated economic imbalance.

It should be noted that Rancière evokes George Sand at a number of junctures in *The Nights of Labor*, including for example her correspondence with and preface to the collected writings of a worker named Jérôme-Pierre Gilland.[46] In the above letter from Gauny, it is none other than Sand's extreme idealist novel *Lélia* that is cited as an example of the terrible reading being advised. Strikingly, the recommended reading is not something on the order of Sand's accessibly realist agricultural story *François le champi*, but of all things *Lélia*, which is an intensely dark antirealist and passionately immaterialist novel, literally illustrating the imbalanced economy of forces of repression. Much in the fashion of the passages cited above from Lyotard, and from Rancière's examples from Gauny, the main character Lélia's much-discussed frigidity is not a problem of impotence, but one of excessive power, and this is precisely what Lyotard and Rancière through Gauny reveal about the worker: that the worker's very bodily subjection is also a form of self-destructive power. Lélia is similarly not without a self-destructive impulse. She has so much power that she is often compared to both God and the devil. If frigidity is a sort of failure in *Lélia*, then it is a sublime one, for it is frigidity, failure, sadness, and suffering that give Lélia her grandeur as a character. She frequently hails this "douleur sublime" (sublime suffering) as the mark of her dignity.[47] So it is in fact entirely apposite that Gauny would recommend *Lélia* (only from the bourgeois perspective would he be recommending something like *François le champi*), and recommend it precisely insofar as it represents the terrible and the sublime. Gauny's "sublime conceptions" as figured in the character of Lélia is a striking marker of imbalance, and in Lélia's case something of a failed repression, to put it in the terms of Freud's economic writings on repression. Freud writes that "repressions that have failed will of course have more claim on our interest than any that may have been successful, for the latter will for the most part escape our examination" and furthermore that "repression demands a persistent expenditure of force, and if this were to cease the success of the repression would be jeopardized."[48] In other words, there must be an inequality of forces for repression to be recognized and brought to the surface. What is terrible in Gauny's writings and recommended readings such as Sand's *Lélia* is the *imbalance* of forces that serves as the impetus to sublime action or inaction. It may produce a subsequent field of equality and of the political, but it seems more fundamentally grounded in the domain of general economy.

Notes

1. Alain Badiou, *Can Politics Be Thought?*, trans. Bruno Bosteels (Durham, N.C.: Duke University Press, 2019).

2. See Alain Badiou, *Manifesto for Philosophy*, trans. Norman Madarasz (Albany: SUNY Press, 1999).

3. Alain Badiou, *Metapolitics*, trans. Jason Barker (London: Verso, 2005), 116.

4. Fredric Jameson, "Lenin and Revisionism," in *Lenin Reloaded: Toward a Politics of Truth*, ed. Sebastian Budgen, Stathis Kouvelakis, and Slavoj Žižek (Durham, N.C.: Duke University Press, 2007), 65.

5. Jameson, "Lenin and Revisionism," 65–66. Regarding the terminology, he notes: "When I use the words economics and economic they have nothing to do with that purely trade-union consciousness and politics Lenin designated by the term economism long ago and in another situation" (65).

6. Jameson, "Lenin and Revisionism," 65.

7. See Michel Foucault, *The Order of Things: An Archaeology of the Human Sciences* (New York: Vintage Books, 1970).

8. Although beyond the scope of this analysis, the advent of the "new spirit of capitalism"—what Badiou will label the "Restoration" of 1980 and Deleuze the "society of control" (and these perhaps situated under the larger headings of neoliberalism and globalization)—seems part and parcel of the shift at issue here from the economic to the political. See Luc Boltanski and Eve Chiapello, *The New Spirit of Capitalism*, trans. Gregory Elliott (London: Verso, 2018).

9. Jameson, "Lenin and Revisionism," 66, my emphasis.

10. See Karl Marx, *Theories of Surplus Value* (London: Lawrence & Wishart, 1969–72).

11. Sigmund Freud, "Repression," in *The Standard Edition of the Complete Psychological Works*, vol. 14, trans. James Strachey (London: Hogarth, 1957).

12. Alain Badiou, *The Century*, trans. Alberto Toscano (London: Polity, 2007), 25.

13. See Sigmund Freud, *Beyond the Pleasure Principle*, trans. James Strachey (New York: W. W. Norton, 1961), chapter 2, and *Moses and Monotheism*, trans. Katherine Jones (New York: Vintage, 1939), part 3, section 1, chapter 2.

14. Karl Marx, *The Eighteenth Brumaire of Louis Bonaparte* (New York: International, 2008).

15. For a more detailed analysis of these sequences, see my "The Desire Called Mao: Badiou and the Legacy of Libidinal Economy," *Postmodern Culture* 18, no. 1 (September 2007), unpaginated.

16. Marcel Mauss, *The Gift: The Form and Reason for Exchange in Archaic Societies*, trans. W. D. Halls (New York: W. W. Norton, 1990).

17. Jacques Derrida, *Given Time I: Counterfeit Money*, trans. Peggy Kamuf (Chicago: University of Chicago Press, 1992), see "The Time of the King," especially: "But, after all, what would be a gift that fulfills the condition of the gift, namely, that it not appear as gift, that it not be, exist, signify, want-to-say as gift?

A gift without wanting, without wanting-to-say, an insignificant gift, a gift without intention to give? Why would we still call that a gift?" (27).

18. See Georges Bataille, *The Accursed Share*, vol. 1, trans. Robert Hurley (New York: Zone Books, 1991), and *Visions of Excess: Selected Writings, 1927–1939*, trans. Allan Stoekl (Minneapolis: University of Minnesota Press, 1985).

19. Gilles Deleuze and Félix Guattari, *Anti-Oedipus*, trans. Robert Hurley, Mark Seem, and Helen R. Lane (Minneapolis: University of Minnesota Press, 1983); Jean-François Lyotard, *Libidinal Economy*, trans. Iain Hamilton Grant (Bloomington: Indiana University Press, 1993); Jean Baudrillard, *For a Critique of the Political Economy of the Sign*, trans. Charles Levin (St. Louis: Telos, 1981); Pierre Klossowski, *Living Currency*, ed. Daniel W. Smith, Nicolae Morar, and Vernon W. Cisney (London: Bloomsbury, 2017).

20. Gilles Deleuze, *Proust and Signs*, trans. Richard Howard (New York: George Braziller, 1972). See especially the chapter "Series and Group."

21. See Jean-Paul Sartre, *Critique of Dialectical Reason*, trans. Alan Sheridan-Smith (London: Verso, 2004), 256–69, in which Sartre uses the example of a group of people waiting for a bus, brought together only in this fleeting and one-dimensional fashion, versus the more focalized praxis-oriented group that comes together for a directed cause but may also quickly recede into a serial formation.

22. Alain Badiou, *Logics of Worlds*, trans. Alberto Toscano (London: Continuum, 2009), 366–80.

23. This might be considered as a form of structuralism—though many of the thinkers in question will distance themselves from structuralism in no uncertain terms—insofar as it attends to the economic forces outlined above through binary rubrics that get collapsed or expanded, condensed or displaced. I would further distinguish simple logics such as these that display a recognizably binary structure from a more radical thought of *structure without structuralism*, gestured toward in certain works of Lévi-Strauss, Lacan, and Deleuze in the 1950s and 1960s.

24. Badiou's work will again provide a certain bridge between these categories of the political if we take his Paul book and in general the heightened interest in Paul and questions of politics that it might be said to have generated, as a certain turn to political theology. Notably, Badiou does not embrace this term, nor does he acknowledge the Paul example as in any way an intrinsically theological one, though multiple critics have wondered why religion is not included as a fifth generic procedure—alongside politics, art, science, and love—that might produce an evental outcome. See Alain Badiou, *Saint Paul: The Foundations of Universalism* (Stanford, Calif.: Stanford University Press, 2003).

25. Jacques Derrida, *Specters of Marx: The State of the Debt, the Work of Mourning, and the New International*, trans. Peggy Kamuf (New York: Routledge, 1994).

26. Jacques Derrida, *The Politics of Friendship*, trans. George Collins (London: Verso, 1997).

27. This shift is arguably inaugurated with "Force of Law: The 'Mystical Foundation of Authority,'" in *Acts of Religion*, ed. Gil Anidjar (New York: Routledge, 2002).

28. Not unlike Badiou's oeuvre, Derrida's work is challenging to squarely situate, since certainly one can find—as Richard Beardsworth in *Derrida and the Political* (London: Routledge, 1996) and others have argued—an interest in the political all along, although what Beardsworth calls political, especially regarding the question of law, I would call economic.

29. Jacques Derrida, *Rogues: Two Essays on Reason*, trans. Pascale-Anne Brault and Michael Naas (Stanford, Calif.: Stanford University Press, 2005).

30. Jacques Rancière, *On the Shores of Politics*, trans. Liz Heron (London: Verso, 1995), 3.

31. For an excellent discussion of Rancière and equality, see Todd May, *The Political Thought of Jacques Rancière: Creating Equality* (State Park: Pennsylvania State University Press, 2008); and *Contemporary Political Movements and the Thought of Jacques Rancière: Equality in Action* (Edinburgh: Edinburgh University Press, 2010).

32. Rancière, *On the Shores of Politics*, 51–52.

33. Badiou, *Metapolitics*, 115.

34. Badiou, *Metapolitics*, 115.

35. Alain Badiou, *Théorie de la contradiction* (Paris: Librairie François Maspero, 1975), 72.

36. Baudrillard, *For a Critique of the Political Economy of the Sign*, 204.

37. The passage in question from Lyotard's *Libidinal Economy*, which I analyze in detail in "The Desire Called Mao," reads: "The English unemployed did not become workers to survive, they—hang on tight and spit on me—enjoyed [*ils ont joui de*] the hysterical, masochistic, whatever exhaustion it was of hanging on in the mines, in the foundries, in the factories, in hell, they enjoyed it, enjoyed the mad destruction of their organic body which was indeed imposed upon them, they enjoyed the decomposition of their personal identity, the identity that the peasant tradition had constructed for them, enjoyed the dissolution of their families and villages, and enjoyed the new monstrous anonymity of the suburbs and the pubs in the morning and evening" (111).

38. Jacques Rancière, *The Nights of Labor: The Workers' Dream in Nineteenth-Century France*, trans. John Drury (Philadelphia: Temple University Press, 1989), 6, my italics.

39. Jacques Rancière, "Afterword: The Method of Equality. An Answer to Some Questions," in *History, Politics, Aesthetics: Jacques Rancière*, ed. Gabriel Rockhill and Philip Watts (Durham, N.C.: Duke University Press, 2009), 276–77.

40. See Pierre Klossowski, *Nietzsche and the Vicious Circle*, trans. Daniel W. Smith (Chicago: University of Chicago Press, 1997).

41. See Klossowski, *Living Currency*.

42. Jacques Rancière, *The Philosopher and His Poor*, trans. John Drury, Corinne Oster, and Andrew Parker (Durham, N.C.: Duke University Press, 2003), 9, my italics.

43. Rancière, "Afterword," 277.

44. Rancière, "Afterword," 277. Notably, this letter is not actually cited in Rancière's collection *Gabriel Gauny: Le philosophe plébéien* (Paris: Maspero, 1983),

but only in *The Nights of Labor,* 19. The French reads, "Ainsi depuis l'*Imitation* jusqu'à *Lélia,* cherche l'enigme de ce mysterieux et formidable chagrin qui travaille dans de sublimes concepteurs" (31).

45. See Rancière, *Gabriel Gauny,* 99–111, and the discussion in *The Nights of Labor,* 84–85. Gauny's and Rancière's affinity for a quasi–desert monasticism is an underground current worthy of exploration. See Rancière, *The Flesh of Words: The Politics of Writing,* trans. Charlotte Mandell (Stanford, Calif.: Stanford University Press, 2004), 79–86; and Alexandre Costanzo, "La puissance de l'égalité," in *La philosophie déplacée: Autour de Jacques Rancière* (Colloque de Cerisy), ed. Laurence Cornu and Patrice Vermeren (Péronnas: Horlieu éditions, 2006), 379–91.

46. Rancière, *The Nights of Labor,* 4, 6.

47. Georges Sand, *Lélia* (Paris: Garnier, 1960); *Lelia,* trans. Maria Espinosa (Bloomington: Indiana University Press, 1978).

48. Freud, "Repression," 153, 151.

All Affects Equal

Tom Conley

Jacques Rancière's fairly recent and aptly titled *La méthode de l'égalité* is composed of transcribed conversations with two informed and astute interlocutors. At first glance the reading resembles an "as-told-to" style of autobiography of the kind aspiring editors craft from conversations with old movie directors or sexagenarian sports figures.[1] At the beginning of "Genèses," the first (and also aptly titled) chapter, Rancière notes that in his adolescence his first training in philosophy began with a reading of Descartes and an impassioned rapport with Sartre and Camus, both of whom had deeply invested relations with film.[2] At its end, seventy pages later, "Genèses" ends with the beginning of a series of copious reflections on cinema.

How Rancière gets there is the vector I hope to draw in the following paragraphs. The itinerary begun in "Genesis" leads to what he later calls a mapping of things possible, a "cartographie des possibles" (255–59). In 1976, recalls Rancière, in a piece titled "L'image fraternelle" ("The Fraternal Image") appearing in the revamped and then-Marxian *Cahiers du cinéma,* he argued for the pleasure that a person feels when isolated in a community of viewers watching a film in a movie theater, a condition that Sartre had earlier described in his praise of the seventh art.[3] Sartre's musings may have pertained to what Rancière first sensed in his relation with film. For the author of *Qu'est-ce que la littérature?* unbeknownst to himself or his own words, cinema may have been the wedge Sartre had been driving between prose and poetry—if only because his experience of the seventh art had never known so wondrous an existential equal.[4]

"Together alone" in the darkened space of the theater, watching any number of films of the moment, we confront what we behold within a welter of impressions and affects present and past. Whether onscreen or off-, these flickerings belong to us; in their instant, no matter what their intensity may be, what we perceive or make of them informs our "situation." Yet somehow, if film brings a commonly shared presence to us all in the confines of the darkened space, a collective force of attraction, indeed of critical conviction, is born and nurtured. In the best of moments, which for Sartre in 1947 might be that of the palette of terror and fear giving way to a frail and fragile sense of hope, we feel ourselves sharing with other spectators in our midst a drive, as he would relate in his famous "L'existentialisme est un humanisme," his upbeat essay betraying the cinematic virtue of his philosophy, to change the condition of the world.[5]

Within Sartre's imaginary theater a film cannot fail to spur memories and reflections at once of "life itself," what as an "every viewer" we have known in our lifelong relation with cinema, in other words, a psychogeography of both individual and collective dimension. In a complementary fashion we realize that film comprises much of our own ideology of experience. As Rancière quickly reminds us, we fashion the chronologies of our lives, the autobiographies that for good fortune we have not nor shall ever have written, from items, such as sports events and movies, to which our imagination refers to order what we think might be the parabola of our subjectivity.[6] Along this line, Sartre's espousal of cinema would have clearly marked anyone of Rancière's generation growing into the political milieus of the postwar years. No doubt, as the recent interview with Rancière reveals, Sartre underpins what he calls the democratic potential of the seventh art.

Now, in 1976, when the editors of *Cahiers du cinéma* had contacted him, his work chimed well with the recent Marxian orientation of the review, especially for "what could be made of it in order, first, to reassess their dogmatic Marxist periods and second, the thematic strands of popular memory" (84; ce qu'on pouvait en tirer pour réévaluer leur période marxiste dogmatique et, deuxièmement, les thématiques de la mémoire populaire). And so too did Michel Foucault and his critique of the *mode rétro*: the editors had him view some left-wing militant cinema that included the Huillet-Straub's *Fortini Cani* and *Leçons d'histoire*, John Douglas and Robert Kramer's *Milestones* (1975), Godard's *Ici et ailleurs* (1976), and a film about the strike in the Darboy printing firm. Ill at ease, Rancière had to think more broadly about what he was being given to see. He needed to go beyond—in other words, below—what the selection revealed to be of a generally Brechtian orientation. In contrast to Straub and Godard, by virtue of Kramer and Douglas's multifaceted study of political action in the wake of Vietnam, Rancière was enabled to refer to

> toute une tradition de cinéma américaine, avec son ancrage historique et sa fiction type, illustrée notamment par le western, l'histoire de l'individu qui finit par adhérer à une symbolique collective. Il me semblait intéressant d'opposer ce type de fiction généalogique à la fiction française avec son rapport à un peuple toujours déjà là, donné dans sa familiarité. C'est par rapport à ça que j'ai été amené à développer cette critique de la fiction de gauche comme fiction familialiste et à opposer une certaine

> fiction de la légende de l'identité à la fiction "sociologique" de l'identité, la fiction qui est là pour que les types sociaux se reconnaissent. (84–85)

> [an entire tradition of American cinema, with its historical anchoring and its fictional type for which the western is a notable illustration, the history of the individual who ultimately conforms to a symbolic collectivity. It then seemed interesting to me to oppose this type of genealogical fiction to French fiction with its pregiven relation with a people given in its familiarity. Through this relation I was led to develop this critique of left-wing fiction as a familial fiction and to oppose a certain fiction of the legend of identity to the "sociological" fiction of identity, a fiction set forward so that social types can be distinguished.]

At this moment, he adds, he felt disgruntled about the concept of popular memory that figured in the manifesto for the journal *Les Révoltes logiques*. Already in the interview in *Cahiers du cinéma* he had marked a distance from what the "famous fiction of the left" had been hailing. In building on a comparison of the two types of fictional representation of the nation—the one American, the other French—Rancière used the iconography of the Revolution of 1848. The left-wing version was based on the oblivion of the memory of those who were vanquished and on how the "left fed itself on the appropriation of those it had gunned down" (85–86). As a result there prevailed among intellectuals on the left a toxic *doxa*, in other words, "everything that was going to sustain the politics of Mitterrand by seeking to appropriate the entirety of popular and working-class memory" (ibid.).

American cinema became a foil, a critical or even post-Brechtian operative. Without quite saying so, Rancière admits that he reached back into his own popular memory when recalling the first time he experienced the pleasure of movies in the midst of his preparation for the entrance exams to the Grandes Écoles. A friend told him

> que le vrai cinéma ce n'était pas Antonioni, Bergman, tous les trucs culturellement légitimes, non, il fallait aller voir *Esther et le roi* [*Esther and the King*, dir. Raoul Walsh, 1960] ou *La bataille de Marathon* [*Giant of Marathon*, dir. Jacques Tourneur, 1960], et c'était le vrai cinéma. Ce cinéma par ses salles comme le Mac Mahon ou des cinémas comme le Ciné qua non ou le Nickelodéon. Ça a été mon initiation au cinéma. C'était aussi l'époque de la Nouvelle Vague, d'un rapport plus ou moins ambigu entre la Nouvelle Vague et toute la grande tradition hollywoodienne. J'ai connu le cinéma en dehors de toute initiation à l'art, à l'histoire de l'art, comme un bloc

d'emblée polémique: l'idée que le vrai cinéma c'était Minnelli, Walsh ou Ant[h]ony Mann et pas les trucs à la mode chez les bourgeois cultivés. (86)[7]

[that the true cinema was not Antonioni, Bergman, all the culturally legitimated stuff; no, it was much better to go to see *Esther and the Queen* (d. Raoul Walsh, 1960) or *Giant of Marathon* (d. Jacques Tourneur, 1960), and yes, that was true cinema, cinema known by its movie houses, like the Mac-Mahon or those like the Ciné Qua Non or the Nickelodéon. That was my initiation to cinema. It was also the moment of the New Wave, of a more or less ambiguous relation between the New Wave and the great tradition of Hollywood. I got to know cinema outside of any initiation to the history of art, much as a generally polemical front: the idea that true cinema was Vincente Minnelli, Raoul Walsh, or Anthony Mann, and not the trendy stuff in the style of the cultivated bourgeois.]

He further recalls that between 1960 and 1968 he became a cinephile but that between 1968 and 1976, when *Cahiers du cinéma* solicited an interview, he never went to the movies. After that, and especially when Antoine de Baecque invited him to become a regular contributor, he once again went to the movies. He avows that he intensely experienced film in spurts, and not "along a line of continuous accumulation" (87). Philosophy and cinema were not "two modes of thought of the same type," but in shifts and ruptures between the one and the other he opened himself onto "territories, pathways, investigations" (ibid.) leading away from a narrowly defined field of political economy. Thus ends a chapter that would have been about the formation of a militant intellectual in dialogue and debate with his mentor Louis Althusser. In the interview the intermittent flickering of cinema in Rancière's early and intensely political years throws light on his difficult relation with Marx. In the middle and late 1970s, perhaps in line with his refusal to toss two minor works—each an epic catastrophe—by two directors of major proportion into a bin of "bad taste," Rancière took to task Louis Althusser, the antithesis of the "ignorant schoolmaster," on the grounds of what seemed to be elitism. Like his master Marx, Althusser espoused the classes from on high, above and beyond the proletariat of which either he knew little or else had to champion in mode of a Romantic hero speaking for it, thus depriving it of voices of its own.[8]

A year before *La méthode de l'égalité*, in the prologue to *Les écarts du cinéma*, reflecting on how cinephilia had linked the cult of art to the "democracy of pleasures [*divertissements*] and emotions," Rancière underscored how much the greatness of film lay not in the "metaphysical elevation of its subjects or the visibility of its plastic effects" but, rather, "in an imperceptible difference in the manner of putting traditional stories and emotions into images."[9] Cinephiles, both he and many of a postwar generation are quick to remember, called it "mise-en-scène" without having an inkling about what the formula really meant. Adepts of the movies did not have an analytical discourse or a lexicon with which they could domesticate or regulate their pleasures, much less turn them into scientific objects of study. Cinephilia, he avows, was what offered access to a democratic sublime, what elsewhere philosophers would brutalize in the concept of an "event," especially where the pleasure of film called into question the categories of modernism, in a "return to a more intimate and more obscure knotting of the marks of art, the emotions of the story and the discovery of the splendor that the most ordinary spectacle could take when projected on an illuminated screen in the middle of a dark room: a hand raising a curtain or that plays with a doorknob" (9).

When did a new equality of affect take place? It was when the crushing beauty of John Mohune's smile in *Moonfleet* (which Rancière takes up in "L'enfant metteur en scène") caused him—like ourselves now, we hope, at a time when neoliberal capitalism conquers all—to ask how a student in the 1960s—or, for the ends of this essay, *hic et nunc*—can negotiate the pleasure of what he was seeing with the common and collective battle against social inequality. In *Winchester '73* the same held for a terrible mix of emotion at the sight of Lynn McAdam (James Stewart) in pain and confusion after he has shot his brother on a rocky hillside overlooking a mesa dotted with saguaro cactuses. Or, too, the close-up of Wes McQueen's (Joel McCrea's) hands joined with those of the wild woman Colorado Carson (Virginia Mayo) beneath the cliffs (near Gallup, New Mexico) in which prehistoric dwellings are nestled, when the forces of law, their bullets riddling Virginia Mayo's voluptuous body, have ruthlessly gunned them down. "What relation could be established between those films and the struggle of the new force of labor against the world of exploitation?" (10).

This undecidable issue seems to be where the political aesthetic of cinema becomes possible—or at least, in the best of worlds, debatable. It is where the *politique de l'auteur*, that had been the rallying cry of aesthetically sanctioned specialists of cinema now turns into what, in the creative drift of Rancière's words, becomes a *politique de l'amateur*. It suffices to see how a give-and-take, a push-and-pull, a movement toward and away from the cinematic object (or, if we can riff on the title of Raoul Walsh, an *Objective: Cinema*) gets drawn into the play of words:

> La politique de l'amateur affirme que le cinéma appartient à tous ceux qui ont, d'une manière ou d'une autre, voyagé à l'intérieur du système

Figure 1. Anthony Mann, *Winchester '73* (Universal Pictures, 1950).

> d'écarts que son nom dispose et que chacun peut s'autoriser à tracer, entre tel ou tel point de cette topographie, un itinéraire singulier qui ajoute au cinéma comme monde et à sa connaissance. (14)
>
> [The politics of the amateur affirms that cinema belongs to all those who have, in one manner or another, traveled within the system of deviations availed by its name and that each and every person can be empowered to trace, between one point or another of this topography, a unique itinerary that enriches cinema both as world and as knowledge.]

Rancière's more recent account of the discoveries that took place at the multiple ruptures between philosophy and cinema are rehearsed in these very pages. When the amateur has traveled in one manner or another within a system of deviations that its name—reference doubling back on *écarts*—"avails" or "disposes," the reader sees how *tracer* reverses *écart*, and how the very word itself, in motion, becomes the site of a topography of productive conflict.

Deviation may be a skeleton key or, better in French, a *passe-partout* in Rancière's writings, where cinema, never directly addressed, bleeds into the prose. The flashbacks to his youth in the movie houses, where

Figure 2. Raoul Walsh, *Colorado Territory* (Warner Bros., 1949).

a relation of passionate affection, ciné-*philia*, fortunately precluded, deferred, or obfuscated the disillusionment that would come with a more reasoned or cultivated appreciation of the seventh art. The relation of pleasure to reason is manifest in other ways and in writings of lesser eminence. As clearly shown in much of Rancière's writing on film, *landscape* is a field where, before the spectator witnesses contradiction, deviations are ubiquitous. In *Colorado Territory* a great rock face displays a crevasse once inhabited by troglodytes. As characters in the film are quick to observe, it resembles a great eye, mouth, or anus of time immemorial. But the film's force of movement is not suspended long enough (speed being the signature of director Raoul Walsh) to incite reflections on a western sublime. The event of the murder of Wes McQueen and Colorado happens *not* to rehearse the myth of Orpheus, nor does it, contrary to what the coda to the film serves up, lead to a happy end—when, in the final credits, the ringing of a bell in a belfry following the discovery of the criminals' stash of money in an abandoned monastery assures its reparation and its rebirth.

Rancière seems to be in concert with what André Bazin had noted about Rossellini's visual parataxis in the narration of events in the sixth and final episode of *Paisà*, which takes place in the reeds and marshes of the Po River delta. Cinephiles recall how the final sequence is the setting for a *fait divers,* an event-of-any-kind-whatsoever in the final days of the Second World War, but also an "image-fact" that is much more than its component elements. In Bazin's words, it is "not the 'shot,' an abstract point of view on the reality [that is] in question, but a 'fact' . . . , a [f]ragment of brute reality, in itself multiple and equivocal, whose 'meaning' [*sens*]" is grasped only in the context of other discernible "facts."[10] Bazin implies that in *Paisà* there results an equality of affective force because, when considered in itself, "each image being only a fragment of reality prior to meaning [*sens*], the entire surface of the screen must present an equal concrete density" (ibid.). All areas of the image are of equal charge and density. No element can be accorded greater value over another. As a consequence the viewer's eye has no single place or detail on which to focus or find an assuring presence. A productive alienation or separation from the image confers on it autonomy irrespective of what the viewer would wish to see within its frame. It is in the same sense of a deviation—an *écart*—that landscapes emerge as cinematic elements at the beginning of Rancière's *Courts voyages au pays du peuple* (1990), in which a foreigner traveling in the countryside of postrevolutionary France could be watching a classical movie. Putting himself in the place of Wordsworth venturing into the French hinterland, he writes:

> De l'autre côté du détroit, un peu à l'écart du fleuve et de la grande route, au bout de la ligne des transports urbains, vit un autre peuple, à moins que ce ne soit simplement le peuple. Le spectacle imprévu d'une autre humanité s'offre sous ses diverses figures: retour à l'origine, descente aux enfers, avènement de la terre promise. Le soleil de juillet qui joue dans le feuillage des arbres devient pour le poète anglais en promenade sur le continent la lumière nouvelle d'une France révolutionnaire accordée à la nature en fête.[11]
>
> [From the other side of the channel, at a slight remove [*un peu à l'écart*] from the major river and main road, at the end of the city transportation lives another people—unless it's simply the people. The unforeseen spectacle of another humanity comes forward in a variety of figures: a return to beginnings, a descent into hell, arrival at the promised land. For the English poet during his sojourn on the continent the July sunshine dappling the trees becomes the new light of a revolutionary France awarded to nature in its festive glamour.]

Rancière notes how Wordsworth's moment resembles that of Mao Tse-tung when the leader takes the initiative to get on a bicycle, leave the city, and be done with the vanity of books to "gather living reality" (ibid.). Adds Rancière, as if harking back to his years of cinephilia, such was "the political experience of our generation" (ibid.). The moment allowed him to see how an illumination—that later develops into the method of equality—emanates from a landscape which a foreigner discovers. Here, at the onset of what Rancière will call the aesthetic revolution, cinema is already incarnate.[12] The observer from the Lake District who reports in words and images what he has seen "shifts angles of view, reworks the initial montage of words and images while, dismantling the certitudes of the places, awakens the present power in each and everyone to become a stranger to the map of the places and the journeys generally known under the name of reality" (10). The writer who mixes words reflecting flashes of light with the wash of clouds upsets inherited political convictions. He constructs images from clichés born of the Revolution itself.[13] He finds a place "in the gap [*dans l'écart*] between images in respect to any promise of common happiness" (10). Rancière avows that some kind of utopian madness in the words and images of his foreign travelers' reports are in slight but telling excess in comparison with the knowledge and political reason that fabricate "reality." An ideal place, which would also be the site of a movie theater, is felt as "a montage of words and images ordered for the sake of establishing the point of recovery, that, is, the point of utopia" (11). The stranger on the road in rural France seeks equality where words and things coincide, but only when the vision of a common identity—an identity of the landscape and its description in words or its unalloyed presentation in a film—is sensed as a possibility of an equivalence of things "all-over," yet an equivalence that cannot ever be counts less than what the difference or gap makes apparent. In this earlier writing where he writes of Wordsworth, Büchner, and Rilke, Rancière finds in their process a method of equality. Its outlines become limpidly clear through the unspoken mediation of cinema, that later is manifest where Hollywood is in question, where Rancière first felt an annoying contradiction between the pleasure westerns afforded and a reasoned assessment of the economy that produced them.

In the "people's country" there remains at the very least one unanswered question. In *Les écarts du cinéma* Rancière observed how cinephilia, what now can be considered as what comes before reasoned reflection about the seventh art while also being what reason cannot do without, casts "artistic modernism" into doubt. It returns to the unspoken yet intimate ties that link the signs of art and manner of narrative to a *genius loci,* the illuminated screen in a dark room that displays "the most ordinary spectacle" (9). Precisely: "a hand that raises a curtain or turns a doorknob, a head leaning out of a window, a fire or headlamps in the night, glasses clinking on the zinc of a bistrot" (ibid.). No sensation could be so banal or, inexplicably, so enthusing. Because it belongs to no one and everyone, in memory it carries incalculable wealth. It unlocks other sensations held within images and verbal shards that we hold within us. It would seem that in having film become a place where there is an uncommon sharing or equal distribution of sensible things it may be because an "equal concrete density" commands the aural and visual field on the screen. Rancière would be refining Bazin for whom the staging of close-ups on a "door button, on the color of house paint, dirt embedded on the panel of a door, the shine of metal, a worn-out deadbolt amounts to so many useless facts, concrete parasites of abstraction that ought to be eliminated" (282), but which, as the cliché goes, "in the final analysis" are not: herein an equality shared among so many details that remains the untold promise of cinema where, in the difference of words and landscapes in the *Courts voyages au pays du peuple*, a mode of equality is felt in concomitant forces of estrangement and attraction.

Without jogging through the rest of either the *Courts voyages* or the *Écarts du cinéma* (especially the percussive reflections in the chapter titled "Politiques du cinéma"), for the sake of economy two unsettling conclusions can be essayed. (1) The old world of the cinephile and the amateur to which Rancière returns time and again to go ahead and to rethink a political aesthetic in postrevolutionary writing and contemporary cinema (and, it can be added here, in its multiple modes of viewing and production) is seductively problematic: how can the politics of the amateur work within a field where cinephilia risks becoming an academic experience? New means of handling the modes of production, including the viewing and making or even the writing of cinema, can be directed along multiple networks that run on the fringes of the museums of art and the archive while also being drawn through them. In this respect it is vital to think afresh the ways that today cinema is (or is not) assimilated: when seen in reduced format on YouTube, on screens on the narrow backs of airplane seats, on cellphones, in miniature, or amid interruption of email and tweeting, the medium becomes immediately accessible and, paradoxically, more remote.[14] (2) For the cinephile it may be that an art of doing, what long ago was called a tactical *art de faire*, may be at issue.[15] The amateur takes cognizance, as was not always the case in the heyday of the auteur, of a loose but finely wrought webbing where affect can be appreciated as such and, in the same breath, distributed along paths that are not pregiven. Rancière sums it up, unwittingly perhaps, when he implies that, much like Jacques Rivette's Paris, the invention belongs to us and to us alone. *Elle nous appartient*: what we do with it belongs to us, and so too it is up to us to devise how we can hold it apart, at a critical distance from ourselves, but in full cognizance of the ways that our amateurism shapes us. If, as the field of reference implied by *La méthode de l'égalité* suggests, weaned on Descartes, Rancière would hope us to realize along the fault lines of politics and aesthetics that the force of affect belongs neither in multiplexes nor in the citadels of sensitivity we call museums and galleries. It is everywhere, and it can be shared equally and well in many shapes and forms, for, in sum, *l'affect est la chose du monde la mieux partagée.*

Notes

1. Jacques Rancière, *La méthode de l'égalité: Entretien avec Laurent Jeanpierre et Dork Zabunyan* (Paris: Bayard, 2012). May this note convey my gratitude to the author for having forwarded a copy when it first appeared.

2. "Au hasard d'un exposé que j'avais à faire sur la distinction du corps et de l'âme chez Descartes, je me suis lancé à corps perdu dans les *Méditations*, les *Objections*, les *Réponses aux Objections*." Rancière, *La méthode de l'égalité*, 16.

3. See Michel Contat and Michel Rybalka, *Les écrits de Sartre: Chronologie, bibliographie commentée* (Paris: Gallimard, 1970).

4. Parts of the decisive postwar essay first appeared in *Les temps modernes* in 1947 before the volume was issued integrally as *Situations II*. Arlette Ekaïm Sartre has recently set under the same title the writings that appeared from the moment of Sartre's famous "République du silence" (in *Les lettres françaises*, published on the heels of the Liberation of Paris in September 1944, in which, consonant with his philosophy, he argues that never were the French so free as under the Occupation) to that of the end of 1946, which includes what was published at the time of his visit to the United States. In her new postwar edition, she is setting *Qu'est-ce que la littérature?* under the title *Situations III*, in which the work of 1947 is to be regrouped. A literary historian would speculate that Rancière would have followed closely the publication of Sartre's postwar writings.

5. First delivered at the Club Maintenant in Paris on October 29, 1945, the essay became a point of reference for the upbeat appreciation of the philosophy he had crafted with the publication of *L'être et le néant*, the opus of 1943 based on his readings of Husserl and Heidegger during his confinement in a prison camp in 1940–41.

6. Of a similar generation, Marc Augé "works through" his relation with World War II and the Occupation when he relates childhood memories to the incursions of those of *Casablanca*. Released in France in 1947, Michael Curtiz's film of 1942, interfering with Augé's construction of his childhood, prompts him to retrieve embedded memories and to reconsider a relation with history. In the postface to *Casablanca: Movies and Memories* (Minneapolis: University of Minnesota Press, 2009) I have sought to draw a broader sense of this kind of relation, a relation that Rancière brings forward in the memories he recounts in the interview.

7. Mention of Mac-Mahon indicates a vector of taste. The theater was known for its ace of diamonds, at whose four corners stood as many directors: Losey, Lang, Preminger, and Walsh. See Antoine de Baecque, *La cinéphilie: Invention d'un regard, histoire d'une culture, 1944–68* (Paris: Fayard, 2003), 214.

8. Oliver Davis tersely observes that "Althusserianism is judged by Rancière to be a condescending philosophy which protects the social privilege of those institutionally associated with it . . . While the working class were the embodiment of the future for Marxist-Leninist theorists, they did not themselves have direct knowledge of their defining role in the historical process," hence the "ultimate effect of Althusser's lengthy crusade against humanist interpretations of Marx was to defend the privilege of intellectuals." Davis, *Jacques Rancière* (London: Polity, 2010), 14.

9. Jacques Rancière, *Les écarts du cinéma* (Paris: La Fabrique, 2011), 8.

10. André Bazin, *Qu'est-ce que le cinéma?*, 11th ed. (Paris: Éditions du Cerf, 1999), 282 (my translation).

11. Jacques Rancière, *Courts voyages au pays du peuple* (Paris: Éditions du Seuil, 1990), 7.

12. Thus the trajectory of *Aisthesis: Scènes du régime esthétique de l'art* (Paris: Galilée, 2011), its title in dialogue with Erich Auerbach's *Mimesis* and *Scenes from the Drama of European Literature*: *Aisthesis* begins with Winkelmann (1763) and goes to Vertov (1926) and writer/film critic James Agee (1936–41).

13. "Cliché" itself is an image and a sound, its origin one of onomatopoeia: "end of the eighteenth century . . . , recalling the sound of a matrix striking metal in fusion" (Oscar Bloch and Walter von Wartburg, *Dictionnaire étymologique de la langue française* [Paris: PUF, 1932/1975], 36). The word is affiliated with presses printing revolutionary pamphlets and posters.

14. Francesco Casetti takes up the vagaries of viewing in *L'occhio del novecento: Cinema, esperienze, modernità* (Milan: Bompiani, 2005), in English as *Eye of the Century: Film, Experience, Modernity*, translated by Eric Larkin with Jennifer Pranolo (New York: Columbia University Press, 2008).

15. Michel de Certeau, *L'invention du quotidien, 1: Arts de faire*, ed. Luce Giard (Paris: Gallimard/Folio, 1990). Reference is made to the French edition, whose title is far more precise than its gauzy English translation as *The Practice of Everyday Life*.

Afterword

Rethinking Theory and Practice

Jacques Rancière

What sense can we make of the expression "practicing theory"? The way it is set up clearly tells us that we should not take it at face value. The point is not how we can apply theory, but how we can think about theory in other terms than in the terms of something that has to be applied. The idea of the "application" of theory has always been thwarted by a suspicion: the suspicion that theory is precisely the kind of thing that has no application, which is of no use in real life. This suspicion has two sides. There is the commonsense opposition of "abstraction" to "reality." But there is also the positive statement that theory has its "reality," its ends and applications, within itself. It appears, then, that "theory" is not simply a matter of the production of systematic knowledge. Nor is practice a matter of the application of knowledge to reality. Theory and practice were initially defined forms of life opposed to other forms of life. In the Greek philosophical tradition, *theoria* is the activity of thinking taken as its own end. As such, it is a form of activity that belongs to a specific form of life: the life of leisure, the life of those who do not have to worry about matters of everyday life. And practice is not the application of knowledge. Practice is a form of activity. There are, in the same Greek tradition, two forms of activity: there is *poiesis*, which produces objects useful for life, and there is *praxis*, which has no end outside of itself, but is concerned with its own perfection. It is clear that this difference is also a difference between two kinds of human beings: those who live in the sphere of means, and those who live in the sphere of ends. In this sense practice is not an application of *theory*. Nor are *theory* and *practice* opposed to each other. They are on the same side: the side of a life which does not have to waste itself in matters of usefulness and necessity.

It is taken for granted that modern times and modern thinking have dismissed this hierarchy of forms of life. Under the name of production, *poiesis* has become the form of activity which determines the life of our societies. The part played by science in determining the conditions of *praxis* seems in perfect accordance with the central position of production. But that perfect connection may hide a gap and I would like to analyze its significance by reexamining two forms of thinking that tried to overstep the theory/practice opposition by linking the modes of production of thought with the forms of social production. I shall start with the theory to which "practicing theory" is an ironical response, namely the Althusserian theory of "theoretical practice." The notion was clearly designed to refute the idea that theory is mere abstraction, estranged from real social practice. (That demonstration has a very practical target that was to demonstrate the necessity for a Communist Party to have a strong and autonomous organization dedicated solely to the study and development of Marxist theory.) For that purpose, Althusser overwhelmingly uses the analogy of production. Theory is practice, comprised in the whole network of social practice, to the extent that it is production. Production transforms raw material into products. Correspondingly, theory transforms raw material into products of its own. It has to do with raw material, that is, with already existing "generalities" (1) that it transforms into new "generalities" (3) by using specific tools, concepts, or generalities (2). The analogy soon proves unsound. The existing givens, concepts, theories, or experiments that are the starting point of the transformation are no "raw material." But Althusser has the answer: yes, precisely. They are not raw material; they are not something that can be worked with ordinary tools. The raw material that "science" has to transform is spoiled material; it is old obsolete science; or it is the opposite of science: ideological beliefs which have encroached on the work of science. The productive work of science is first and foremost the work of unraveling and eradicating those encroachments. Now the question is: where do those encroachments come from? And the answer is loud and clear: they come from social practice and notably from "productive practice": the "agents of production" are hindered by their very place and practice in the productive process from understanding this process and the part they play in it. On the one hand, theory is practice because it is production; it transforms raw material into products, as workers do. On the other hand, the ordinary practice of transforming "raw material" into products makes those who do it unable to perceive the social and historical process inside which they operate. It encloses them in a lived world of beliefs and illusions about what they do and what they are. Theoretical practice then is theory because it escapes the illusions born out of the activity of production. Its task is the task that no social practice can perform: the dissipation of the illusions that social practice produces. This duplicity takes up the old Platonic duplicity: the philosopher uses paradigms borrowed from craftsmanship the better to separate the business of philosophers from the business of craftsmen. The affirmation of equality (we are all producers) is coupled with an affirmation of inequality which is an inequality in the capacity for "*theoria*" in its most literal sense: the capacity for seeing. There is a majority of "producers" who, like the prisoners in Plato's cave, look at shadows in front of them and are unable to perceive the machinery at their back. And there is a minority of producers who see the truth because they can embrace the mechanism of social production as a whole. This relation is not casual, it is structural. It is not a question of knowing more or less. It is a matter of knowing or ignoring. The relation is a topographical one. The place of material production is a place where it is impossible to see, impossible to move to the place for seeing, impossible to share the leisure of "*theoria*." The distribution links positions and timelines with aptitudes and inaptitudes. There is a time and a place in which practice means ignorance, and there is another time and place in which it means science. This relation is both an abstract one and an empirical one. As Althusser stated, Marxist science had been possible because it had been produced by "the theoretical practice of intellectuals possessing a very high degree of culture . . . and 'introduced from without' into proletarian practice."[1] On the one hand, the "high degree of culture" is a form of understatement which means in reality "the hill of truth"; on the other hand, it assimilates "science," seen as the viewpoint from the top, with "culture"—a notion which equates knowledge with "leisure," which means the privilege of those who are not entrapped in the time and space of ordinary social practice.

Now the point is that the Platonic opposition of the hill to the cave was in line with an idea of science as the knowledge of a celestial sphere governed by the mathematical rule opposed to an earthly world governed by randomness and opinion. Philosophers and ignoramuses did not see the same world and the "application of theory" in the world of the artisans and ignoramuses amounted to organizing it, as far as possible, in accordance with the mathematical rules of proportion governing the movements of the stars. But when it comes to modern theoretical practice, things become more intricate. The hill is the viewpoint from which the theorist sees the same world where he lives and where the producers and ignoramuses live. The difference is that the former sees the connection of the laws that govern this world while the latter only see the effects estranged from their cause: the reflections that this world, as a lived world, produces in their restricted field of vision. This distribution of positions entails a presupposition: the presupposition that the nexus of social causes is a totality which can be embraced by the theorist. The theorist is both inside (as a man of practice) and outside (as a seer). (This duality is reflected in the relation of science to the objects and notions of the "practical world": scientific concepts are said to be entirely different from empirical notions, even when they bear the same name.) But there is another problem: the application of science to the transformation of society is no more the task of the philosopher as a lawmaker, as it was with Plato. It is the task of the producers. It is the task of those who are structurally unable to live in the world of theory. Theory must give them the tools for that transformation. Now the tool that theory can give them is a viewpoint—the viewpoint of the place which is inaccessible to them due to their very position. The effect that theory produces outside itself is awareness. What awareness means is the transformation of the consciousness of those who live in the cave of social practice and normally produce the contrary of science which is ideology. The product of theory outside itself is "ideological struggle." But if the production of science consists in the correction of the errors of vision that are unrelentingly produced by the social machinery and if its effect outside itself also is the correction of those errors, it turns out that the practice of science is only the ceaseless staging of the difference between science and its other, the staging of the difference between the sun of the Idea and the shadows of the cave.

"Theoretical practice," then, is the name of a desperate attempt to constitute theory as a practice without questioning the distribution of positions which sustains the very notions of theory and practice—and notably the basic presupposition: there are two opposite ways of seeing, two opposite ways of speaking, two opposite ways of using senses and of making sense of their givens. What is at the core of the issue is the very cartography of the perceptible and the thinkable. This issue was clearly set up in the well-known conversation between Foucault and Deleuze in 1972 on "Intellectuals and Power." What has been mostly remembered of that conversation is the metaphor of "theory" as a "toolbox." I am not sure that this metaphor breaks away from the traditional idea of theory, as it does not question the very issue of the relation between "theory" and "usefulness." What's most important is the reconfiguration of the space where theory and practice are located. This reconfiguration calls into question the distinction between two time-spaces. It calls into question the structure in which "modern" thinking has relocated that distinction: the structure of the totality that can be embraced from a privileged point of view. There is only one space, and there is no point in that space from which the global nexus of causes could be given. The point, then, is not to put theory into practice. Theory and practice are the names of two ways of tracing paths and drawing maps in that space. This is what is summed up by the apparently disconcerting statement Deleuze made: "A theory is always local and related to a limited field, and it is applied in another sphere, more or less distant from it."[2] There is no knowledge of the nexus of causes from which one can deduce what people have to do in a given situation. The act of theorization always starts from that given situation—it stems from the specific field of tensions that makes a situation. We cannot theorize power from an idea of the logic of social domination and of the effects that must be produced on its subjects. We can theorize power from the techniques that are applied in a specific set of relations, the discourses that legitimize them, the effects that they produce, the resistance that they provoke, and so on. A theory of power is a form of expansion of what is at play in those situations. But that is not all. Not only is any theory local, but the field in which it becomes effective is not the field where its elements have been gathered and linked together. A "theory" is a discourse in-between, the product of an experience that may provoke new and unexpected effects at another moment in another field of experience. Or, if we stick to the idea that theory means "vision," theory is the view that can be taken in the course of a journey within a territory of the perceptible and the thinkable. Now the journey and the view are not only manners of finding one's way by locating points on a map, they contribute to a new mapping and a new territory.

This rethinking of theory entails a rethinking of practice and of the theory/practice relation. The conversation between Deleuze and Foucault revolved around a specific practice: the action carried out by the Prison Information Group created by Foucault to investigate the situation in prisons. In the conversation Foucault strongly emphasizes their difference with the view of militant action as an application of theory through the mediation of "awareness." Prisoners or other dominated groups don't lack knowledge. "When the prisoners began to speak, they possessed an individual theory of prisons, the penal system, and justice."[3] That which subjects groups of human beings to power is not ignorance. The invisible that the practice of intervention has to bring to the fore is not the hidden law of the structure; it is the ordinary violence of the system. It is not a matter of illusion; it is a matter of secrecy. "Practicing theory" then is not deducing forms of action from a theory of the penal system. It is breaking the law of silence, fighting against the system of power which "blocks, prohibits and invalidates" the prisoners' discourse and knowledge.[4] In this kind of action, Foucault says, it is not a question of explaining the causes of a situation. The right question is not the usual question to which the theorist has the answer in store: Why? The right question is: Who? Who does this or that in this or that place? Practicing is naming. Naming is speaking, but speaking in this case can no longer be opposed to "action." Naming is an action that disrupts the traditional relation between "thinking" and "doing": the relation that consists in providing the knowledge that makes things understandable. There is nothing to understand. It is just a question of naming, locating, and identifying: for instance, the practices of humiliation that are exerted in this prison or the frozen blankets in that other one. These are the kinds of situations that have to be pinpointed: situations in which power is naked, in which it becomes concretely its own abstraction. And this is what the target of action is: making this nakedness appear in the open. This is the openness which in turns allows prisoners to rise up, and prisoners did rise up in several French prisons a few months after the creation of the Prison Information Group. Its creation had not given them any knowledge about the penal system, its place in society, and the ways to rebel against it. It had created a space where prisons were visible, what happened inside prisons had become a public affair, and prisoners themselves could be seen as citizens affirming their rights. The act of naming had created another mode of visibility for their acts. And their rebellion in turn contributed to a new mapping of the possible.

The relation between "theory" and "practice" thus seems to be redistributed in a series of performances each of which is both "theoretical"—since they deal with matters of visibility—and "practical"—as the transformation of the relations between the visible and the invisible establishes a new mapping of the common and a new landscape of the possible. There is the work of the researcher who delves into the archives of confinement and draws out of this research a new form of visibility of society which does not so much refer social domination to an invisible global mechanism as refer it to singular spaces and mechanisms. There is the action of the militant investigator who designates specific points in those spaces and draws into the open forms of power aimed at creating silence and working in silence. There is the collective action of the prisoners who rebel against their living conditions and by the same token transform the closed space of the prison into a public stage. The general form of the relation between these different actions is not the cause-effect relation. Instead, it is a complex set of relations: parallelism, proximity, condition of possibility, action from a distance. There is no direct consequence from any of those actions to any other. Now this lack of consequence can be interpreted in two ways. It can be interpreted as the disruption of the theory/practice relation. But it can also be interpreted as a form of divergence. I think that it is worth pointing out what is at issue in that alternative.

For this examination, I shall start with the statement that Foucault once made when he said that his work as a theorist bore no relation to his action as a militant investigator. In a first sense, we can interpret it as a distinction between two practices. Between the work of a researcher writing books on the history of confinement and that of a militant in a Prison Information Group, there is a leap. What makes the leap possible does not stem either from the necessity of the theoretical demonstration or from the development of the empirical situation. It is just a feeling: the feeling that something is intolerable. What is intolerable for Foucault is first and foremost our tolerance: the way in which we accept the division between good and evil, the sound and the unsound, the normal and the pathological. The same refusal underpins the set of questions generating the work of research and the punctual interventions of the militant. Up to this point the statement of the separation between the practice of research and the practice of intervention is faithful to the rethinking of theory and practice as two practices both separated and unified by the same logic.

But there is a point where the difference becomes a divergence and a divergence which reinstates a logic of separation and opposition. This point is the writing of theory: the form of concatenation of significations that transforms the products of research into a consistent totality. This problem falls under what I have called a poetics of knowledge: the choice of the plot within which the combination of narration and argumentation adds up to the knowledge of a domain or the form of intelligibility of a process. The issue can be set up by looking at the first chapter of the book that systematizes Foucault's research on the penal system: *Discipline and Punish.* This chapter starts with two material scenes. The first one is the spectacle of the execution of a French regicide, Damiens, drawn by horses and quartered for his attempted murder of King Louis XV. The second is the timetable of an institution for young delinquents eighty years later: two material facts, two ways of dealing with the criminal body and with the visibility or invisibility of punishment. The whole question is how you move from one scene to the other. At this point, Foucault makes a choice. He chooses the strong causal plot, which is usual in the writing of theory after having been a criterion for poetic excellence in the Aristotelian tradition: the determination of a global direction—a goal to be attained—that determines the means to attain it and the effects that they produce. The two scenes are here to evince a historical shift. And this historical shift witnesses an entire rethinking of the imposition of power over bodies. From this point on, the itinerary that the book traces is that of a transformation that makes the penal system an instrument of action on the souls of the criminals, more precisely an instrument that gives them "souls." What it describes is a system of production of knowledge and formation of individualities whose effect goes past the task of repression just as it goes past the borders of the prison. But that strategic model soon proves incompatible with the idea of the theory as "local," as the movement from one relay to another. It sets up a radical difference of scale between the functioning of the machine and the events that may happen at this or that point on the map. What kind of proportion can there be between the global logic of the production of souls and the "tiny" material things and events that disclose power in its nakedness and provoke rebellion? Moreover, the great lesson of the book is that we must stop thinking power in terms of repression. We must think of it in terms of the production of knowledge, thoughts, and habits.

But, for their part, the reasons of rebellion and the forms of militant investigation have to stick to those little things in which power appears naked, in all its pettiness and absurdity. Between the rationality of the global system as an object of knowledge and the rationality of the intervention in a local and punctual situation, there is only one relay left, the abstract notion of what the system wants to destroy and what resists its endeavor: namely the notion of resistance which is the other side—the blind side—of the strategic dispositif and of its knowledge. "Resistance" designates the "outside," the absent cause which gives its form to the system of social domination. But for this reason it becomes impossible to give it a status either within the writing of theory or in the relation between writing and public action.

A new divorce thus appears between the reasons of science and the reasons of revolt. There is no relation between my two practices, said Foucault. This is true if it means that the writing of theory does not provide tools in the Marxist way. But it is false to the extent that theory is a mapping of the possible. That which connects the writing of theory, the militant investigation, and rebellion is a certain mapping of the possible. The revolt of May '68 had created a map of the possible where the leap from a theory of confinement to a militant investigation was possible, the militant investigation had created a mode of visibility of the prison within which a revolt of prisoners acquired a new meaning and a new import. That revolt created a new idea of what the struggle of the "subaltern" meant. *Discipline and Punish* in turn was an intervention reframing, along with the thinkability of the prison, the thinkability of intervention and revolt. But that intervention apparently re-created the point of view of the theorist embracing the whole machine from the hill. As a matter of fact, the publication of *Discipline and Punish* provoked a great number of historical and sociological studies on the technologies of power and the disciplinarization of bodies. But those studies were no longer committed to echo the revolts of those who were subjugated to those techniques. Instead they tended to show how the technologies of disciplinarization had been invented to domesticate rebellious popular bodies and how they succeeded in that endeavor. This means that they reintroduced the viewpoint from the hill of science on the machinery of the cave. Needless to say, that view did not prove very inspiring for fostering the spirit of rebellion. Instead it was absorbed in the general mood, which transformed the forms of critical thinking into the description of a huge machine of power seizing on anything that claims to challenge it.

I don't want to elaborate on those effects. I just want to outline the core of the problem. Foucault was often accused at that moment of using only the archives of power instead of listening to the "voices from below." But it is not a question of political inclination. It is a question of theoretical plot, a question of a politics of knowledge. The plot of the constitution of disciplinary power had to rely on the archives of power. There is no archive of resistance that might be contrasted with the archives of power. There is no symmetry. Inequality also structures the practice of keeping traces and archives. The appeal for opposing the voices from below to the archives of power is still a way of confirming the hierarchical distribution. To challenge the point of view from the hill, you first have to rethink the cave, to rethink what is meant by "the voices from below." The prisoners, Foucault said, had their own theories about the penal system. We should take it seriously, and possibly more seriously than he did. Having theories doesn't only mean having explanations. It means living in the time and space of theory. Those in the cave—prisoners or other groups dominated by a form of power that assigns them a definite time-space—take possession of theory as a form of disruption of their normal timetable. Prisoners transform the time of confinement into a time of leisure within which it is possible to see the prison as a system and not only as the walls of the building where they are confined. They "possess theories": this means that what they say can no longer be reduced to a "prisoners' voice" as opposed to theories of the penal system. It is no longer possible to distinguish two forms of vision and two modes of discourse. What is in the background is the Aristotelian distinction between the animal voice which expresses pleasure and pain and the human logos which discusses issues of justice and injustice. Aristotle also said that slaves understand language but don't "possess" it. To emphasize that prisoners or members of any similar group "possess" their own theories is to say that it is no longer possible to separate two kinds of speaking beings: those who express their pain and those who account for those pains. No longer possible to separate the speaking beings who are the object of theory and those who are the producers of theory. The "theoretical" link between the practice of the theorist, the practice of the investigator, and that of the rebels is the link of equality: what I named after Jacotot the presupposition of the equality of intelligence. Now equality in the world of inequality works as dissensus: as an interruption of a normal timetable, which means a rupture of the normal order of things.

The idea of dissensus and its place in a rethinking of the "practice of theory" can be highlighted by comparison with another concept used by Foucault, the concept of "infamy." I said earlier that the analysis of the disciplines in *Discipline and Punish* tended to constitute "resistance" as the other side or the blind side—the absent cause—of the strategies of power. Now the blind side takes on a positive figure elsewhere, when Foucault deals with the "lives of infamous men." "Infamy" means two things: it means shameful behavior, but it also means the lot of those who are not famous, who are not visible, not audible. Infamy thus designates the fact that those who should never appear, those who should never be seen and heard become "famous": visible and audible. But in Foucault's view the only way for them to be famous is to be famous as infamous: as criminals or monsters. He assumes that this violent apparition of obscure lives on the stage of "glory" evinces a new status of the "fabulous" which finds its accomplishment in literature. Modern literature, he says, is born by substituting for the old fabulous stories the new fable that makes the unseen abysses of obscure life appear in the open. This is why Foucault invites us to read the stories of the "infamous men" as we read literary pieces. This means two things. First, Foucault locates the "fame of the infamous men" in a form of writing specifically committed to the manifestation of the "outside." He keeps them outside theory, in literature. But he also includes literature and its way of giving fame to infamy in the global logic through which power obliges life to tell itself. Literature, he says, belongs to "that great system of constraint by which the West compelled the everyday to bring itself into discourse."[5] I think that we can take a different view of the relation between "infamy" and literature. What is important in the case of the "infamous men" is how people who are not supposed to tell their life and make arguments to justify their deeds set out to do so—for instance when Pierre Riviere, the parricide who was the subject of a collective book directed by Foucault, writes his long report to explain his conduct and justify it. Transgression is not so much the anomaly of behavior with respect to the norm. It is a shift in position. Pierre Riviere is a son of peasants and he is deemed an idiot, yet he writes this long text to give the reasons for each of his three murders and prove his right with reference to the Bible. People speak when and where they are not expected to do so, and in the form that is not expected from them. And this is what literature means: the anarchical circulation of written words, the disruption of the normal link between the circulation of words and stories and the distribution of social positions. Infamy can thus be rethought as dissensus. The general notion of dissensus is the notion of a disruption of the normal distribution of bodies into places where they are supposed to have a specific occupation and the sensory equipment fitting that occupation. There is dissensus when those who are supposed to stay in the silent anonymity and invisibility of "everyday life" break away from that assignment. It is not only a question of becoming visible or audible. It is about acquiring another sort of look and another mode of speaking than those that fit your "condition." Dissensus occurs when those who are supposed to be only able to voice their pain affirm their capacity for speaking about justice and injustice. It is not the dramatic confrontation of a body with power as Foucault stages it. Dissensus is not an opposition of forces. Instead it is a confrontation of worlds. It is the confrontation between the world where a worker or a prisoner is just a worker or a prisoner, using the words, gestures, attitudes that are suitable to their condition and the world in which they break away from that distribution of the possible. They take the time that they do not have to do what is "none of their business." They become spectators and interpreters of their own lives. They get rid of the ways of being and speaking that are suitable to their condition. They borrow the "language from above," take on a point of view of artists on the landscape of their workplace, they play the parts of philosophers or strolling propagandists, and so on. It is on these imperceptible deviations of a body from the gestures, attitudes, and words that are suitable to its condition that I focused when I wrote *The Nights of Labor.* I did not focus on spectacular forms of workers' struggles or popular deviance. I focused on what I saw as the core of any proletarian subversion: the subversion of the normal round of day and night, work and repose. To be exact, I did not focus on that subversion out of a preliminary theoretical decision. I focused on it when I had to give a structure to the mass of documents that I had collected during years devoted to the reading of archives, manuscripts, and all kinds of printed sources. In other terms, it is the process of writing that created the obligation to construct a plot, to "start from somewhere" and draw a thread leading from that original place to another place. To construct a plot first means to make a decision on a mode of concatenation of events. This is what I mentioned about the first chapter of *Discipline and Punish.* My own politics of knowledge consisted of three main operations.

It entailed first the constitution of a specific archive. By "specific," I mean a kind of archive disrupting the normal distribution of the parts, staging on the one side the written records of the operations of power and, on the other side, the "voices of the people." That specific archive thus is an archive of the "writing of the people." Such an archive does not exist. It has to be constituted. And the constitution of that archive was intertwined with the writing of the book. I selected a number of heterogeneous documents coming from different sources: articles in workers' newspapers or public manifestos but also poems, little stories, letters, and so on. An archive of "workers' writing" means a collection of written texts witnessing the rupture through which those who are not supposed to write get into the world of writing. Now those texts witness that process to the extent that they perform it, they enact it.

The construction of the plot entailed a second operation: the selection of a specific theoretical unit. The unit on which I constructed the logic of my plot is the *scene*. This is certainly something that I had learned from Foucault: the focus on the scene as an example which is more than an example, since it contains in itself the set of relations and tensions that constitute its "meaning." The scene describes an event to us which is more than an event; an event which at the same time shows us the border between the event and the nonevent, between what is ordinary and what is not, what has its place in a given order of signification and what is outside or in between. I focused on scenes of writing that are scenes of dissensus. Scenes of dissensus may be scenes of quarrel: the argumentative protocol displayed in a strike, a debate between two workers' journals about communism, a polemical way of phrasing the condition of workers or of reacting to another formulation. But they are first and foremost scenes that witness and perform the crossing of the border, the entry into the universe of writing and the reorganization of the look, the attitudes, the gestures, the timetable with which it is connected: a modification in the way of living the day at work or the night of rest, the narration of a Sunday walk, the invention of a little story, the very act of handling a pen to write at midnight, and so on. As a "theoretical" form, the scene is the staging of the process through which a life affirms its capacity to be an object of thought for itself. By the same token it is the staging of the question: how can we take this process into account? Not to account for this, but to take this into account? Breaking the borders separating theory from profane experience in order to show how the whole of the theoretical question is at work in those little stories? The scene is the mode of presentation in which the very difference between the words and sentences of knowledge and the words and sentences of those who are its "objects" is suppressed. Both appear to belong to the same language and to the same capacity for thinking. There is not a language for empirical narration and a language for theoretical explanation.

There is one language and one intelligence. In other words, the form of theoretical presentation cannot be separated from the form of literary narration. The theoretical plot is a literary one. It is the construction of scenes and the expansion of the internal power of meaning of the scene.

This consequence defines the third operation: the mode of connection of scenes inside a plot. The scene does not need to be explained. It is not an example showing a certain state in the development of a global process that gives it its meaning. Its connection with other scenes cannot be a chain of causes and effects. Each scene has its meaning in itself. Each scene is about the whole theoretical issue, about the distribution of the capacities of seeing, thinking, and saying attached to this or that form of life, about the crossing of the border separating those who are in the cave from those who stay on the hill. The scene needs no explanation. It only needs intensification. Its potential for making things perceptible and thinkable has to be intensified. This implies that the connection between the scenes is a fabric of writing constructing the sensorium within which the potential of each is intensified by its contact with other scenes. Proust once said that we should use his book as a lens through which we can look at our own life and experience. The scene can be viewed as a little optical machine allowing us to look into the other scenes and make what is at issue in them appear in the foreground. But it is not only a question of better seeing. It is also a question of liberating the subversive energy encapsulated in those scenes, the energy of the crossing of the border. Scenes deliver their energetic potential only if one frees them of the causal plot, if one makes them freely resonate into other scenes, if they can mirror one another and echo one another in the open sensorium or the egalitarian sensorium of their coexistence. This is how it happened to me that I wrote a strange book called *The Nights of Labor*, or, more exactly, *The Night of the Proletarians*, a "theoretical book" only consisting in narration without a word of what is usually called theory.

I said "it happened to me." The fact is that the operations that I have just spelled out were never planned. I can describe them and elaborate on their meaning as an example of the "practice of theory" today, thirty years later. But there was no plan, no choice. It happened in the process of writing. It happened as the result of a double constraint. The first constraint was the constraint of the evolution of the world around me. I was writing at a time that was the time of the ebb of the leftist tide, when those discourses about the machine of power and the impossibility of escaping its grip were in vogue. I was trying to find the ways for resisting this ebb of the tide, for keeping the breach open. The second constraint was the constraint of the archival material itself: the letter of the Saint-Simonian worker to his friend imposed the fact that a harmless Sunday walk in the countryside could be a subversion of the logic of domination. It imposed the fact that this subversion was not a matter of resistance to power, that it was a much deeper experience of confrontation with the possible and the impossible in a condition. In the long run, it imposed the structure of the scene, of the plot, and of the mode of intelligibility of the plot. It imposed a certain politics of writing that became mine: the politics that focuses on a few little scenes—the description of the Sunday walk of the Saint-Simonian workers or the glance of the joiner through the window of his workplace; the love story of a young seamstress and a utopian theorist; the argumentation of a tailors' strike; the rewriting of the secession of the plebeian on the Aventine—the politics that focuses on those little scenes and makes them constantly knock against the dominant discourses on society, power, politics, or aesthetics so as to reopen the breach, to reopen the space of another sensible world within the sensible world structured by the forces of domination. The writing of theory belongs to the form of rationality described by the thinker of intellectual emancipation, Joseph Jacotot: the form of the intellectual adventure starting from anywhere and moving forward step by step in a continuous process of learning which is also a continuous process of "ignorance": not knowing where you go, just feeling the impulse that urges you to move forward. What I have tried to do is just to go back over some paths in my own intellectual adventure.

Notes

1. Louis Althusser, "Theory, Theoretical Practice and Theoretical Formation," in *Philosophy and the Spontaneous Philosophy of the Scientists*, ed. Gregory Elliot, trans. James Kavanaugh (London: Verso, 1965), 16.

2. Michel Foucault and Gilles Deleuze, "Intellectuals and Power," in *Language, Counter-memory, Practice: Selected Essays and Interviews*, ed. Donald Bouchard, trans. Donald Bouchard and Sherry Simon (Ithaca, N.Y.: Cornell University Press, 1977), 206.

3. Foucault and Deleuze, "Intellectuals and Power," 209.

4. Foucault and Deleuze, "Intellectuals and Power," 207.

5. Michel Foucault, "The Life of Infamous Men," in *Michel Foucault: Power, Truth, Strategy*, ed. Meaghan Morris and Paul Patton (Sydney: Feral Publications, 1979), 91.

Contributors

Benjamin Arditi is a professor of politics at the National University of Mexico (UNAM). He is the author of *Politics on the Edges of Liberalism: Difference, Populism, Revolution, Agitation* (2007) and the coeditor of the book series Taking On the Political. His current research focuses on posthegemony and postliberal politics.

Nico Baumbach is an assistant professor of film and media studies at Columbia University. He is the author of *Cinema/Politics/Philosophy* (2018).

Pheng Cheah is a professor of Rhetoric and chair of the Center for Southeast Asia Studies at the University of California, Berkeley, where he has taught since 1999. His most recent book is *What Is a World? On Postcolonial Literature as World Literature* (Duke University Press, 2016). He is currently completing a book on biopolitics and human rights and another book on globalization and Chinese world cinema that focuses on the films of Jia Zhangke, Tsai Ming-liang, and Fruit Chan.

Tom Conley, Lowell Professor of Romance Languages and Visual and Environmental Studies at Harvard University, is the author of *À fleur de page: Voir et lire le texte de la Renaissance* (2016), *An Errant Eye* (2011), *The Self-Made Map* (1996/2011), *Cartographic Cinema* (2007), and other titles. With T. Jefferson Kline he has coedited the *Wylie-Blackwell Companion to Godard* (2014). He has translated writings of Marc Augé, Michel de Certeau, Gilles Deleuze, and others.

Sudeep Dasgupta is an associate professor in the Department of Media Studies at the Amsterdam School of Cultural Analysis (ASCA) at the University of Amsterdam. His research and publications focus on visual culture and aesthetics, critical theory, globalization and postcolonial studies, feminist and queer theory, and political philosophy. Recent publications include "The Aesthetics of Indirection: Intermittent Adjacencies and Subaltern Presences at the Borders of Europe," *Cinéma & Cie* (2017); "The Spare Image in an Unsparing World: Framing the Soldier in an

Indeterminate War," in "Rancière and the Senses," special issue, *Transformations* (2011); and "Jacques Rancière," in *Film, Theory and Philosophy: The Key Thinkers*, ed. F. Colman (2009). Book publications include the volume (coedited with Mireille Rosello) *What's Queer about Europe?* (2014) and *Constellations of the Transnational: Modernity, Culture, Critique* (2007).

Scott Durham is an associate professor of French and comparative literature at Northwestern University, where he is also Director of Graduate Studies in French and Francophone Studies. He is the author of *Phantom Communities: The Simulacrum and the Limits of Postmodernism* (Stanford University Press) and editor of a *Yale French Studies* issue on Jean Genet, "Genet: In the Language of the Enemy." He is currently writing two books, with the working titles *Between Rancière and Deleuze: Aesthetics, Politics, Resistance* and *Eurydice's Gaze: Historicity and Memory in Postwar Film.*

Jason Frank is the Robert J. Katz Chair of Government at Cornell University, where he teaches political theory. He is the author of *Constituent Moments: Enacting the People in Postrevolutionary America, Publius and Political Imagination*, and the editor of *A Political Companion to Herman Melville.* His current book project investigates the aesthetics of popular sovereignty and is titled *The Democratic Sublime: Assembly and Aesthetics in the Age of Revolution.*

Dilip Gaonkar is a professor in rhetoric and public culture at Northwestern University, where he is also Director of the Center for Global Culture and Communication. He is also Director of the Center for Transcultural Studies, an independent scholarly research network concerned with global issues. He was closely associated with the journal *Public Culture*, serving as the executive editor (2000–2009) and as editor (2009–2011). Gaonkar has two sets of scholarly interests: rhetoric as an intellectual tradition, both its ancient roots and its contemporary mutations; and global modernities and their impact on the political. He has published numerous essays on rhetoric, including "The Idea of Rhetoric in the Rhetoric of Science," which was published along with ten critical responses to the essay in *Rhetorical Hermeneutics: Invention and Interpretation in the Age of Science*, edited by Alan G. Gross and William Keith (1996). Gaonkar has edited *Globalizing American Studies* (with Brian Edwards, 2010), *Alternative Modernities* (2001), and *Disciplinarity and Dissent in Cultural Studies* (with Cary Nelson, 1995). He has also edited several special issues of journals: "Laclau's *On Populist Reason*" (with Robert Hariman, for *Cultural Studies*, 2012), "Cultures of Democracy" (for *Public Culture*, 2007), "Commitments in a Post-Foundational World" (with Keith Topper, 2005), "Technologies of Public Persuasion" (with Elizabeth Povinelli, 2003), and "New Imaginaries" (with Benjamin Lee, 2002). He is currently working on a book manuscript titled *Crowds, Riots and the Politics of Disorder.*

Eleanor Kaufman is a professor of comparative literature, English, and French and Francophone studies at the University of California, Los Angeles. She is the author of *The Delirium of Praise: Bataille, Blanchot, Deleuze, Foucault, Klossowski* (2001), *Deleuze, the Dark Precursor: Dialectic, Structure, Being* (2012), and *At Odds with Badiou: Politics, Dialectics, and Religion from Sartre and Deleuze to Lacan and Agamben* (forthcoming); and coeditor of *Deleuze and Guattari: New Mappings in Politics, Philosophy, and Culture* (1998). Funded by UC President's and Guggenheim Fellowships, she is embarking on a new study titled "Structure: A Counterhistory of Twentieth-Century French Philosophy."

Giuseppina Mecchia is an associate professor of French and Italian at the University of Pittsburgh. Her numerous publications include essays, edited volumes, and translations in the field of cultural politics and literary and cinematic critique. Among others, she has recently published on Stendhal, Marcel Proust, Elsa Morante, Jean Baudrillard, Jacques Rancière, Paolo Virno, Franco "Bifo" Berardi, Michael Haneke, and Michel Houellebecq.

Codruţa Morari is an associate professor in the Program of Cinema and Media Studies and the Department of French at Wellesley College. She is the author of *The Bressonians: French Cinema and the Culture of Authorship* (2017).

Jacques Rancière, born in Algiers (1940), is an emeritus professor of aesthetics and politics at the University of Paris VIII, where he taught from 1969 to 2000 in the Department of Philosophy. He also taught at the European Graduate School and in several American universities. His work crosses the fields of social history, politics, aesthetics, film studies, and literature. He is the author of more than forty books, most of which have been translated into English, including, notably, *The Ignorant Schoolmaster: Five Lessons in Intellectual Emancipation* (1991), *Disagreement: Politics and Philosophy* (1998), *The Politics of Aesthetics* (2006), *The Future of the Image* (2007), *The Emancipated Spectator* (2009), *Mute Speech: Literature, Critical Theory, and Politics* (2011), *Proletarian Nights: The Workers' Dream in Nineteenth-Century France* (2012), *Aisthesis: Scenes from the Aesthetic Regime of Art* (2013), *The Intervals of Cinema* (2014), and *The Lost Thread: The Democracy of Modern Fiction* (2017).

Joseph J. Tanke is an associate professor in the Department of Philosophy and Director of the International Cultural Studies Program at the University of Hawai'i at Mānoa. He has published widely on topics in nineteenth- and twentieth-century European philosophy, including *Foucault's Philosophy of Art: A Genealogy of Modernity* (2009) and *Jacques Rancière: Philosophy, Politics, and Aesthetics* (2011). He is the editor of the series Global Aesthetic Research. Recently he has been interested in exploring the relevance of Kant's *Critique of Judgment* for the purposes of discussing contemporary art and literature. To that end, he has just published a philosophical reading of Marcel Proust's *À la recherche du temps perdu,* "Communicability without Communication: Kant and Proust on Aesthetic Pleasure," in the journal *Diacritics.*

Index